THE LEGEND 4

Mick the Miller

THE LEGEND OF
Mick the Miller

SPORTING ICON OF THE DEPRESSION

MICHAEL TANNER

PHOTOGRAPHIC ACKNOWLEDGMENTS

Section 1 – Popperfoto; 1 top, 4 bottom: British Film Institute (BFI):
1 bottom; Michael Greene: 2 top and bottom, 3 top; British Library:
3 bottom, 4 top, 6 bottom, 7; author's collection: 6 top; Getty Images: 8.

Section 2 – National Greyhound Racing Club (NGRC): 1 top, 3, 5 bottom,
8 top left and bottom; author's collection: 1 bottom, 2 top left and centre;
4 top; Popperfoto: 2 top right, 5 top, 6 bottom; British Library: 2 bottom;
Mirror Syndication: 4 bottom; BFI: 6 top, 7 top and bottom; Frank Hill:
8 top right.

Published in paperback in 2004 by Highdown,
an imprint of Raceform Ltd
Compton, Newbury, Berkshire, RG20 6NL
Raceform Ltd is a wholly-owned subsidiary of Trinity Mirror plc

First published in 2003
Copyright © Michael Tanner 2004

ISBN 1-904317-67-7

Designed by Fiona Pike
Printed by Cox & Wyman, Reading

CONTENTS

AUTHOR'S NOTES

John Ford's elegiac Western movie *The Man Who Shot Liberty Valance* ends with the line, 'When the legend becomes fact, print the legend.' So it has always been with The Legend of Mick the Miller. For 70 years or more, the story of the solitary canine to merit mention alongside Rin-Tin-Tin and Lassie as an icon in the eyes of the British public has been shrouded in a miasma of half-truths, hearsay and endlessly recycled inaccuracies.

I have attempted, wherever possible, to shine a light through the haze and separate fact from fable. Occasionally, this has resulted in a few myths being debunked. Was Mick auctioned on the terraces of the White City after his sensational English debut in 1929? Not in the correct sense of the word. And Mick only contested the re-run of the 1931 Derby at the insistence of the future Edward VIII? Not so. The future King was many miles away.

The myths surrounding the genesis of Mick's wonderfully alliterative name and his brush with the killer disease distemper are two further instances. We have been asked to believe that the name Mick the Miller derived from either: (1) his being farmed out as a pup to the local baker where he was found frolicking in some flour; (2) being named after his owner-breeder's odd-job man called Mick Miller; or (3) in recognition of the mill-wheel in front of the said owner's property. There was no mill-wheel at Millbrook House and the only odd-job men who fit the bill were called James Hill and Michael Greene. The testimony of Greene's children, Michael and Kathleen, is therefore the most tangible primary evidence available regarding this early period of Mick the Miller's life, and I'm happy to concur with their explanation regarding the dog's nomenclature in the absence of anything more concrete or credible.

The time, place and duration of Mick the Miller's bout of distemper is another case in point. The popular story that Mick became ill in 1927 before he was a year-old and was sent to Shelbourne Park in Dublin to be tended by the vet Arthur Callanan is highly implausible. Callanan did not take up his post there until 1928 when Mick was 18 months-old. Furthermore, had the dog contracted such a disease at the young age habitually stated, he would have been routinely destroyed: there was no earthly reason to send an ordinary young pup to Dublin. The only reason he could have come into Callanan's care was if he was already in training at Shelbourne. If he had already shown some promise (which he had), trying to save him thus became an option. My interpretation is based on three points: (1) Mick's sudden disappearance from track action after 11 May 1928 until coursing in the autumn – he was certainly not a sick dog for a full ten months as some have inferred owing to his not resuming track racing until 25 March 1929; (2) his owner's determination to offload him throughout the late summer of 1928; and (3) a brief report in the lead up to the English Derby in July 1929 to the effect that 12 months earlier Mick the Miller had been an invalid at Shelbourne.

Thus, I have resorted to fable only where it appears to support the facts or lends inescapable colour to them. And yet, even after restricting literary licence to the bare minimum, the story of Mick the Miller still assumes legendary status.

That this is the first full-scale monograph on the subject of Mick the Miller remains as much a surprise (and a mystery) to me today as it did way back in 1960 when I first enquired of my local village librarian about the existence of such a volume. In bringing at long last this labour of love to fruition, I must straight away extend a debt of gratitude to the guiding lights at Highdown, namely Brough Scott and Julian Brown, who shared some – if not all – of my conviction that a book about a dead dog was worth writing and, more crucially, worth financing.

The list of thanks thereafter is a long one, but without each and every one of the following individuals or organisations the task of even getting close to the bottom of the Mick the Miller story would have been immeasurably harder than it was.

For published secondary sources on the greyhound I enjoyed the luxury of being granted unlimited access to probably the most extensive private library on the subject in the country, namely that belonging to Sir Mark Prescott. Mindful of my own reluctance to allow anyone to remove books from my reference library makes me all the more grateful for Sir Mark's generosity in this respect. Sir Mark's complete set of British and Irish Stud Books was a vital source of information regarding not only Mick's antecedence but also his initial career in the coursing fields of Ireland. Other publications of particular usefulness in furthering my knowledge of the greyhound, its breeding, rearing and training were: *The Book of the Greyhound* (Ash); *Greyhounds and Greyhound Racing* (Culpeper Clarke); *All About Greyhound Racing* (Tompkins and Heasman), *The Book of the Greyhound* (Wimhurst), *The Complete Book of the Greyhound, and A Complete Study of the Modern Greyhound* (Edwards Clarke); finally, a rare copy of the 1935 book *British Sports and Sportsmen: Racing and Coursing* contained a profile of WE Washbourne detailing the sale of Macoma and Mick in August 1928 and a letter subsequently received from Father Brophy.

Facts and figures about greyhound racing were obtained from various copies of the *Irish Coursing & Greyhound Racing Annual*; *Irish Greyhound Annual*; *Irish Greyhound Review*; *Greyhound Racing Encyclopaedia*; *Racing Post Greyhound Year*; *Sporting Life Greyhound Annual*; *Daily Mirror Greyhound Fact File*; *Who's Who in Greyhound Racing*; and *The NGRC Book of Greyhound Racing*. John Kearny's three books on the Tullamore district, especially *The Long Ridge*, were invaluable aids in outlining the historical background to Killeigh.

Details of Mick's brief excursion into the world of cinema were fleshed out by reference to the autobiographies of Michael Balcon (*Michael Balcon Presents...A Lifetime of Films*), Michael Powell (*A Life in Movies*), Evelyn Laye (*Boo To My Friends*), Bud Flanagan (*My Crazy Life*), and Jessie Matthews (*Over My Shoulder*). Patricia Warren's *British Film Studios* and Pam Cook's compendium of essays entitled *Gainsborough Studios* also proved invaluable in this regard.

Among the staff of numerous libraries I must thank, are especially those of University College Dublin; the National Railway Museum in York; the British Library, St Pancras; the Royal Archive, Windsor; the Lincolnshire Archive; the West Sussex Record Office in Chichester; the Offaly County Library in Tullamore, particularly Mary Larkin and Siobhan Butler; Chris Smith at the Norfolk Heritage Centre in Norwich;

and Mandy Holloway in the Zoological Department of the Natural History Museum, South Kensington. Katherine Dixon and Hilary Tanner (no relation) smoothed the way for me to view Mick's 1934 movie Wild Boy and attendant material at the British Film Institute; British Pathe Ltd dug out Mick's 1931 gazette feature for my perusal.

Last, but by no means least, I extend my thanks to the staff at the British Newspaper Library in Colindale who answered the incessant calls for copies of musty newspapers and dodgy microfilm. Among countless sources consulted, the following were particularly valuable: The Sporting Life; The Sporting Chronicle; The Grahound Daily Mirror (later The Grahound/Greyhound Evening Mirror and The Greyhound Mirror and Gazette); Greyhound Express; Greyhound Outlook; Greyhound Magazine; Irish Independent; The Irish News; Cork Examiner; Belfast Telegraph; Belfast Morning News; The Star; The Times; The Scotsman; Western Mail; Daily Mirror; Daily Mail; Daily Express; Daily Sketch; Daily Herald; Sunday Sportsman; Sunday Dispatch; Evening Standard; Evening News; Pictorial Weekly; Film Pictorial.

The sincerest thanks of all are reserved for those individuals who went out of their way to grant me personal interviews or assistance above and beyond that which any writer might reasonably expect. Several members of the Catholic Church in Ireland lent me assistance: Father John Stapleton, the current parish priest at Killeigh; Father John McEvoy of Carlow College; and Brother Linus Walker at the Bishop's House in Carlow. I am particularly indebted to Father Pat Ramsbottom, parish priest at Coolearagh, for kindly allowing me to make use of Monsignor Maurice Browne's unpublished manuscript Dogs and Men which records the circumstances surrounding the projected sale of Mick the Miller to Moses Rebenschied in 1927.

My research also benefited from interviews and conversations with several other denizens of the Emerald Isle: Michael Greene's children, Kathleen and Michael, told me tales of Mick and their father, in addition to unearthing the rarest of photographs to go with them; Frank and John Hill did likewise about their father James, and Frank took the time to provide me with a special recording of The Ballad of Mick the Miller, which he co-wrote with Danny Coughlin (former All-Ireland accordion champion and landlord of Killeigh's bar); Matt Bruton kindly put me in touch with Elizabeth Tobin who related memories of her uncle, Arthur Callanan; Michael and Adrian Horan answered a whole host of questions about their father; and Gerry McCarthy proved on more than one occasion that his reputation as the fount of all knowledge on matters pertaining to the Irish greyhound scene is no exaggeration.

On this side of the Irish Sea, I was fortunate to speak with three people who actually saw Mick the Miller race: Harry Rothbart (who has seen every English Derby); former trainer Jimmy Brennan; and Sidney Orton's son Clare, whose recollections of Mick and his father were particularly welcome; as were Norah McEllistrim's of her father. The doyen of greyhound vets, Paddy Sweeney MRCVS, patiently answered all my technical queries pertaining to whelping and distemper; Ian Stevens and his sister June reminisced at length about Arundel Kempton, a lifelong friend to their father Con Stevens, who was associated with the Wimbledon track as racing manager and director of racing for almost 50 years; Edward VIII's biographer Philip Ziegler helped unravel HRH's contentious whereabouts at the time of the 1931 Derby; Bob Rowe at Wimbledon and Emma Johns at the British Greyhound Racing Board fielded all my enquiries with good grace; and Jim Cremin at the Racing Post helped open a few doors. Finally, an immense debt of gratitude to Tony Smith at the National Greyhound Racing Club for not only taking the trouble to root out the scrapbooks and assorted memorabilia belonging to Mr and Mrs Arundel Kempton but also arranging for me to make copious use of such an unexpected treasure trove.

Posterity will show just how successfully I have moulded this material and these memories into a narrative worth reading. Any failure is mine, not the story's. My abiding hope is that I've somehow contrived to do justice to this most noble, magical and magnificent of animals: the peerless, the incomparable, the one and only Mick the Miller.

Michael Tanner
Sleaford, Lincolnshire. July, 2003

PROLOGUE

Life can be thrilling when you're 11 years of age. For my own part, back in 1958, not only had I just won a place at the local grammar school but I'd also acquired my first job.

My Uncle Bob lived close by my new school, in Littlemore on the southern edge of Oxford, and he had just given a home to yet another greyhound. Uncle Bob never seemed to be without a greyhound. He took in cast-offs from the Cowley track, five minutes round the corner, and ran them on the 'flappers'* at Swindon and High Wycombe. For such expeditions he needed transport: he had none. Cue my dad, who did in the form of an old 1937 Hillman. So, that got one of the Tanner family onto the team. 'What about the boy, then?'

After some head-scratching, it was agreed that, since I had reached the grand age of 11, I could be the new dog's kennel-boy. My duties were simplicity itself. One: sit in the back of the car keeping it quiet to and from the races. Two: stop off en route to school every morning to give it a walk round the block. Half-a-crown (two shillings and six-pence or 12½p in today's money) a week sounded good to me.

I was introduced to my charge and given a tutorial in the early-morning routine I was to adopt. Eddy – for that was the black-and-white beast's pet name – lived out back of Uncle Bob's council estate semi in the coal-shed which had been converted to meet his needs.

'Hold the end of his collar in your left hand and unlock the door with your right and as he pokes his head out, slip the collar underneath', explained Uncle Bob, 'and then grab it with your right hand and fasten it at the back of his neck.'

Now, my Uncle Bob was a lovely man, mild-mannered and on the small side (not much bigger than me I thought), so, when I watched him nimbly execute this procedure as effortlessly as if he was doing it in his sleep, my new responsibilities seemed money for old rope.

I turned up for my first morning's work resplendent in posh new school uniform – natty grey short trousers, garish pink blazer and cap

*Flappers is a racing term for tracks with poor facilities.

– looking a real toff. Taking Eddy's collar and the coal-hole key off the nail by the back door, I prepared to re-enact Uncle Bob's every move with equal dexterity.

As soon as the key went into the lock, I heard a noise like a combine harvester start up from within; all swirling straw and assorted banging. I edged the door ajar and bent low, my right hand gingerly poised to grab the end of the dangling collar and lasso Eddy's white head as it appeared. Perhaps Eddy picked up a whiff of my fear in his nostrils because he exited the coal-hole as if the traps had just opened on his last stab at greyhound immortality. His head and chest struck me like a runaway train and before I had got the collar under his neck, let alone around it, he was up on his hind legs with his front paws on my shoulders and his warm, wet tongue all over my face.

Fortunately for me, Eddy was a big softy. Company, not escape, had been his priority. Unfortunately for me, his affection left souvenirs on my beautiful new blazer that were richer and more odorous than mere mud. I was in deep trouble. My new school was going to be singularly unimpressed, and I could already feel my ears positively throbbing at the prospect of my mother's stinging rejoinder. My eyes were beginning to fill with tears as Uncle Bob was drawn from the kitchen by all the commotion. The situation was self evident. 'Don't worry, Michael, you'll soon get the hang of it,' Uncle Bob said reassuringly.

My humiliation at Eddy's paws was far from over, however. After a series of training runs on the school field, plans for the first betting coup were duly hatched. The chosen venue was High Wycombe, where every Saturday a farmer held decidedly unofficial races in one of his fields. The track was marked out with a length of baler twine (stretching from one end of the field to the other) which had a nasty habit of billowing in the breeze, thereby ensuring a tricky passage for any 'railler'; the hare was a rugby ball painted white onto which a powder-puff had been glued to act as an enticing tail. This 'lure' was attached to another length of twine and hauled up the track using distinctly Heath Robinson principles and apparatus: the twine was reeled onto a bicycle wheel positioned at the top of the field and powered by some furious hand-pedalling on the part of the farmer's son. Consequently, this particular hare tended to provide a quarry both lively and erratic enough to bamboozle even the wiliest coursing greyhound let alone the assorted collection of crocks and has-been trackers that Wycombe threw up.

However, there were other considerations of far weightier import. A couple of bookmakers always attended; and all races were 'graded' by the farmer. You did not need the intellect of Stephen Hawking to work out what Uncle Bob was up to. Even an 11-year-old rumbled the scam pretty quickly.

The first couple of Saturdays my dad would halt in some quiet spot after he had finally coaxed our old jalopy up the A40 to the summit of Stokenchurch Hill so that Uncle Bob could treat Eddy to a hearty snack and a bellyful of water. Suitably gorged, Eddy was thus guaranteed to perform with all the dash of a Saint Bernard climbing the Eiger – therefore demanding he be downgraded. Goodness knows how many others were perpetrating the same subterfuge every Saturday, but a high success rate was assured so long as the farmer knew the score and was able to get his money on the one dog in each race that was patently running beneath its true class yet which was actually primed to run for its life.

Came the day. No pause for canine elevenses on Stokenchurch Hill this Saturday; just the slow crawl up followed by the customary free-wheel down the other side when dad switched off the ignition: 'No point wasting petrol, son,' was always his motto. Eddy may have looked dead to the world as he lay slumped on the back seat alongside me with his head in my lap but we knew he was really a coiled spring on the very brink of wallet-filling action.

It goes without saying that a weighing machine was conspicuous by its absence at High Wycombe's finest dog track. Ditto kennels. There were no amenities, full stop. All competing dogs were confined to a holding area bounded – surprise, surprise – by yet another length of baler twine. 'Michael, you stay in here with Eddy,' says Uncle Bob, 'your dad and me are going up there.' He was pointing in the direction of the van parked near the winning post from which an enterprising publican sold bottles of beer. 'Now, whatever you do, look after him.'

This was the first occasion I had been entrusted with sole care of Eddy around other dogs. I began to grow anxious. I looked around me at this sea of brindle, fawn and black. Remarkably, it was surprisingly tranquil. The sound of silence was broken only by a chorus of panting and the occasional yawn. Obedience reigned. No need to worry, then?

Once the opening race got closer I took a tighter hold of Eddy. No way am I not going to 'look after him'. However, the instant those first six dogs left the boxes the atmosphere in the holding pen changed alarmingly. It was as if someone had flipped a switch. Every dog began howling and rearing and tugging at its leash. I held onto Eddy's collar for dear life.

The rugby ball suddenly appeared, zig-zagging its way up the field from one tuft of grass to another followed in similarly demented fashion by its six canine pursuers. Amid mounting panic, I gripped Eddy tighter and tighter. Big mistake. I should, of course, have been cutting him a little slack. As the racers scampered past us, he went up on his hind legs and with a serpentine wiggle of his neck, slipped his head out of the taut noose I was kindly providing for him so misguidedly. All of a sudden I'm left looking down at an empty collar. And there are now seven dogs in the race because Eddy has sped away to join in the fun.

The finish line was too distant for me to see or hear the reactions of my dad and Uncle Bob as a familiar black-and-white shape crossed the line in playful pursuit of its new pals, but if they did not splutter something unprintable into their beer I'd be flabbergasted. At least the pair of them had not 'done their money', but weeks of Machiavellian scheming had gone up in smoke thanks to their gormless kennel-boy. Nor was the sight of the said cretin running toward them waving collar and lead and jabbering incomprehensibly exactly calculated to curry favour. I managed to sway beyond dad's swinging right palm – but there was still Uncle Bob's ire to contend with.

'Don't you fret, Michael,' he said with that characteristic good grace of his which in the prevailing circumstances must have been terribly difficult to summon up. 'This dog will make it all worthwhile, you wait and see. You mark my words, this dog is going to be the next Mick the Miller.'

I hadn't a clue who this Mick the Miller was but I was damn well going to find out. He had a lot to answer for. What I found out opened up a whole new world.

THE BALLAD OF MICK THE MILLER

Mick the Miller, this famous dog, his name it is renowned;
He is the most famous dog of all the greyhounds.
He was owned by Father Brophy, in his kennels beside the mill-race,
In this lovely village of Killeigh, you could pick no better place.

Let's sing the praises of this dog,
Sing them low and high.
Let's give three cheers to good old Mick
As he goes flying by!

Father Brophy brought Mick to England, 1929,
To enter him for the Derby, that great race of all times.
Mick ran a blinder, the best ever seen in time,
Left all the other wonder dogs beaten far behind.

Let's sing the praises of this dog,
Sing them low and high.
Let's give three cheers to good old Mick
As he goes flying by!

While the Killeigh folk were overjoyed when they heard
of Mick's great win;
They went and told each other that a party would begin.
They all assembled on the green and a bonfire they did light,
They gave a twilight procession and a welcome home that night.

Let's sing the praises of this dog,
Sing them low and high.
Let's give three cheers to good old Mick
As he goes flying by!

This wonder dog ran again, winning the great St Leger;
He ran so well, you could almost tell, his name would live forever.
Then one day he passed away, and to keep his name a treasure,
Mick was preserved by a great expert so he would last forever.

Let's sing the praises of this dog,
Sing them low and high.
Let's give three cheers to good old Mick
As he goes flying by!

Frank Hill

CHAPTER ONE
CONCEIVED IN THUNDER

'James, will you give us all a rest from that infernal mouth organ and go down to the pub and fetch a bottle of whiskey.'

'Certainly, Father. Straight away, Father.'

James Hill thrust the offending instrument in his trouser pocket and, running a nervous hand through his shock of jet-black hair, hurriedly made his way through the kitchen of Millbrook House and out into the backyard.

You definitely didn't want to get on the Father's wrong side, for he could be the crossest priest you ever saw. Why, wasn't it said round the village that he once punched a parishioner on the arm in a fit of temper, and didn't the unfortunate man lose the use of it? These were volatile times and the times were full of volatile people.

Hill was accustomed to this sort of request when his employer, Father Martin Brophy, was hosting what he termed 'a big dinner'. To be sure, the curate in County Offaly parish of Killeigh boasted a deserved reputation for infinite philanthropy when it came to replenishing the glasses of his guests with alcoholic beverage! As a rule, Hill's duties at the priest's grand residence only extended to overseeing the livestock; at other times you'd find him up on the bog digging the peat which he'd dry and then make a few bob selling from the back of a donkey-cart on the streets of Tullamore. But on occasions like this he would stay on at Millbrook House into the evening to lend the housekeeper a hand. After all, he'd only recently wed his sweetheart, Mary Kelly, and every penny was doubly welcome. Each and every job counted in the Ireland of 1925.

Tonight's 'big dinner' was a celebration in honour of Father Brophy's good friend and counterpart in the nearby parish of Clonbullogue, Father Michael Kennedy, who had just been elevated to the position of parish priest at Myshall. The local tipple, Tullamore Dew, would be flowing tonight all right, thought Hill, as he marched the half a mile or so down the lane into the village with the brisk, ground-devouring gait of the First World War combatant he had once been.

Hill turned up the collar of his jacket to combat the cold autumn rain that was scudding across the fields into his face. Jaysus, wouldn't this be a grand place to live if it didn't rain every other day? The stark and imposing crenellated tower of St Patrick's Church loomed up on Hill's right as he quickened his step toward his destination that lay dead ahead, overlooking the village green. He entered Corcoran's pub and strode purposefully up to the bar.

'A bottle of Tullamore Dew, if you please,' said Hill, instantly causing the odd eyebrow to rise among those who knew him to prefer a night in with a good book to a night out on the drink. 'No, best make that two bottles. Father Kennedy's coming over from Clonbullogue and they'll be after talking greyhounds well into the night. The Father will only be sending me down again for another bottle. I may as well get it in advance and save myself another journey! Who in their right mind wants to be out on a night like this?'

After lodging a whiskey bottle securely into each of his jacket pockets, Hill began to retrace his steps back to Millbrook House. The gathering gloom through which he trudged seemed to exemplify the brooding forces presently menacing his homeland. It was seven years since 'the war to end all wars', in which he had volunteered to fight (illegally and underage) for king and country with the Royal Dublin Fusiliers as a 16-year-old, was brought to a close.

Those intervening seven years had not been kind to Ireland. Rebellion and civil war had reduced it to a troubled isle. Even though he had willingly signed-up to fight for his King (promptly 'bought out' by his sister, the gung-ho youngster merely rejoined and saw active service with the Royal Artillery in the Middle East), Hill was nonetheless sympathetic to the Republican cause: indeed, he would in time become secretary of the local branch of the Fianna Fail party that espoused Republicanism. But he had seen enough of his countrymen die in the Great War (some 40,000 Catholic Irishmen gave their lives for the Empire) to want to get involved in further conflagration.

"Ah, away with such negative thoughts!" He lifted his tempo and began whistling *'Show me the way to go home'*, one of the year's most popular tunes. Then, remembering what he'd read lately about some New York professor saying that whistling was 'a sign of a vacant mind', he switched to quietly singing the words instead.

On the surface, Killeigh was an unremarkable village in an unremarkable part of Ireland. Delve a mite deeper, however, and that peculiarly Celtic tapestry of legend, myth and history could be found etched on every rock, building and tombstone in the area.

County Offaly had escaped relatively lightly from not only the bloody struggle for independence from Britain between 1916 and 1921 but also those nine painful months following the creation of the Irish Free State in 1922 when Irishmen spilt the blood of fellow Irishmen. Even so, the tide of national events had not bypassed Offaly completely: a strategic location slap-bang in the Irish heartland saw to that. 'Top brass', like Michael Collins, frequently passed through during the War of Independence and were always requesting the necessary protection to ensure safe passage.

Communications for everybody else were not so reliable or safe, since Republican units made a habit of blowing bridges and blocking roads in pursuit of the cause. In April 1920 one such unit went further and attacked Killeigh's Royal Irish Constabulary (RIC) barracks. Finding it deserted but for Sergeant Small's wife and children, they evicted the terrified family and burned the building to the ground. Two years later, during the Civil War, members of Offaly's Number 1 Brigade of the IRA ambushed a party of Free State soldiers at Scrub Hill, just north of Killeigh, as it returned to Tullamore after acting as a guard of honour at the funeral in the village of Private Joseph Lawlor.

Then there were the 'Black and Tans'. This notorious band of special constables – a collection of mainly ex-British servicemen hired in 1920 at a rate of ten shillings (50p) a day to assist the beleaguered RIC – were reviled throughout the country for their indiscriminate brutality and, thus, were constantly in danger of ambush wherever they presented themselves. Killeigh's neighbouring village of Geashill, for example, gave the Black and Tans a very hot reception.

The streets of Tullamore, Offaly's county town lying some five miles to the north of Killeigh, were often no safer. In April 1920 British troops shot and killed Matthew Kane off Church Road. Six months later, Republicans exacted some kind of retribution by gunning down Sergeant Henry Cronin of the RIC on his own doorstep, his wife cradling the policeman's head as he lay dying.

Killeigh's final brush with death came in the very last month of the Civil War, May 1923, when Free State troopers under Lieutenant Jack Drum searching Corcoran's for 'Irregulars' (supporters of Eamon de Valera's Republican faction) were fired on from the yard. Drum was shot in an arm, which had to be amputated.

The creation of the Free State had scarcely lifted the ever-present threat of violence.

Even now, in late 1925, despite an amnesty being declared for all convicted in connection with the Civil War, no Irishman could assert with any degree of confidence that the last drop of Irish blood had finally been shed. On 11 July 1927, for instance, James Hill picked up a copy of the Offaly Independent to read that no less a personage than the Vice-President of the Irish Free State, Kevin O'Higgins, had been assassinated the previous morning after attending church in a Dublin suburb. Struck by shots fired from a waiting car, the minister slumped to the ground, whereupon more gunmen pushed through the gathering crowd to pump his body full of bullets as the he lay dying on the street. In one fell swoop, talk of a renewed civil war was on everyone's lips.

People like Hill needed no degree in history in order to appreciate the circumstances that had brought Ireland to the very brink. It was common knowledge that the sore that was Ireland's unrest and discontent had been a long time weeping. County Offaly, for instance, had been a hot-bed of political intrigue and insurrection for centuries and had only recently regained its historic name after existing for over 350 years as King's County thanks to English colonisation in the 16th century.

Things were not always so turbulent. The settlement of Killeigh itself was a religious foundation, established in around 520ad by Saint Senchall, a direct descendant of Cahir More, High King of all Ireland. Killeigh's very own patron saint was the first man to be baptised by Saint Patrick and chose to build his abbey on low-lying ground between two ridges, which at least rescues the village from the physical monotony characteristic to most hereabouts. However, the Monettia Bog to the south and, further to the east, the vast expanses of the Bog of Allen, did nothing to lessen the area's general bleakness and sense of isolation, which only served to add further mystery to what was a landscape already steeped in the supernatural.

Another legendary name familiar to Hill was that belonging to Saint Senchall's kinfolk, the O'Connor Faly, whose members occupied many a plot in Killeigh's graveyard. This warrior clan ruled the ancient territory encompassing not only the county which carried its name but also Laois (traditionally spelt Laoighis) and Kildare throughout the lengthy period when the only English-speakers in Ireland were within a few miles of Dublin, the region known as 'The Pale'. The O'Connors held sway until their fortress at nearby Daingean was overwhelmed by Henry VIII's troops in 1537, resulting in several of them losing their heads and every one of Killeigh's religious houses being reduced to the assorted ruins visible today.

In 1599 the O'Connors were humiliated in battle one last time and driven into the bog-lands. In company with the rest of the country, central Ireland slowly slipped beneath a rising tide of simmering resentment and barely repressed hostility. With its lands lorded over by English aristocrats and its laws administered by English civil servants, Ireland's somewhat retarded national psyche found no more vivid expression than in the tale of the Dublin merchant who, while his English cousins were lining their pockets with the products of an increasingly urban and commercial society, went into business selling second-hand poems.

Life in the Irish countryside was never less than a struggle. Bog-fires that periodically destroyed both crops and homes were bad enough, but the potato famine of the 1840s proved the last straw, causing the death of possibly a million people and the dispersal to other countries of two million more. The populace stared into an abyss of despair. According to Killeigh's parish priest of the time, 'the general condition of the poorer classes is much deteriorated since 1815,' with most of the 262 inhabitants living in squalor. Some of the tiny, sod-constructed, 5-feet high and two-roomed cabins housed two families; adult males could only expect to find work for six months of the year if they were lucky; and children were being abandoned as the parents left in search of a better life. As emigration began to gather momentum, the village of Killeigh, like its neighbours, began to die. Its population fell to 87 by 1871 and had only just scraped back into three figures at the dawn of the 20th century.

The seeds of discontent were being well watered once more. It was only a matter of time before they grew into open rebellion. In 1914 Geashill's curate, Father Thomas Burbage, was moved sufficiently by the plight of his parishioners to pen the following verse:

> *We have to get the land*
> *Where the bullocks now do stand,*
> *And we never will give up the fight*
> *Until we get the land.*
> *So now my boys get ready,*
> *Have your hazel cut and dry,*
> *The time is fast approaching*
> *When we'll win our cause or die.*

That November, 24 agitators were arrested after shots were fired at a local demonstration, as a result of which several received prison sentences with hard labour. Ireland was rumbling toward a fateful period of self-destruction. Not lightly did the great poet WB Yeats liken the rocky path to nationhood as 'a terrible beauty is born'.

Thus did the 1920s mature into volatile times. And yet, although many a priest became actively embroiled in the turmoil that tore Ireland apart (Father Burbage, for example, was arrested in January 1921 and interned on Spike Island in Cork Harbour for subversive activity), surprisingly no finger of suspicion was ever pointed at one member of the Offaly clergy who seemed congenitally unable to sit on a fence, namely Father Martin Brophy.

Father Brophy hailed from a clerical family in Shankill, Paulstown, in County Kilkenny, that provided the Church with at least four other recruits. He was appointed to Killeigh in 1923 at the age of 47, having previously served as curate at Mountmellick (1901), Portarlington (1902), Abbeyleix (1908) and Baltinglass (1914). Curates enjoyed far greater latitude than their immediate superiors, the parish priests, who were bogged down with all manner of routine chores and commitments. Killeigh's curate exploited this privilege to the ultimate degree. He revelled in the freedom resulting from the customary provision of accommodation quite separate from that of the parish priest. While Father William Phelan lived in the village proper, his curate resided at Millbrook House, in splendid and convenient isolation outside the village, just off the lane leading up to Graigue.

It was not long before James Hill – and anybody else in Killeigh who had their eyes and ears even half-open – detected what made the new curate tick. Father Brophy not only bore a strong silver-haired, facial resemblance to Wilfrid Hyde White (though somewhat better nourished) but also shared the English actor's penchant for a bet. The Father was an inveterate gambler. He loved his sport, but was never happier than when he could wager on its outcome. Every August Bank Holiday, hundreds of people would flock from far and wide to attend the Killeigh Sports. All were eager to eat, drink and be merry to the music of the Clonaslee Pipe Band and while demonstrating their allegiance to the standard bearers of Geashill, Killurin, Tullamore or wherever throughout the afternoon's programme of athletic events, especially the running and cycling, which was held round the circular track on Fair Green. And who is it that stands centre stage for the photographer amid this throng? None other than the unmistakable figure of Father Martin Brophy wearing his trademark black Fedora, rather than his immediate superior, the parish priest William Phelan.

It would be a surprising if the odd bet was not being struck on the outcome of the blue-riband events, such as the cycling in which Billy Colton was invariably a 'sure thing' for the Talbot Cup – and an even greater shock to the system if Father Brophy had not availed himself at a decent price. It was frowned upon for any member of the clergy to become involved in sports other than those of the Gaelic Athletic Association, but Father Brophy somehow managed to drive a coach and horses through any restrictions imposed by canon law. His passions lay elsewhere, and the licence afforded by his junior status and separate roof enabled him to pursue them with a vengeance.

Millbrook House card schools, for one, quickly became the stuff of local legend. And members of his flock were just as likely to spot him at Punchestown Races as at Saint Patrick's Church. Not within the confines of the racecourse, naturally, but, in company with several like-minded brethren, atop 'Priests Hill' which overlooked the track. Or he could as likes be found at Mullingar and Maryborough 'following the flags' in the coursing field, that historic battleground where two greyhounds demonstrate their speed, agility and cunning in pursuit of the hare. Yes, Father Brophy loved his greyhounds. So much so that despite the Church's censorial attitude toward direct involvement in gambling sports he couldn't resist the lure of ownership and, while serving in Baltinglass in 1917, he had registered himself with the Coursing Club as the owner of the dog Crom Abu.

Crom Abu was, in one sense, the worst thing that could have happened to Father Brophy. The black son of Topsman proved to be a gold mine, winning 16-dog stakes at Baltinglass and Slyguff in his first coursing campaign of 1917-18. The priest was smitten. He was the proud possessor of his very own punting vehicle. Flushed by this instant success, he bought another dog, An Toglac; followed by three bitches from a July 1921 litter bred by Kiltegan's PM Kelly. The trio, who were named Roseen Breac, Slan Availle and Na Boc Lei, were the outcome of a mating between the ultra-game Let 'im Out and Talbotstown III.

Three of Crom Abu's successors were disappointing but Na Boc Lei became the cleric's pride and joy, belying her Gaelic name, which roughly translates as 'Ignore her' or 'Don't bother with her'. Shortly after Father Brophy took up residence at Millbrook House in 1923, the bitch showed she possessed more than the just the white-and-brindle markings of her illustrious sire by winning the 16-dog Portlaoghise Stakes at Maryborough on 23 November.

Such was Father Brophy's passionate involvement with the sport of coursing – its track racing cousin would not commence in Ireland until 1927 – that he now took steps to conceal it. The birth of the Irish Free State had also seen the creation of a separate Irish Coursing Club, and in the resultant first volume of the *Irish Stud Book* Father Brophy chose to re-register himself under the pseudonym of 'Mr B Murphy', even though a handful of other priests continued to own and race in their own names.

Na Boc Lei's litter brother Kill 'im Dead had also demonstrated a fair amount of ability that same season of 1923-24, dividing stakes at Harristown and Celbridge and reaching the final of the Leahy Challenge Cup at North Kildare and the Irish Purse at the prestigious Irish Cup meeting at Clounanna before running up (losing) in both. Now seemed the opportune moment for Father Brophy to cash in on the success of the siblings by breeding from his prized bitch.

For her first consort Father Brophy chose Jedderfield, who stood at a fee of seven guineas up the road in Kildare, and in April 1924 Na Boc Lei whelped a litter of five pups. One was named Mr Miller, establishing the letter 'M' and the obvious reference to his 'milling' abode, which was henceforth to become a recurring theme in Father Brophy's choice of names – whether he bred them or not – right up until he finally quit the sport. The following summer, for example, a pup acquired from Joseph Gowing of Philipstown was christened Musty Miller (he developed into a useful dog, dividing one stake in 1928 and winning two others, notably the all-aged Westmeath United Stakes at Killucan); three purchases in 1929 were christened Mighty Miller, Musical Miller and Miller's Maiden, and as late as 1931 he registered Miller's Question.

There was one other, more oblique, reason for the adoption of the 'Miller' reference. Na Boc Lei's grandam, the indelicately named Bag o'Slack, was by Merry Miller II; she traced to the unbeaten Coolmassie, the dual Waterloo Cup-winning bitch of 1877-78, who was subsequently acquired by a Mr HG Miller. Coolmassie bred six litters, one of which contained Posada who turned out to be Bag o'Slack's fifth dam.

Clearly, Na Boc Lei deserved the best mates Father Brophy's pocket could run to. He intended to discuss the list of possible suitors which he had drawn up for her 1926 mating with Father Michael Kennedy over this celebration dinner. They were enthralled by the findings of the Augustinian friar Gregor Mendel whose experiments in the mid-19th century with peas, and later bees, in his monastery garden at Brno in Moravia had revolutionised thinking about the laws of heredity. Both men pored over the intricacies of breeding and the significance of some bloodlines over others, and the walls of Millbrook's study were dotted with charts showing the lineage of both outstanding greyhounds and outstanding racehorses.

The two Fathers had a picture in their mind's eye of the kind of dog that would fit the bill. After all, had not the 'Propeteis of a goode Grehound' been identified as long ago as 1481? In *The Boke of St Albans,* attributed to Dame Julia Berners and one of the earliest printed works, the good prioress of the nunnery of Sopwell listed the desired traits as follows:

> *Heded like a Snake.*
> *And necked like a Drake.*
> *Foted like a Kat.*
> *Tayld like a Rat.*
> *Syded lyke a Teme.*
> *Chyned like a Beme.*

The nimbleness of foot for the chase; those flat sides carrying not an ounce of superfluous flesh; a sinuous neck adept at striking its prey. But, how did one set about realising this paragon of swiftness and agility in flesh and blood?

As the debris of a typical Millbrook House 'big dinner' was gradually cleared away, the two friends began to dominate the post-prandial conversation, holding forth once more on the subject of 'Mendelism', the theories of the Austrian monk Gregor Mendel, with which they were much taken. Might not it be possible to replicate Mendel's famous triumph of selective breeding that created a more productive strain of honeybee in the rest of the animal world. With greyhounds, for instance?

The discussion ebbed back and forth. The pros and cons of this bloodline and that bloodline were each analysed and debated. Was in-breeding and line-breeding to common ancestors in order to concentrate desired qualities preferable to introducing new blood via an out-cross, for instance? 'In-breed to strength but out-cross from weakness', was the golden rule to follow.

In this regard, Father Brophy craved nothing less than any other breeder. That potent fusion of speed, stamina and pluck was the ultimate brew. Any two of these three precious qualities might just suffice and provide the ingredients for a successful career. But, prized above all, reasoned the two priests, was pluck. They could ill-afford to breed back to a 'soft' one, the kind of flagrant 'chucker' who quits when the going gets tough. The courageous dog will prevail, they insisted, where the faster coward succumbs. For God surely hates a coward. Yes, courage was the holy grail they must seek.

The host brought the discussion to a close. 'Michael,' he said, 'we could go round the houses discussing this till the sun comes up! It boils down to two things. One: like begets like. My bitch was as honest and true in the field as the day is long and she possessed wonderful working powers. Plus, they say courage comes from the dam's side. So we can always be sure of that from Na Boc Lei. Wasn't her father Let 'im Out the bravest of the brave? Did he not contest the finals of the Cork, Tipperary and Irish Cups all in the same year!'

'Yes, Martin, for sure, he possessed the heart of a lion.'

'And wouldn't you agree that nothing succeeds like success? Na Boc Lei traces back in direct line on her dam's side to no less than Coomassie, who was only a scrawny little thing and yet she was the unbeaten winner of two Waterloo Cups!'

'She was a game bitch, and no mistake.'

'So, Michael, I'm left thinking that I'm looking for speed to complement that family courage.'

Father Brophy ran his finger down the list of potential mates he had written out on a piece of paper. His eyes fixed on one name. Turning to the copy of the *Irish Greyhound Stud Book* resting at his elbow, he flicked through its contents until he found the page he was looking for, and pushed it across the table toward his guest.

'Michael, this is the one. Believe me, this is the dog to bring the best out of Na Boc Lei.'

Kennedy picked up the book and read out aloud the advertisement his friend was indicating:

'Glorious Event, a brindle dog of 76lb, whelped June 1918, winner and divider of several stakes, unluckily beaten in the semi final of the Midland Cup but the winner of the All-Ireland Cup 192, run as a substitute for the Irish Cup. The glorious son of the mighty hawk – Osprey Hawk (now dead), himself winner of the Irish Cup in 1919 and a direct descendent of the legendary Master McGrath, three times winner of the Waterloo Cup. A beautifully-framed dog with the best of legs and feet and a splendid constitution, considered the fastest, cleverest and gamest dog in Ireland. Sire in his first season of the champion puppy Moon Queen and eight others (from just 16 puppies to run) who won or divided 14 stakes, a record for a Stud Dog in his first season. Fee eight guineas. Apply James Conroy, The Kennels, Maryborough.'

'Well, Michael, what do you think? Pretty impressive, eh? I've studied the pedigree this mating would give at great length. As well as that bottom line tracing to Coomassie, there would be no fewer than 22 contributions – 22 mind! – from Master McGrath. Now, if THAT isn't a formula for success breeding success, I don't know of one. And we'll be cutting our coat according to our cloth with Glorious Event standing just down the road. So, is Glorious Event the dog for Na Boc Lei or not?'

A rhetorical question if ever there was one. His friend was in full flow. It was no time for disagreement or prevarication. 'Yes, Martin, yes. Glorious Event will suit Na Boc Lei nicely.'

'Capital!' exclaimed the Father, hands thumping the table in delight. 'We'll drink to it then.'

The host got to his feet. 'Here's to the union of Na Boc Lei and Glorious Event! May the gods look kindly on their offspring!'

The glasses tinkled into action around him.

'Who knows, perhaps they'll bless me with a dog to match Sceolan or Doilin or even Coinn Iotair!' he added in pointed reference to the fabled hounds of Irish legend.

'And before I sit down, I've one further thought. Let's not forget to honour that other individual without whom there'd be no sport at all!'

Raising his half-empty tumbler in salute, Father Brophy began to intone a poetic homage familiar to all around his table:

> 'When coursing men gather,
> The speech is of hounds.
> And I myself would like to see
> A long tail fly as swift
> As a falling star across the midnight sky.
> But then I think of the guy who leads the outfit
> And should the laurels wear,
> The little gentleman in brown,
> The gallant Irish hare!'

To a chorus of 'hear-hears', the gathering drank to the health of the 'gallant Irish hare'.

'Now,' said Father Brophy in the act of pushing back his chair, 'I'll get some more whiskey! And let's play some cards!'

The curate's head peered round the dining room door. This was the moment Hill had been anticipating.

'James, will you go again to the pub for another bottle!'

'I have it here, Father,' answered the perspicacious Hill triumphantly.

'Good thinking, James!'

The priest took the bottle and returned to his guests. Hill heard the conversation once more rise to a concerted babble. It was going to be a long night.

'Tell me, Martin,' he could just make out someone asking above the din, 'how is it that two brothers, two clerics, can be so different to each other? Your brother Larry is such a devout and reserved man, while you're so outgoing and into everything. It's extraordinary. How are you so different?'

'Well, I really don't know, but, for what it's worth, I'll tell you what my mother often told me. She said Larry was conceived during a holy Mission – and I was conceived during a thunderstorm!'

Truly, Na Boc Lei's next litter would be born under a mystical sign, her pups touched by thunder. And one of their number the gods would dip in magic dust.

CHAPTER 2
'YOU'RE A RIGHT MILLER!'

The pensive-looking figure paced up and down the cobbles with the slightly manic air of a condemned man awaiting his execution. All of a sudden he stopped. Then he began again, only this time it was a circle he traced, albeit demonstrating just the same combination of anxiety and energy.

'Mick! Will you go easy, now!', called Father Brophy through the kitchen door that lay ajar in the oppressive heat of a late June afternoon. 'You'll wear the leather off those boots! She'll whelp when she's ready.' Then, with a resigned shake of the head, he added: 'You're a right "miller" of a boy, and no mistake!'

'Milling' has always been associated with a never-say-die, all-action style of fighting (and still is in the Parachute Regiment of the British army) but to refer to anyone or anything as 'a miller' in these parts of Ireland was more a sign of admiration or respect or endearment – occasionally even all three. 'A miller of a dog or hare' in the coursing field was a game animal; 'the miller of a player' on the hurling field was one worth watching, a non-stop performer, one always milling around.

This particular exponent of perpetual motion was Michael Greene, whose responsibility it was to look after the curate's greyhounds. Tullamore born and bred, Greene had worked with dogs for most of his 26 years. Short of stature and quiet of personality, the tousle-haired Greene came to life most when in the company of his beloved dogs. Quite the ideal man to graft the requisite day-to-day care and expertise onto the priest's idealism and frequent flights of fancy. It was he who had escorted Na Boc Lei to her date with Glorious Event back in the last week of April 1926.

Greene had driven the 20 miles to Maryborough (not yet restored to its original Irish name of Port Laoise) in his employer's Ford, with Na Boc Lei stretched out contentedly along the back seat. Lately she had been living the life of Riley; taking next to no exercise for a dog once accustomed to precisely the opposite, while tucking-in to a hearty diet of meat, vegetables and unlimited supplies of fresh milk. She had come into season ten days ago. On arrival at the kennels, Greene took Na Boc Lei for a short stroll, and once he was sure she had emptied her bladder, he muzzled her in readiness for the mating. Glorious Event knew his job. Greene held Na Boc Lei firmly at her head with his right hand while running his left along her back and applying a little pressure at the base of her tail. The tail rose and twitched to one side. Na Boc Lei was ready and willing to receive her mate. The 'tie' lasted for a minute or two. A second service was deemed unnecessary. Mission accomplished. After allowing Na Boc Lei a few hours rest, Greene chauffeured his charge back home to Killeigh.

The journey presented Greene with the chance to contemplate the litter this liaison might bring. It was easy, he thought, to become bogged-down in all this pedigree mumbo-jumbo. One morning, for instance, the Father had laid out on the kitchen table a large sheet of paper on which a five-generation pedigree of the new litter was neatly written out in capital letters. Now how complicated was that? Surely, most of the dogs on that paper were never going to influence the outcome of this mating?

Some of the names meant absolutely nothing to Greene. However, he could recite chapter and verse the exploits of the immediate ancestry: Glorious Event victorious in the

All-Ireland Cup, the 1921 substitute for the Irish Cup cancelled owing to 'The Troubles'; and his sire, Osprey Hawk, winner of the 1918 Tipperary Cup and 1919 Irish Cup; while the recent death of Na Boc Lei's sire Let 'im Out revived memories of his gallant failure in the Irish, Cork and Tipperary Cups of 1918. Greene had heard the stories of how this dog had caught rabbits for a living before he ever saw a coursing field, yet he still possessed the unbridled enthusiasm to collect the scalps at one time or another of dogs like Osprey Hawk and Holgarth, who had denied him the Irish Cup victory he so richly deserved. His obituary in the *Irish Greyhound Stud Book* made the pertinent assertion that, 'through his bitches, the great qualities the old champion possessed will be transmitted and be of great account in future pedigrees.'

The more distant elements of the pedigree were much less familiar to Greene. But a couple of things had lodged in his mind.

The Father had pointed out one name which appeared in the ancestry of both Na Boc Lei and Glorious Event; Royal Jessie, a black and white bitch whelped in 1904 who traced back through Posada to the legendary Coomassie. You see, Father Brophy had said, she was not only the dam of Bag o'Slack but also the mother of Royal Tim, the sire of Glorious Event's grandam Royal Leily. Therefore the new litter, stressed the Father, will be inbred to Royal Jessie.

'That doubling-up of Coomassie "blood" might prove significant. The female input is always more important than the sire. Do you see, Michael?' Greene's instinctive nod denoted more deference than conviction.

Then he'd watched as his employer ran a finger down the 32 names on the right-hand side of the page that comprised the fifth generation: 22 of these 32 animals, he said, contained the mighty Master McGrath in their pedigrees. The English legend Coomassie *and* the Irish legend Master McGrath in your family tree was some kind of inheritance to savour.

Just like Let 'im Out, Coomassie initially worked as a rabbit dog before running her first course at Beckhampton in October 1876. This tiny 42-44lb fawn and white bitch was never beaten, and but for sustaining a broken leg in a trial would quite probably have completed a hat-trick of Waterloo Cups in 1879. The fifth litter she produced for HG Miller (that of 1884 by Peter) included the red bitch Posada (the only winner in the litter) who became the fourth dam of Royal Jessie, and therefore the seventh dam of Na Boc Lei.

Master McGrath was the most famous greyhound of them all. A black and white dog (ticked with white over his back 'as if a shower of hail had fallen on him') only 10lb heavier than Coomassie at 54lb, he made up for any lack of substance with immense heart. And in more senses than one, because his heart was found to be twice the size of an average dog and more than that of the average man! 'Dixie', as he was known, lost only one course out of 39, when during a frosty 1870 Waterloo Cup he jumped into the River Alt and got trapped momentarily beneath the ice. He returned to Altcar 12 months later to add a third Waterloo Cup to those secured in 1868 and 1869, and according to the *Liverpool Post* he looked 'as if he were supercharged'. Such was his fame that Queen Victoria requested he be taken to Windsor Castle, and a cheering guard of Eton schoolboys lined his route from the station. 'All the family greeted the dog and were pleased to pat him,' recorded the Queen in her daily diary, 'I gather he is the most famous dog of all time.'

Master McGrath had relatively little opportunity to pass on his outstanding genes because after just nine months at stud he caught pneumonia, dying on Christmas Eve 1871. 'All Ireland went into mourning as the bells tolled,' wrote a contemporary correspondent; a memorial was erected in his honour adorned the Irish sixpenny-bit. Master McGrath's memorial was raised in the grounds of Colligan Lodge, his birthplace in County Wexford – but was subsequently moved to the crossroads at Ballymacmague.

So, mused Greene, as Killeigh at last came into view, this union could indeed turn out to be a marriage made in heaven.

All that was a good nine weeks back. Today, Tuesday 29 June, Greene needed no advice from 'His Master's Voice' on the subject of an impending whelping. Na Boc Lei's 63-day gestation period was up and he recognised full well the signs of a bitch on the verge of giving birth. She had been restless all day, constantly tearing and shredding her paper bedding, and had not touched her feed. For some time she had been panting. And just now he'd noticed the onset of a slight vaginal discharge.

Greene stole one last look inside the former coach-house he'd especially converted to cater for every need of the expectant mother and her new litter. All possible sources of draught had been sealed off and the floor covered with plenty of loose straw. In one corner, some 6 inches off the ground, Greene had constructed a wide bench from strips of wood, being careful to leave gaps in between, which eased the passage of any droppings onto the floor. He'd placed plenty of old newspaper over the bench ready for the whelping. Once Na Boc Lei had completed her task, the paper would be burned and replaced with some straw-filled sacks and an old mattress Greene had snaffled to provide additional comfort for mother and offspring. Too much paper posed potential problems: new-born pups had been known to hurt themselves slithering about on a surface of soiled paper or, worse still, even become so tangled-up in the wet strands they strangled themselves

Na Boc Lei was beginning to strain. This, Greene knew, could go on for anything up to two hours or so. He slipped on her collar and leash. A gentle walk to relieve herself (she'd also benefited from a laxative some days beforehand) would help matters progress. Then it would be up to her. The bitch would be left alone to complete nature's work. A short walk round the yard had the desired effect. He ushered her back toward the bench. Taking a cloth from a bucket of warm water, he cleaned her teats one last time and, after giving her one final fond stroke down the neck, turned and closed the door behind him.

Greene looked at his watch. It was now past 6 o'clock. Thankfully, the summer sun had begun to lose much of its power. The first pup, Greene reckoned, ought to be on its way in around three hours.

Greene maintained a constant vigil, albeit taking great pains not to disturb the mother-to-be. She didn't need his help: nature made the best midwife. Every now and again he'd interrupt his aimless to-ing and fro-ing to steal a peep through the coach-house window. At last he was able to distinguish the outline of a new-born pup. Then another. And another. The speed of delivery suggested Na Boc Lei was in the process of whelping a decent-sized litter.

When Na Boc Lei had finally ceased straining and pushing, Greene gently eased open the door and tiptoed toward the bitch. She was already licking, cleaning and drying the small bundles of wriggling, whimpering new-born life. Greene's eyes took a slow, deliberate census. There were ten of them, an above average litter and Na Boc Lei's biggest, though some way short of the 16 that some bitches had been known to produce.

One of the whelps, a brindle with a little white patch on his chest like a penguin's waistcoat, seemed slightly smaller than the others. It was not unknown for the punier whelps in a large litter to be put down at birth; that way, the limited supply of mother's milk could be directed toward fewer, more promising, mouths. Nor did the colour of his coat exactly boost his chances of survival. Once upon a time, the brindle coat – a mixture of fawn, black, red and white – was so distrusted by coursers that whelps of that hue were frequently destroyed. On the other hand, he did boast a proportionately longish body which grey-hound folklore insisted was a sure sign of future swiftness. The key question, however, was whether he'd live long enough to test the hypothesis.

Greene gently washed Na Boc Lei's hindquarters where she lay, before going off into the house to give his employer the news. He returned with a bowl of warm milk fortified with beaten egg to replenish Na Boc Lei's strength. Then he left her alone to nurse her family and to get some sleep whenever she could.

Apart from briefly acquainting himself with the litter, there was next to nothing Father Brophy could do for either whelps or mother. It was essential that the pups became accustomed to humans, but that rapport was best established with one person only. That person was Michael Greene.

He was soon able to identify each and every one of the ten. The litter was evenly divided. The five bitches comprised one brindle and white (the dominant colour always listed first), one red and fawn, one fawn and two brindles; the five dogs comprised two white and fawn, one fawn and red, one white and brindle... and the single brindle who sported a white tip to his tail and that curious white waistcoat very reminiscent of his father, Glorious Event.

There was little for Greene to concern himself for a week or so. The pups would then begin to open their eyes and he'd need to clip the toenails of their forefeet to stop them scratching their mother's teats when suckling. But ten mouths were a lot for Na Boc Lei to feed and there was bound to be slim pickings for some of the whelps. Dispersal was the obvious solution, particularly as it also counteracted total loss from one outbreak of disease. Thus, most of them were eventually billeted with friends of Father Brophy (Miss Nevins, Pat Brady, the Yarrs and the Corbetts) in and around Killeigh; two went to Mr PJ Meehan, the owner of Glorious Event, who was a solicitor in Maryborough. Not the brindle dog, however. He was going nowhere.

From the outset Greene had set about lavishing all the care and attention he could muster on this undersized whelp in order to build him up. He set about giving the brindle regular feeds with warmed and slightly diluted unskimmed milk from a bottle as if it were a pet lamb. At night the pup was allowed to snuggle up with his mother, but during the day he was to be found safely ensconced in the kitchen of Millbrook House awaiting his next bottle. Thanks to the devotion of its surrogate parent the weedy youngster began to thrive.

As a general rule, the weaning process commences after 10-14 days when the bitch's milk may no longer be enough to satisfy the pups. So, in order to encourage his adopted pup to lap from a bowl, Greene began rubbing its lips and gums with the lukewarm milk prior to dipping its nose into the dish. This Greene repeated every three hours. Gradually, he added a little bread or even porridge to the liquid, taking care to feed little but often. Soon the increasingly podgy pup began exploring his immediate environment on unsteady legs, enjoying the first feel of warm Irish sunshine on his back.

Bit by bit Greene increased the amount of time mother and pup were kept apart until a natural separation was finally effected. At six months, permanent teeth had replaced his milk teeth and he was augmenting a copious intake of buttermilk by happily wolfing down raw meat, boiled potatoes and bread – topped off by the occasional dose of cod liver oil to put a sheen on his coat. Technically speaking he was now a sapling. The trickiest phase of his development was at an end.

One problem had been overcome. Yet another loomed. It was inconceivable that Millbrook's master would retain all ten of Na Boc Lei's latest pups. He had no need of such numbers and – more importantly

– they represented a welcome source of revenue to bolster his finances. But which would be sold and which would be retained?

Greene was on tenterhooks. He had been asked by the Father for his opinion regarding each individual's prospects and had duly obliged, but there was no knowing how much sway his input would have.

'Michael, I shall be dispensing with four of the litter. The fawn bitch, the two white and fawn dogs and...'

Greene's heart was fair jumping through his shirt.

'...the red dog. The other six will stay and I'm presently completing their registration forms for the Stud Book. I'm sure you'd like to know what they'll be called? Each one will carry our letter "M" signature. The brindle bitch is Magical Maud; the red and fawn bitch is to be Mitella; the white and brindle bitch will be called Meconic and I think we'll have Millbrook for the brindle bitch. Now, for the two dogs. I've decided on Macoma for the big white and brindle, who looks every inch like Na Boc Lei and her father...'

The priest executed a perfectly practiced dramatic pause worthy of his doppelganger Wilfrid Hyde White before fixing his expectant employee with an impish glare. Greene shifted uneasily from foot to foot.

'And as for that little friend of yours you think so much of, all things considered, I'm thinking there's only one name for him. He can't be anything other than Mick the Miller.'

CHAPTER THREE
THE HAND OF GOD

The news Michael Greene dreaded most arrived like a thunderbolt one morning the following June. His employer informed him that a Father Maurice Browne was motoring over from County Kildare with a view to buying some of the saplings.

The six retained pups had all prospered through the lazy days of summer and come through the winter of 1926-27 without mishap. The first year is the crucial period in the development of any greyhound. A good wholesome diet and a home that combines the liberty to frolic by day with the security to sleep as 'snug as a bug in a rug' at night strikes the perfect balance. What better environment than rural Ireland in the 1920s?

If the saplings were not running free in the wire-meshed paddock constructed by Greene at the rear of Millbrook House, they were as like to be seen walking the roads around Killeigh – that over Gorteen Bridge to Killurin was a particular favourite – in order to toughen their pads and build-up muscle. The groundwork provided by pounding the roads was invaluable. Greene also introduced them to the thrill of the chase and the rudiments of how they would be expected to earn their living one day.

First of all, he whetted their appetite by standing in the centre of the paddock with an old slipper tied to a length of rope which he'd proceed to swing round in circles for the pups to chase. Then, later on, safe in the knowledge that the chasing instinct was present and correct, Greene took them to a decent-sized field where they could be 'slipped' off the leash for a gallop. It was important to teach the dogs how to run and compete without resorting to playing, 'leaning on' or fighting. Such playful bad habits, if not eradicated, would assuredly finish their competitive careers in the coursing field before they had even got started. To this end, Greene galloped a pair together but he would not release them simultaneously. While James Hill stood a couple of hundred yards away up the field twirling the slipper, Greene held the two dogs by the collars in readiness to loose them one after the other, seconds apart.

Consequently, the six saplings that awaited Father Maurice Browne's inspection were not only in the pink of condition but also on the brink of being ready for active service 'in slips'.

Besides their common calling, Father Brophy knew of Maurice Browne through the success of his coursing dog Lugnagun, which had divided a stake at Kilmoganny the previous October before losing in the final of the prestigious Belsize Cup at Killucan the following month, even though Father Browne also resorted to a racing pseudonym. In Father Browne's case an unfortunate choice, since 'William Twyford' earned him notoriety as 'The Jacks Man' based on the Irish slang for the lavatory and the fact that the firm of 'Twyford' manufactured virtually every toilet bowl in the country!

Fifteen years Father Brophy's junior, the 36-year-old Browne was a scion of an equally clerical family rooted in Grangemockler, County Tipperary, within which he always claimed to be 'the least brilliant of the lot'. Given that one brother, Patrick, was a noted mathematician and linguist who went on from the priesthood to become Professor of Mathematics at Maynooth College and later President of University College, Galway, while a second, Michael, joined the Dominican Fathers and rose to the exalted rank of Cardinal, working in the Vatican for Pope John XXIII, Father Browne may have had a point. However, he himself was a man of many parts. In time he would write three books using the *nom de plume* Joseph Brady: *Big Sycamore, My Presbytery Window* and *In Monavalla* – this last-named centred on the village of Hollywood in the Wicklow Hills where he was for so long the parish priest.

Father Browne had only recently developed an interest in greyhounds, and then only by chance. Up until returning from serving in a parish in Brooklyn, New York, his preferred pastimes were more along the lines of a wee *dorun* of Irish whiskey accompanied by an unbroken chain of cigarettes. This fondness for nicotine led to an embarrassing *faux pas* as soon as he'd arrived at the house of his Brooklyn host. Promptly lighting-up, he began regaling fellow guests with tales of the 'old country' as he lent confidently against the mantelpiece – on which he spied a receptacle obviously put there for the deposit of cigarette ash since it was already half-full. After using it for his own by-product throughout the ensuing hour and umpteen further 'gaspers', he was to be mortified when his host entered the room and, picking up the urn, for that was what it was, exclaimed: 'My heavens! The old man is putting on weight!'

If the truth be told, Father Browne was more attracted to gun-dogs than greyhounds. Then fate took a hand and directed him down the road which ultimately brought him to the gates of Millbrook House. Unlike himself, Father Browne's close friend and the curate in the parish of Kill, Father Andrew Farrell, was a greyhound fancier. In May 1924 he had two pups out of the bitch Actress XIII by Jedderfield. Sadly, Father Farrell was in poor health and was shortly leaving for Denver, where the mountain air of Colorado would be beneficial for his tuberculosis. He was anxious to offload the two pups to good homes before he left and pressed the reluctant Father Browne, much against his better judgment, into accepting one.

Father Browne called his white-and-brindle dog Lugnagun (Gaelic for 'Hill of the Greyhound') and, lodging it with Mary Behan on the Curragh, duly erased all thought of the pup from his mind. However, reality resurfaced once he received a letter from the dog's custodian which read:

'Please remove your greyhound. He has us persecuted. Whenever anyone opens the door of the shed in which we keep him, he's off like a shot to chase sheep.' Although suitably chastened, Father Browne was soon won over by the sight of his Lugnagun chasing swifts through the Wicklows 'with the poetry of motion' and he decided to put him into training with Jedderfield's owner-breeder, Tom Harte, the proprietor of Kildare's Commercial Hotel.

Harte was no fool. Within an hour of setting eyes on Lugnagun he tried to buy him. But, nor was Father Maurice Browne a fool. If Tom Harte was that keen to get his hands on Lugnagun, the dog must have a future and he was better off keeping it for himself. The affable Harte bade his visitor farewell with sound advice: 'Give this lad a four-mile walk every evening and before you bed him down for the night soak his pads in water that has been left over from the boiling of salty bacon. For his evening meal, give him a basin of brown bread soaked in milk and finish it off with a pound of minced beef.'

Lugnagun repaid Father Browne's faith in the potential Harte had intuitively divined. Others soon began to appreciate Lugnagun's qualities once he began excelling in the coursing field. One such was Joseph Tierney, then acting as a buyer for Mr Moses Rebenschied of 1140 Broadway, St Louis, Missouri. Racing greyhounds after an artificial hare around an enclosed oval track was in the process of taking America by storm – St Louis's track had opened in 1921, for example. All the sport lacked was racing greyhounds. Where better to acquire top-quality stock, thought the ambitious Rebenschied, than the Irish countryside?

Rebenschied cabled an offer of £200 for Lugnagun. Needless to say, the offer – an astronomical sum for a comparatively untried dog – was accepted without delay. Lugnagun did not disappoint his new owner. In the spring of 1927 Rebenschied wrote saying: 'Lugnagun has broken three track records at St Louis. He is the idol of the racing fans. Is there any hope you could send me two more prospective Lugnaguns? I leave it to your judgement to select them. My agent, Joseph Tierney, will pay you any price you consider reasonable.'

Father Browne knew exactly where to go in search of his two 'prospective Lugnaguns'. He immediately contacted Father Martin Brophy. 'Come to Killeigh and take your pick of a bunch of saplings, for the greyhounds have me broke,' came back the anguished reply. 'I intend to sell off every one of them.' No second invitation was needed.

Seller led buyer through the kitchen of Millbrook House and out into the yard, where the anxious figure of Michael Greene was waiting for them by the doors of the old coach house. 'All right, Michael, let them out.'

The six saplings burst out of their confinement and instantly set off in pursuit of the various fowl happily scratching and pecking in the yard, scattering them hither and thither in fear of their lives. A large Silver Sussex cock was slower than the others to retract his undercarriage and found himself snapped up in the jaws of a white-and-brindle predator who refused to relax his grip even after Father Brophy's housekeeper appeared and began belabouring him with her broom. Via a combination of whistling and waving, Greene and Father Brophy got all the dogs back in the coach-house with the notable exception of the individual careering about the yard with the squawking cock in its mouth.

'Pay whatever price you like,' said Father Brophy to his fellow priest who had stood motionless amid the mayhem. 'My first choice is this white-and-brindle fellow charging about here – Macoma.'

'I'm happy to take your advice,' replied the buyer. 'What about the others?'

The two priests walked across to the coach house and peered through a window. After a moment's reflection, Father Browne announced his selection. 'I'll take that powerfully built brindle over there.'

'An excellent choice, Maurice. That's Mick the Miller.'

The agreed price was £100 the pair with Father Brophy undertaking to keep the two saplings until the necessary travel arrangements that would see them depart for St Louis had been finalised. Father Brophy escorted his guest back to his car. 'If Mr Rebenschied likes them, I'll send the rest of the saplings to him at a reduced price. I've told you, the greyhounds have me broke!'

Within a few days Rebenschied had authorised the deal and Father Browne wrote out a cheque for £100. However, no sooner was he congratulating himself on a job well done than proceedings took a nasty turn. He received another cable from Rebenschied. Its message was stark and unwelcome: 'Don't purchase dogs. Stop. Writing. Stop'

Rebenschied's letter arrived a few days later. 'The Hand of God is warning me against greyhounds. On the tenth day of June a tornado struck St Louis and blew the roof off my kennels, killing 27 dogs including Lugnagun. My son Rube was on his way from the railway station with four dogs and the storm overran the van and killed the four dogs.

Rube escaped with a broken nose. I repeat, the Hand of God is warning me against greyhounds. Sorry for giving you all that trouble.'

Father Maurice Browne was now the owner of two dogs he did not want. He broke the news of the collapsed deal to Father Brophy as a matter of course – and was stunned by the response it elicited. 'It would not be fair to stick you with the saplings,' said the priest. 'We'll forget the deal was ever made.' Father Browne heaved a sigh of relief.

'If I'm candid,' he wrote toward the end of his life, by now a Monsignor, 'I was glad the bargain had been amicably called off. But, it was a terrible unfortunate thing that I didn't hold on to Mick the Miller.'

Father Browne's sadness may be easily understood in the light of his subsequent involvement in the sport of greyhound racing. Later on, 'The Jacks Man' owned a winning bitch called Gosha Bead whom he eventually bred to Inler; this 1933 mating produced Ataxy who, after being sold on, smashed track record after track record and won the 1935 English St Leger and 1936 Cesarewitch. Then a 1936 union between Inler and one of Gosha Bead's daughters called Tranquilla yielded Talist, who set an Irish record for 525 yards of 29.90 (the first sub-30 seconds round Shelbourne Park) and, granted luck in running, would almost certainly have won the Irish Derby of 1938 but for a bizarre injury (Talist broke two toes when pouncing on the hare that had inexplicably fallen off its trolley) sustained whilst leading his first round heat.

What Talist failed to achieve, was more than made up for by his full brother from Tranquilla's 1938 mating with Inler. Named Tanist, Browne sold him to Dublin-based Londoner Arthur Probert for £200 with a £100 contingency should he win either the English or Irish Derby. Tanist proved so fast from the traps that he found it almost impossible to negotiate the first bend at Wimbledon (where he'd been sent to be prepared for the English Derby) without being knocked for six by the other runners. Returned to Dublin without an English victory to his name, he bettered his brother's Shelbourne time with one of 29.66 before earning Browne the additional £100 through collecting the Irish Derby by six lengths. Even though the track was rain-soaked, this amazing brindle dog still managed to record the first sub 30-seconds time in the final, stopping the watch at 29.89. Tanist went on to add further lustre to his reputation by being the first to duck below 30 seconds at Clonmel on his one and only visit to the track.

Then, with no further track opportunities open to him during the winter of 1940-41, Probert entered him for the Tipperary Cup as a warm-up for a crack at nothing less than the Irish Cup, the holy grail of Irish coursing. Tanist reached the last four in both Cups, losing to the eventual victor on each occasion. Probert immediately retired his dog, who commenced an equally illustrious stud career that saw him sire Classic winners, such as the Irish Derby winner Daring Flash, and the great sprinter Mad Tanist. Fittingly, Tanist's 29.66 record stood at Shelbourne for five years until lowered by his own son, Smartly Fergus.

Even if Father Maurice Browne did just own Mick the Miller by proxy for a week or so, it inspires almost unconditional belief in the power of the Church to think that one humble country priest could go down in history as being the owner of Ireland's two most exalted greyhounds from the first half of the 20th century.

In the summer of 1927, however, Father Martin Brophy was still looking to sell his saplings. Pretty soon the English came calling. For years they had been plundering the fields of Ireland for hunters and steeplechasers, and with track greyhound racing now a year old it was inevitable that the new breed of English greyhound fancier would soon be on the prowl, open chequebook in one outstretched hand and a thick wad of banknotes waving in the other.

The infant sport was booming. The trailblazing English season of 1926, inaugurated at Belle Vue on 24 July and restricted to the Manchester track, had drawn total attendances of around 400,000; 1927 would see racing take place at 30 venues with crowds soaring to a staggering 5.6 million. Thus, if the mushrooming sport was to encounter any problem it was more likely to be its ability to ensure a constant stream of competitors into the traps rather than spectators through the turnstiles. An eight-race card required 56 dogs and with three meetings per week that left each track needing a notional total of 168 dogs in its kennels. Multiply that figure by 30 tracks and the sport was looking at a working population of around 5,000 greyhounds. The number of litters being registered bore out this increased demand but, significantly, in Ireland the figure increased by over a third to 1,013 compared to only 686 in England. Accordingly, the same qualities that had attracted Moses Rebenschied to Irish stock were bound to tempt potential buyers from England.

First to leave Millbrook House were Magical Maud and Meconic, sold for 60 guineas each to Thomas Addy, landlord of The Woodman Inn, Rotherham. So taken was Addy with his new acquisitions that he determined not to leave Killeigh without their mother. For a further 60 guineas he became the owner of Na Boc Lei. How well she fared in Yorkshire is not known. *The Stud Book* has no record of any more litters after that of February 1927 resulting from a mating with Tom Harte's Hidden Rock. Of the seven pups, Metalloid won for Father Brophy at North Kilkenny on Boxing Day 1928.

Who would be next out of the gates was anyone's guess. Michael Greene didn't want to think about it. Macoma and Mick the Miller were by a long chalk the most promising of the bunch – as evidenced by their selection for Rebenschied. If the Father could get 60 guineas apiece off the English for the likes of Meconic and Magical Maud, what on earth were the best two worth?

Greene did not want to think about the unthinkable. Instead, he concentrated his mind on preparing Mick the Miller to fulfil his legacy in the coursing field, his destiny since the moment of his conception.

CHAPTER FOUR
GOING TO SLIPS...

In the summer of 1927 every owner of a greyhound dreamt their kennel might be housing a dog capable of winning the Waterloo Cup. The slumbers of Father Martin Brophy were similarly disturbed.

The Belsize Cup...the Irish Cup...then the Waterloo Cup. All things were possible at this hope-springs-eternal stage. As fellow priest and coursing *aficionado* Joseph Pelly famously remarked, 'There was never yet a greyhound puppy which was not a Waterloo Cup winner – on the hearthrug!' In Mick the Miller and Macoma, Father Brophy knew he had his best chance to date of fielding a contender for the big cup events at home, and perhaps even one fit to cross the Irish Sea for the 'Blue Riband of the English leash'.

Using greyhounds in the pursuit of game was a pastime as long as history itself. According to 'Proverbs, chapter 30', King Solomon included greyhounds in his 'four things which are comely in going', and they appear in numerous Egyptian and Greek murals dating from the centuries before Christ. The breed, a prototype Saluki, originated in the deserts of southern Arabia and eventually spread westwards via the civilisations of Egypt, Greece and Rome to Britain. A brace of greyhounds and their Saxon owner, Elric of Mercia, features in an illuminated manuscript of the 9th century, for instance.

The name is almost certainly a misnomer. Although Flavius Arrianus referred to the soft grey eyes and grey coat of a favourite hound in the 2nd century AD, the prefix 'grey' may well originate from the Icelandic for dog, from the Anglo-Saxon 'gre' or 'grieg' meaning 'first in rank', or possibly from the Greek description of them as 'gazehounds' due to their ability to hunt by sight. Evidence suggests there were two distinct types in Britain, the long-haired 'gagehound' used for stalking deer and the short-haired. 'gazehound' favoured for coursing hare.

> *See'st thou the gagehound, how with glance severe*
> *From the close herd, he marks the destined deer;*
> *How every nerve the greyhound's stretch displays*
> *The hare, preventing in her airy maze.*

Whatever the precise genesis of their name, these dogs were already being coursed under guidelines which had elevated the activity from a massacre to something approaching a true sport. 'The true sportsman does not take out his dogs to destroy the hares,' stated its trailblazing chronicler Flavius Arrianus in his treatise *Cynegeticus* in AD 116, 'but for the sake of the course and the contest between the dogs and the hares, and is glad if the hare escapes.' By the 2nd century AD coursing was widely practised throughout Europe and, if Arrianus is to be believed, was thriving among the Celtic and Pictish nations that made up the Roman Empire's western outposts. For instance, the boat bringing Saint Patrick to Ireland, it is said, was entrusted with a far more precious cargo: greyhounds.

Ownership of a greyhound conferred social status. In the 10th century the value of a greyhound and a hawk equalled that of a man, and in 1016 a law of King Canute decreed none but 'a gentleman' was allowed to keep a greyhound since it was common knowledge that, 'you may know a gentleman by his horse, his hawk and his greyhound'. That grasping skinflint, King John, was even prepared to accept greyhounds in lieu of taxes; while as many as three castles once changed hands in return for ten greyhounds. Edward III had a greyhound incorporated into his seal, and it was during his reign that Chaucer first wrote in *The Canterbury Tales*: 'Greihounds he had as swift as fowl of flight.' Later on, Henry VIII considered no aspiring nobleman's education complete unless he was skilled in the art of raising and preparing greyhounds for the course.

Oh! What a noble chase!
See how they twist and turn and fleetly race.
Turning to scorn the critics who declare
'Poor is the triumph over the timid hare.'

Coursing was taken to a new level during the reign of Henry's daughter Elizabeth. The sport was put on a firmer footing and public awareness increased. Dr Caius, Court Physician and founder of Caius College Cambridge, included the greyhound in his book *Englishe Dogges* and, at Elizabeth's personal command, the Duke of Norfolk drew up a set of rules for coursing. The Duke's 'Code' demanded two dogs only were to be coursed, with a slip of 240 yards being afforded the quarry, and 'skill not kill' to be the vital component of the judge's decision. The Virgin Queen herself is known to have watched coursing in Cowdray Park in 1591 and there are a dozen references to the sport in Shakespeare's plays. In *The Merry Wives of Windsor*, for example, one character responds to taunts about his greyhound being 'outrun' by explaining, 'it could not be judged...he's a good dog and a fair dog, can there be more said?' There are also few more oft-quoted lines than those uttered by Henry V before the walls of Harfleur when he exhorts his troops to stirring deeds with the words: 'I see you stand like greyhounds in the slips, straining upon the start.'

The introduction of a bulldog 'cross' by Lord Orford in the 18th century was an attempt to bring the breed to the point of functional perfection – though some breeders were unimpressed by the emergence of certain bulldog traits, such as the proclivity of some pups to sit around like so many useless frogs. Nevertheless, Orford's pioneering work created the now familiar brindled coat and one of the early successes of the 'bulldog cross' was King Cob, who eventually featured on both sides of Master McGrath's pedigree.

The actual appearance of these 'greyhounds in the slips' tended to reflect the circumstances under which they were asked to compete. By the 19th century, five distinct varieties were recognised in Britain, ranging from the smaller, muscular type seen to its best advantage chasing the lighter, short-running hares of Wiltshire to the larger dog in its element across the wider, flatter plains typical of Lancashire or the country around Newmarket. The classic Irish variety – developed from the rough-haired wolfhound of Celtic legend, the largest of the lot who weighed in at 120lb, twice the size of the eventual coursing *beau ideal* – likewise grew more refined with the incorporation of English bulldog blood.

With less and less onus being placed on obtaining food from the kill, the *raison d'etre* of coursing gradually shifted toward the test of sporting skill propounded by Arrianus. In 1776 the first coursing club was established at Swaffam by Lord Orford, to be followed four years later by the formation of Lord Craven's committee to run the meeting at Ashdown Park. Clubs subsequently sprang up the length and breadth of England, prompting the formation of the National Coursing Club in 1858.

The most renowned club of them all dated from 1825. The Altcar Coursing Society was founded by Viscount Molyneux to hold meetings on the estate of his father (the Earl of Sefton), on the Lancashire coast near Southport. The Society's Waterloo Cup, named after the Liverpool hotel where it was first mooted (rather than the battle), was contested for the first time in 1836 and was won by Molyneux's own bitch Milanie, whom he'd loaned to the hotel's owner, William Lynn, especially for the purpose. Ireland had to wait 32 years before the legendary Master McGrath broke the country's duck by winning the first of his three Waterloo Cups in 1868. A further three Irish dogs were to emulate him by 1927.

Naturally, Ireland had its very own roster of clubs and cups by 1927. It was known that coursing had taken place on the plains of the Curragh for centuries (the local landowners were paid half a sovereign for every hare put up) and five clubs were in existence by 1900; within ten years the number had soared to over 30, making the formation of a separate Irish Coursing Club in 1916 a formality. A framework of major events was put in place to support the holy grail of Irish coursing, the Irish Cup, first run at Clounanna, near Limerick, in January 1906 and won by Peerless de Wet.

If Mick the Miller could win at Clounanna – if not the Cup itself, the minor prizes of Purse or Plate for early eliminations would suffice – Father Brophy would enter heaven a very, very happy man. However, before Mick could be put to the test, Michael Greene had to get him ready.

Both Mick the Miller and Macoma had been introduced to the chase as saplings prior to their projected sale to Moses Rebenschied back in May 1927. By common consent, a dog reached maturity at 18 months (two months earlier than a bitch) which, as late June whelps themselves, suggested they would be ready to course by the end of the year. Irish country folk tended to be less patient. Greene's brief was to have the pair fit to enter slips when the season opened in early October.

Their preparation was stepped-up accordingly in mid-August. First of all, Greene ensured they were free of vermin and gave their innards a good cleansing by worming them with the traditional remedy of pow-dered glass mixed with butter. He also began to modify their diet by reducing the amount of dry food – the bread, toast or biscuit – in favour of increased protein in the form of more meat. Once Greene was satisfied with their condition, the two dogs commenced a six-week training programme designed to bring them to racing readiness.

Walking, as ever, formed the basis of this process. All their excess fat had to be burned off – but slowly. Five miles a day over a period of three to four weeks gradually achieved this objective. At one and the same time, their muscles and pads were all the while hardening and strengthening. So, enough exercise to tire them out but not so much as to induce staleness was the nub of Greene's strategy. If, once they'd received their post exercise massage and were put back in their kennel, they made straight for their benches with a contented sigh ready for sleep, Greene knew he had got things in the right proportion.

Greene's final task was to give the two dogs a couple of gallops. A twirling slipper at the end of a rope would no longer suffice on these occasions. Only a live hare would do. Millbrook's field of cabbages was a deliberately planted bounty to attract a steady supply. There was no point slipping Mick and Macoma together. They would as likely get in each other's way as learn anything. No, Greene would pair them with Millbrook's older and wilier inmates, Mr Miller and Musty Miller. And to ensure his young dogs first experience of the genuine article was not gruellingly protracted and potentially off-putting, Greene chose a field which allowed the hare an easy escape: a course of up to 30 seconds would be sufficient to give them the taste of things to come.

As October drew to a close the brothers were deemed ready to make their debuts. The meeting chosen was the Laoighis County Coursing Club's meeting at Maryborough's Clonreher running ground on Tuesday, 1 November.

There are two types of coursing venue: open and enclosed. The latter is commonly referred to as park coursing. The former more closely approximates to natural conditions than the latter. Open coursing depends on a hare being driven by a team of 'beaters' from its natural habitat onto the running ground whence it makes its escape as and where it can. Park coursing, on the other hand, involves a hare being released into an enclosed field at the top of which lies an artificial escape route (called a sough), a bank or hole in a hedge, with which prior acquaintance has made it familiar (park hares are frequently trained within the running ground so they soon learn exactly where the 'escape' is located). Since the greyhound hunts by sight only, it quickly gives up once the hare has disappeared from view. Consequently, park coursing seldom lasts a minute before the hare duly exploits its escape route, whereas open courses often exceed 11/2 minutes, until such time as the hare is killed or the dogs have succeeded in running themselves to an exhausted standstill. Your dog could wind up in the next county if you were unlucky. Put another way, open coursing places a premium on stamina; park coursing rewards speed. Clonreher was park coursing.

All coursing events, then as now, are nothing more than simple knock-out competitions, just like a tennis tournament, for example. Dog against dog until all bar one is eliminated. Thus, in order to win the 16-puppies National Breeders' Trial Stakes (worth £22 and five shillings), Mick the Miller needed to win a total of four courses.

Each course would be decided on a points system. The judge (usually mounted so he might follow the action more closely – though one was once noted to be so inert he was nicknamed 'the fossilised judge') was charged with deciding all courses upon one uniform principle: the

dog that does most toward killing or 'working' the hare during the con-
tinuance of the course should be declared the winner. It was up to him
– and he alone – to estimate the value of the work done by each competitor and award points accordingly. In short, contrary to much public
perception, coursing is not a contest to the death: death is not so obligatory as it is in the bull ring. As Arrianus had written centuries earlier,
'The true sportsman does not take out his dogs to destroy the hares, but
for the sake of the course and the contest between the dogs and the
hares, and is glad if the hare escapes.'

So, it was unlikely either Mick the Miller or Macoma would taste blood
on their first visit to the running ground. Although the day's official card
advertised, 'Dead hares sold after meeting, 2/6d each,' they would be in
short supply because only one in seven courses results in a kill.

Despite the existence of a well-defined points system, the eventual
decision of Clonreher's arbiter, Mr PJ Kennedy, would, as is always the
case in sporting endeavours reliant on human judgement, be prone to
subjectivity. He could award points as follows; leading by three lengths
on the run from slips until the hare is initially turned (the 'run-up') was
worth up to three points; turning the hare by more than 90 degrees
gained one point, but turning it by less than 90 degrees (termed a
'wrench') warranted only half a point; to turn or kill the hare after passing your opponent in a straight run or on the arduous outside circle
(described as a 'go-bye') was also worth a maximum of three points;
tripping or 'flecking' the hare earned no more than one point.
Ironically, a kill merited no more than two points, and then on a
descending scale in proportion to the degree of merit displayed, which
could amount to no points whatsoever if the dog only achieved it
thanks to the assistance of its rival rather than through any superior
dash on its own part.

Clonreher was much like any other Irish running ground of the park
variety. It was a meadow about 500 yards long by about 200 yards wide,
bounded by hedgerows and wire netting, with a home for the hares
at the bottom and a ready-made escape of at least 50 yards width – a
natural bank or planted fence – for them at the top. Given the

circumstances – the confinement, the regulation 60-80 yards run-up afforded the hare before the slip (known as 'law') plus its knowledge of the terrain – seldom would more than half a dozen turns be executed before a successful escape was made. Speed from slips was therefore of the absolute essence because the dog who dragged its heels in the run-up to the hare had precious little time thereafter to wipe out the points deficit courtesy of any superior working powers it might possess. Indeed, that initial turn and the subsequent re-start tends to rob both dogs of so much energy that the initiative passes to the hare, which is why she so frequently affects a successful escape.

It was just as well Maryborough was only a short drive from Killeigh. Ireland had been plagued by a week of gales and it was a wild and windy day as Mick the Miller and Macoma left Millbrook House. Accompanying them was Musty Miller. A year older than the brothers, he was down to compete in the Duffer Stakes, the ungraciously named fixture of every meeting that was confined to dogs who had never won more than two courses in any one event. The stake for puppies (dogs not yet two years of age) came first, and it constituted one of 64 such 'trials' leading to a grand final (the forerunner of what in later years became the Derby) at the National Meeting held in the spring at Clonmel's Powerstown Park. Bad weather or not, a typically huge crowd made its way to the running ground by car, donkey cart, jig, horseback and on foot – armed with all the necessary alcoholic fortifiers just in case of emergency.

The first brace of dogs was due 'in slips' at 12.30. Today's slipper was Ed Cleere, of Templetuohy, County Tipperary. One cannot overestimate the importance of the slipper. He was the most significant official on the field. Concealed from the approaching hare by his 'shy' (merely a portable screen), it was Cleere's responsibility to release each brace on an even keel, with each dog having a good sight of its prey. This was not a straightforward procedure even when the hare entered the running ground from directly behind his shy, but if it tore across his eyeline from left or right like a duck in a shooting gallery it could develop into a nightmare because he would be forced to vacate the shy and edge laterally in order to preserve a fair start, no easy matter with up to

10 stone of yapping, bounding greyhound straining at the leash.

Mick the Miller was drawn six, in the third brace. His opponent was Hidden Jew, a dog belonging to Tom Harte that, crucially perhaps, had the benefit of previous experience, having won three courses at Kilmoganny before dividing – splitting – the stake with his final opponent, a promising animal called Odd Blade, about whom much more would be heard in the Mick the Miller story. Since Hidden Jew was also a brindle, he and Mick were obliged to wear distinguishing woollen collars equating to their number in the draw and, ultimately, the colour of handkerchief raised by the judge to denote the eventual winner and then conveyed to the crowd by a flag steward: red for the odd-numbered top dog in each pair who goes into slips on the left of the slipper; and white for the even-numbered bottom dog who enters on the right.

Michael Greene eased the flimsy white-knitted collar over Mick's head. Having seen, heard and smelt two other courses, Mick was tugging and whining for permission to get on with the job. Taut as a drawn longbow, every muscle in his body quivered in anticipation. His bright eyes darted hither and thither in search of his quarry. From the sidelines Father Brophy watched Greene deliver his dog to the slipper. 'Good luck to you, Father,' he vaguely heard someone say. 'Your boy looks ready to run for his life, so he does!'

All eyes were now riveted on the bottom end of the field, waiting for the first glimpse of the hare, watching for clues in the demeanour of the slipper and the behaviour of the two dogs in his care. A scatty looking hare zig-zags in from the left. Perhaps she is bothered by the wind. Both dogs instinctively lunge forward, pulling like billy-o. Cleere's body leans slightly backwards to absorb the tension whilst his right hand grips the leash controlling the twin-collared slips even tighter. He must not release the dogs until the hare has been given its 'law' of at least 60 yards. On the point of slipping his dogs, Cleere sees the hare unaccountably veer off back to the left – perhaps perturbed by the wind – and eventually vault the boundary fence to safety. Damn! He'll have to wait for another hare.

Denied their quarry, Mick and Hidden Jew have added bemusement and frustration to their natural eagerness and excitement. Fortunately, they don't have long to wait before a fine big hare suddenly appears, almost brushing the shy on its way past. On this second time of asking Cleere gets the dogs away. But Mick is soon languishing. Whether his previous disappointment or just sheer tardiness from slips in the face of a more experienced rival is the prime cause, he has no answer to Hidden Jew in the run-up. The voice of the judge, Mr PJ Kennedy, is heard calling 'Red two' which meant the award of two points to the dog on the red collar (only one collar is ever scored at a time, on an increasing or decreasing scale).

Mick had to do something quick if he was to overcome his poor run-up and pull the score back to level. Try as he might, there was to be no fairytale conclusion to Mick the Miller's first course. Kennedy waved his red handkerchief. Up went the steward's flag. Hidden Jew had got the decision.

Macoma fares a little better. He was victorious in his first course against Wee Musician, but in the next round he, too, was put in his place by Hidden Jew. What with Musty Miller not getting beyond round one in the 'Duffer', it was neither an auspicious nor profitable day for Millbrook kennels and its owner. A disappointing walk to his car was punctuated only by the odd consoling comment, 'Hard lines, Father. There'll be plenty of other days.'

There would indeed be plenty of other days during the remaining four months of the season. In Mick the Miller's case, the twin highlights were his outings at Roscrea on Wednesday, 28 December and at Kilbeggan four weeks later which saw him 'divide' on each occasion.

Mother Nature played an instrumental part in the proceedings at Roscrea, a little town 20 miles to the south west of Killeigh, on the Tipperary border. A bitterly cold and frosty morning delayed the start of sport, so that by the time the main events were concluded there was only sufficient daylight remaining to complete the first two rounds of the Parkmore Stakes, which had attracted seven other puppies beside Mick the Miller. Mick dispatched Nice Alarmer and Town Pride, before dividing the spoils with Glen Beha.

The Millbrook dogs seldom strayed too far from their native Offaly, and Kilbeggan was another short hop, just a few miles the other side of

Tullamore. The Belmont Stakes featured on Kilbeggan's inaugural card of Wednesday, 25 January 1928, and was a 16-dog event for two-course maidens (that is, dogs like Mick and Macoma who had never won more than two courses in any one stake). Both were entered, and both made it through the opening two rounds before the stake was divided four ways at the semi-final stage.

Clearly, the two pups were learning fast and were soon sure to gain winning brackets. But Father Brophy was already setting his sights on other targets. Track racing had come to Ireland when Belfast's Celtic Park opened its doors for the first time on Monday, 18 April 1927, soon to be followed by Dublin's Shelbourne Park a month afterwards. Quickly establishing itself as a commercial success for owners, trainers, spectators and punters alike, track racing constituted an irresistible magnet for owners wishing to keep their charges – and source of revenue – ticking over throughout the lengthy coursing off-season which in the 1920s stretched between St Patrick's Day (17 March) and October.

However, in order to maximise the potential of his young prospects, especially with a second Dublin track about to open at Harold's Cross, it struck Father Brophy as a wise move to place them with a licensed trainer attached to a track. In charge of the Shelbourne Park kennels for that groundbreaking year of 1927 was a man well known to him from the coursing field. Why, had the man himself not slipped Musty Miller the day he won the Westmeath United Stakes at Killucan only this January? Indeed, this 30-year-old from Trim was generally regarded as the premier slipper in the country. Now, as one of Shelbourne's four freshly licensed trainers, he was weaving his magic preparing greyhounds for the track. Moreover, he seldom had a bet, so he was not the kind of loose-lipped confidant liable to spoil the odds for any of his owners who liked a punt. He was just the man, decided Father Brophy, to train the two brothers. His name was Michael Horan.

CHAPTER FIVE
...AND INTO THE TRAPS

When the Black and Tans boarded his train in West Clare, Michael Horan knew fear for the first and last time in his life. Like everyone else in Ireland that autumn of 1920, he knew all about the Tans whose unsavoury reputation went before them. Horan had read the grim details of how they had descended upon County Clare in recent weeks to burn and pillage Lahinch and Ennistymon. On this occasion, however, the Tans targeted victims even more defenceless than usual, contenting themselves with taking indiscriminate pot-shots out of the carriage windows at any unsuspecting cattle, sheep and pigs that took their fancy.

After the train's unwelcome passengers had eventually disembarked, a relieved Horan sucked in lungfuls of invigorating air. The colour flooded back into his wan features. He reached for the hip flask inside his jacket containing the brandy and port he always kept by him to combat the numbing chill of raw, hand-chapping days spent slipping greyhounds on some windswept running ground. The tension finally melted away and a thin smile reluctantly began to tug at the corners of Horan's mouth as his mind automatically returned to the matter in hand. He searched his memory for the words of the popular doggerel which contained the slipper's perennial lament:

> We're mad to be here in the cold and the dirt,
> The rain's going through me and its down to my shirt!
> This coursing's for idiots not right in the head,
> Much saner at home, and all cosy in bed!

Horan raised the flask to his lips and took a deep, celebratory swig. Ah, now, perhaps slipping greyhounds isn't such a bad life after all. Even though he stood 6 feet 3 inches tall and could handle himself in the event of a 'donnybrook' breaking out around him, Michael Horan was no fool. No one willingly mixed it with the Black and Tans.

This was one experience Horan was glad not to see replicated on the annual Irish odyssey he undertook during the coursing season in his role as one of the country's foremost slippers. He knew the railway timetables backwards. So much in demand was he (at £4 a day plus expenses), that by the time Mick the Miller entered his life in 1928 that his photograph was wont to stare out from the sports pages three or four days a week between October and March. Moreover, training greyhounds for the new game of track racing was by then providing the 30-year-old with a job for the other six months of the year. Aside from that unexpected brush with the Black and Tans, life could not have worked out sweeter for Mick Horan.

When he wasn't roaming the Irish countryside for weeks on end, Horan went home to his farm at Agher, between Enfield and Summerhill, barely 30 miles out of Dublin to the west. Invariably smartly attired in dark suit and tie, silver watch-chain dangling from his waistcoat, alert eyes peering out from beneath the rim of a soft hat that concealed a fine head of hair, he had been slipping greyhounds on the coursing fields of Ireland since the age of 17. His father had been groom to Enfield's affluent Hope Johnstone family, who owned land in Scotland besides County Meath, and it was on the recommendation of Miss Alice Hope Johnstone (herself the winner of two Irish Cups) that young Mick was given his first opportunity in the shy when the appointed official one day failed to put in an appearance.

Horan developed a distinctly individual style of slipping to meet the demands of the period. What the coursing greyhounds of the 1920s may have lacked in size compared to today's protagonists was more than offset by their wilful and headstrong nature in slips. Like most of his colleagues, Horan was a shrewd judge of a hare, knowing intuitively how it would run and, consequently, the precise second to release his dogs. However, few of his colleagues could match his powers of control. Unlike the majority who restrained their brace using only one hand, he leashed his dogs from left to right using both hands, with the leash doubled under their stomachs. In this way, he felt better able to release the pair without them bumping or colliding. Furthermore, his height enabled him to stand tall over the dogs, squeezing them between his legs, thereby maintaining near perfect control. Shorter slippers, by contrast, ran the risk of frequently ending up 'wheelbarrow men', the apt – though somewhat cutting – description of their ungainly posture as the brace pulls away from them demonstrably out of control, a scenario evoking muttered renditions of the old lament:

> *That slipper's no good, he can't balance a dog.*
> *He runs too far, or stands like a log!*
> *He gives too much 'law', or he slips 'em too short;*
> *Can't get 'em in line – he'll ruin the sport!*

Not so when Mick Horan was in the shy. And as a finale to the performance, as if just to remind his audience that they were watching the maestro at work, Horan tended on releasing his dogs to throw up his right arm with a flamboyant theatrical flourish that quickly became his signature. The only day Michael Horan's mind wasn't totally focused on the job in hand was the occasion at Killucan when an attractive farm-girl in the adjoining field caught his eye. Her name was Rose Reilly – and, in time, he would marry her.

Horan's contacts were extensive. Anybody and everybody went coursing in the 1920s, and he also enjoyed the priceless asset of being introduced to a constant stream of influential people in the Hope Johnstone mould by his brother, the steeplechase jockey Bill Horan. Brother Bill, who became rather well-heeled in the wake of his victory in the 1924 Irish Grand National aboard Kilbarry, invested in greyhounds and horses and was soon mixing with the high and mighty. He taught the legendary amateur Aubrey Brabazon, the eventual partner of Vincent O'Brien, stars such as Cottage Rake and Hatton's Grace, how to ride and he was once entrusted with escorting the future Edward VIII on a morning spin across the gallops. Consequently, as one local succinctly commented, 'The Horans weren't just a family in County Meath, they were an institution!'

Michael Horan rarely gambled, even though he invariably knew the time of day. This is not to say he lacked the courage of his convictions. Occasionally, however, an opportunity would present itself that only the certifiably insane could ignore. One day, for instance, he would invest £1,500 on a dog of his at Celtic Park because he knew it could not possibly lose based on the times it was clocking down at Shelbourne. You had to get up pretty early in the morning to get one over on Mick Horan.

As with the successful trainer of any animal, Horan enjoyed an uncanny rapport with his charges, in his case a form of canine green fingers. Blessed with a photographic memory, he knew every hair on the head of every dog in his care. He'd spend hours with his dogs, walking them across the fields, talking to them, all the while chewing on a straw and trying in every way possible to get inside their heads so that each could be treated as an individual.

He ran his Agher kennel like an army camp. Every paw was examined and washed; every nail filed; every tooth brushed with baking soda; every coat combed, oiled and rubbed down; every constitution dosed with syrup of blackthorn boosted by a dash of Powers whiskey. This was a man who would always choose to stay at the North Star Hotel adjacent to the main railway line whenever he brought dogs to Dublin because, although its human clientele was virtually guaranteed a sleepless night, the hotel possessed a set of kennels for the comfort of his beloved dogs. The dogs always came first with Michael Horan.

Thus, the name of Michael Horan quickly sprang to mind when the Irish Coursing Club (who governed the sport until the creation of the Bord na gCon in 1958) addressed the task of identifying suitable candidates for the first batch of trainers to be licensed at Shelbourne Park; alongside Horan's, were ranges allocated to Paddy Quigley, Billy Donoghue and Ben Scally.

Shelbourne Park duly opened to a fanfare of publicity: 'A £1,000 reward will be paid,' ran the advertisement in the *Irish Independent*, 'to any person or persons who can prove to the satisfaction of the Directors of the National Greyhound Racing Company Limited that the Dublin public have not heard of Greyhound Racing at Shelbourne Park.' A crowd of 8,000, who paid up to five shillings (25p) for the privilege, turned out on Wednesday, 14 May 1927, to witness a six-race card made up of four flat races and two over hurdles. The box-man for the very first race at 7.30pm – over 500 yards on the level and won by the 5/2 joint favourite Morning Prince – was none other than Michael Horan.

Attempts had been made for some years to establish a form of greyhound racing using an artificial lure. Back on 11 September 1876, for example, *The Times* carried a report of a 'trial' near The Welsh Harp at Hendon in which greyhounds chased 'a sham hare, an apparatus like a skate on wheels fitted to rail hidden in the grass, for a distance of 400 yards in a straight line, like so many kittens after a cork.' Fourteen years later, a British patent for an oval circuit – one that might reward ingenuity on the turn, in the manner of coursing, as well as pure speed in a straight line – came to nothing through lack of finance, and it was left to the American coursing enthusiast Owen Patrick Smith to kick-start the sport.

Smith was wont to entertain weekend guests to a spot of coursing in an enclosed paddock at the back of his house in Oklahoma. The success of his pastime attracted so many gatecrashers that his neighbours complained about the disruption and he was eventually charged with the offence of coursing live rabbits in an enclosed space. However, Smith's business antennae twitched to the obvious commercial possibilities of adapting the sport (and appeasing his detractors) to involve an artificial rather than a live quarry and a circular track rather than the open spaces afforded by a field.

Smith's prototype lure amounted to nothing more than a stuffed rabbit hauled by a motorbike, but by 1919 and the opening of his track at Emeryville, in California, the mechanism had been refined to a motorised trolley. Further tracks quickly sprouted. The St Louis venue patronised by Moses Rebenschied appeared in 1921 alongside others in Tulsa, Houston and Miami. By the time Smith died in 1927 he was the owner of no fewer than 25 tracks. More importantly, he had lived long enough to see his brainchild take its first teetering steps on the other side of the Atlantic.

The leading lights behind that opening day at Belle Vue, Manchester, on Saturday, 24 July 1926 were Charles Munn and Major Leslie Lyne Dixson. The former was an American businessman from Philadelphia, the latter a much respected vet and judge in the British coursing world. Munn had shrewdly acquired the British rights for the fledgling sport and set about gathering supporters and finance. One was easier than the other. Britain had a million unemployed and a general strike was looming. Eventually, a consortium headed by Dixson, Brigadier-General Alfred Critchley and Sir William Gentle (a retired chief constable of Brighton) scraped together by hook or by crook the necessary £22,000 to form the Greyhound Racing Association Limited and set about constructing Belle Vue on a disused clay pit in the Gorton district of Manchester, a city with an acknowledged predilection for whippet racing. When the directors added up the takings at the end of that first night, which had attracted just 2,166 paying customers, they found themselves £50 in the red. However, at the conclusion of the first season, encompassing just three months and 37 meetings, both spectators (averaging 11,000 a fixture) and money were rolling in, causing the company's shares to rocket from the equivalent of 5p to a staggering £37.50.

It was never going to be more than the merest blink of an eye before a similar enterprise saw the light of day in the land where every kennel invariably contained a greyhound and every working man fancied a bet. In the autumn of 1926, Belfast bookmakers Hugh McAlinden and Joe Shaw accompanied by Paddy Joe Ryan visited Manchester with a view to arranging for the sport to be brought to their city. Not that they knew it at the time, but a second triumvirate, made up of Paddy O'Donoghue, Jerry Collins and Ballybunion bookie Jim Clarke, were keen to see the sport established in Dublin. Once the two groups became conversant with each other's plans, they joined forces to set up the National Greyhound Racing Company with McAlinden as chairman and Ryan as secretary. McAlinden was also a director of Belfast Celtic AFC, whose Celtic Park ground and facilities paved the way for the relatively easier introduction of the sport in Ulster on Easter Monday, 1927. Dublin comprised more of a problem since a site was harder to find. Hopes for the hurling citadel of

Croke Park fell through, and the new venture, christened Shelbourne Park, was born on virgin land at Ringsend in the city's eastern docklands.

Having taken charge of his two new acquisitions from the coursing field, Horan needed to sharpen them up in readiness for the differing demands of the track. Working on their fitness was no problem; walking the roads – with the odd day on grass to prevent scorched pads – saw to that. But developing their trackcraft was another matter altogether. To prevail at the conclusion of a day's coursing, a dog would need the stamina to have run something approaching 2,000 yards. Mick and Macoma would be running a quarter of that distance on the track. Bullet-from-a-gun speed off a standing start in the traps was the crucial ammunition in this arena. Yet that was not all. Shelbourne was 500 yards in circumference, of which the two straights comprised only 240 yards. Raw pace would not suffice. To be seen to best advantage the two brothers would need to be taught how to harness their speed both approaching and negotiating the bends. Horan could ill afford to have a 'chocolate dog' (one that melts on the corners) on his hands.

Horan began the process of drawing out the latent pace in Mick and Macoma by occasionally giving them a gallop of 400 yards or so across the big fields surrounding Agher. However, fine judgment was called for because too many such gallops would make them go stale. Horan would hand-slip them, one after the other, to chase after someone trailing a hare carcass or waving a handkerchief. One warm day, so the story goes, Mick evaded immediate capture and was ultimately apprehended in the chapel grounds at Trim availing himself of a drink of holy water. When told of his dog's sacrilegious escapade, Father Brophy's irreverent response was typical: 'Well, the devil won't catch him now!'

In truth, Mick was showing all the signs of a greyhound in scant need of assistance from the Almighty. During the same telephone call from his trainer reporting Mick's sacrilege, Father Brophy heard words suggesting his prayers had been answered.

'Father,' said Horan, 'Mick is a natural. I don't have to give him much work. He's ready to go to Shelbourne. Mark my words, this dog is a natural!'

The two brothers went to Shelbourne in late March 1928. To begin with, hand-slipped gallops around the turns were used to build upon Agher's numerous dummy runs, but the duo soon progressed to dress rehearsals incorporating every facet of the genuine article: the muzzle; the momentary darkness; the whirr of the oncoming hare; the bang of the lids opening; the sudden rush of light; the glimpse of a bobbing white tail disappearing into the distance. Almost every facet. The one thing missing was the noise of 5,000 people roaring on their fancy.

Wednesday, 18 April 1928 was the night chosen for their debuts. Mick was first on the track, contesting the Punchestown Stakes over 500 yards at 8.55pm, which was worth £10 to the winning owner. Two hours before race time Horan delivered him to the Shelbourne kennels to be weighed and checked over by the vet, Arthur Callanan. Here he stayed until Horan returned with his race jacket – red, for trap one – prior to having him join the parade in the paddock. Mick's twitching nose and darting eyes betrayed the gamut of new sensations he was now experiencing. Lots and lots of people; a cacophony of different voices and sounds; strange smells and aromas he could not associate with any food or drink he knew. From somewhere the sound of a bugle cut through the air. This was the call to the track.

Mick was listed on the racecard as Mick the Millar with an 'a', and was not expected to trouble the odds-on favourite Seregawn housed in trap five. If Father Brophy was keen to indulge himself, 4/1 was freely on offer among the line of bookies.

On this occasion, the familiar sequence of sensations in the traps was accompanied by a hubbub of noise which swelled to a crescendo as the lids flew upwards. Mick vacated his box like a quarrel from a crossbow. Checking onto a left-leg lead, he held his place round the first two turns, shot down the back straight glued to the inside rail, assumed a winning position round the final turn and sped away to cross the line two lengths in front of Kyle Boy. It was all over in a flash. Mick had completed the 500 yards in 29.60 seconds.

Macoma ran in the next race. If Father Brophy wondered whether this was going to be a case of taking candy from a baby, he had good reason. Slightly taller and some 8lb heavier than his brother, Macoma had performed with more success in the coursing field. Besides that division at Kilbeggan, for example, he also reached a semi-final at County Carlow in February before dividing a 'Duffer' at Castletown and the Ossory Stakes at Maryborough in March. Furthermore, on the racetrack time is king, and in their Shelbourne trials Macoma had clocked a time tantamount to six or seven lengths better than Mick the Miller's. So highly did Horan regard Macoma that, in order to keep the brothers apart, he suggested to Father Brophy that Mick the Miller should be directed toward a career over hurdles since he had been tried and tested to be highly proficient in this sphere. The owner wouldn't hear of it. The hurdles in use at the time were exceptionally stiff, little different to horserace hurdles, and Father Brophy was concerned his dog might injure himself.

Macoma's perceived superiority manifested itself in his elevation to a tougher heat. However, looking on the bright side, should he continue to demonstrate a half-second superiority over Mick the Miller, a time of 29.10 might conceivably give Dick's Son, the favourite and popularly acclaimed 'Kilkenny Crack', something to worry about.

So much for theory. As things transpired, a time approaching 29 seconds proved perfectly sufficient to upset Dick's Son – but it was not Macoma who clocked it. Both Dick's Son and Macoma were trounced by an old thorn in Macoma's side from the coursing field in the shape of Mutson, who ran the distance in 29.20. This really did rub salt into the Millbrook wound. Mutson came fresh from winning the Midland Cup at Maryborough where he'd eliminated Mr Miller in round one before beating Musty Miller in the final.

Five days later Macoma raised his game to reveal his true potential by defeating Kreisler courtesy of a sensational performance. Kreisler, who was a year older than Macoma and a namesake of the world-renowned violinist, came to the track boasting outstanding credentials from the running grounds where he'd been tagged as a 'fast youngster'. He'd had two successes at Clonmel and Kilsheelan, in addition to four other divisions, including one at Kilmoganny the previous month, all of which suggested he could not be beaten by a novice such as Macoma. Furthermore, it was Kreisler who held the world record for the 500 yards. Yet Macoma thrashed him by six lengths and lowered the record to 28.80 into the bargain.

The next port of call for Horan's two flyers was to be Celtic Park on Wednesday, 25 April, for the heats of the Abercorn Cup, a three-round competition over a distance just short of 527 yards named in honour of the Governor of Northern Ireland. The brothers took their first train journey from Dublin to Belfast the day following Macoma's scintillating display against Kreisler, and were lodged overnight in the kennels Horan kept at Celtic Park. The previous week, a free-for-all amongst the runners had reduced one race to farce, so the Celtic Park executive was mightily pleased to watch all three heats for its big spring event pass without a hitch. Each favourite obliged: Dick's Son (7/4 on) took heat one in a track record of 30 seconds dead; Macoma (11/4 on) landed the second heat in 30.40; and Mick (5/1 on) won the third by a proverbial street in 30.80.

The brothers stayed at Celtic Park in readiness for the quartet of semi-finals. Only the winner of each went through to the four-dog final. Macoma was drawn in the first semi, on 4 May and, despite the opposition containing Dick's Son, he entered the traps the 11/10 on favourite. Macoma disappointed. He could finish only third to Dick's Son and was out of the final.

However, Macoma still had a vital role to play at Celtic Park. His brother's semi-final was still three days away, and Macoma would provide a wonderful running mate for Mick the Miller's final track gallop, a sharpener over 375 yards.

As the whine of the approaching hare ignited Macoma's competitive instincts, the big white-and-brindle dog grew more and more frantic in his anxiety to get on with the job. He began pawing the bars of his box but only succeeded in getting one of his forelegs stuck in the wire mesh. When the lids sprang, poor Macoma was unceremoniously yanked upwards along with them. By the time Horan reached the stricken dog, it was apparent Macoma had sustained a broken hock.

The loss of Macoma in such freakish circumstances was a grievous blow to both Horan and his owner. All Father Brophy's hopes now rested with Mick the Miller. His principal rival was Mullawn, and the two of them vied for favouritism.

The race proved an eye-opener. Mick broke fast from trap two, but the dog on his inner – Happy Jamie – was even swifter. However, rather than pounding into the first bend hell for leather and contest every inch, Mick seemed to concede right of passage to his opponent in the red jacket and then proceeded to follow him through the second into the back straight. Happy Jamie continued to maintain a comfortable two-length advantage, which was only just starting to be whittled away as he leant into the third bend.

Then something extraordinary happened. Mick, as if he'd been biding his time all the while, suddenly dived behind the leaders hind quarters to reach the inside rail for the final bend. This seemingly conscious manoeuvre acted like a form of jet propulsion that catapulted Mick clear, and he crossed the line half a length to the good.

'It was,' said the *Irish Independent*, 'the best race of the evening.' More specifically, the Belfast crowd had been privileged to witness the unveiling of that peculiar brand of racing intelligence, that nous, which would become synonymous with the name Mick the Miller and distinguish him from all other canines.

Animal psychologists, let it be stressed, are of one accord on the subject of canine behaviour: dogs act on instinct, full stop. One instinctive action triggers another, and so on and so forth. Dogs do not reason. They do not plan ahead. At Celtic Park that night, Mick the Miller served first warning to boffins everywhere that if there is one certainty about any rule it is that there will always be an exception to it. Crazy as it may sound, even as early as the third race of his track career, Mick the Miller had already worked out the object of the exercise and how best to go about achieving it. Here was a greyhound imbued with a form of racing intelligence not evident in his contemporaries.

Mick was immediately trained back to Dublin for the first round of the Spring Show Cup, commencing at Shelbourne two days later. He won his heat effortlessly by two lengths but, more significantly, he equalled Macoma's mark of 28.80 in so doing. Four races in three weeks had knocked some of the rough edges off the young dog. Clearly – as the clock's impartial evidence testified – he was improving with his racing.

However, the final of the Abercorn Cup was only 48 hours away, and there was yet another journey north to be negotiated in between. On the time test, Mick needed to be jumping out of his skin if he was to have any chance of beating Dick's Son and the local hope Moorland Rover, who had both recorded faster semi-final times. The market went evens Dick's Son, 11/8 Moorland Rover, 5s Mick the Miller and 33/1 Mourne Flapper in the four-dog final. At the conclusion of a thriller, the Celtic Park patrons went wild as the Ulster dog pipped the 'Kilkenny Crack' by a short head. Mick was just half a length adrift.

This first reverse in five starts could conceivably be blamed on all the travelling Mick had endured during the week leading up to the Abercorn Cup. On the other hand, Father Brophy and Mick Horan could console themselves with the thought that when all was said and done their dog had been defeated by two decent animals. Moorland Rover was good enough to have won a ticket to Powerstown for the National Breeders' Stakes through a victory at Kilkeel in January, while inside three months Dick's Son would carry off the English Cesarewitch, one of the Classics. And, of course, there was still the Spring Show Cup to come.

There was much for owner and trainer to look forward to. That is, until the morning Horan opened the door of Mick the Miller's kennel to be met by a sight every dog-man dreads.

CHAPTER SIX
SICK AND FOR SALE

Mick the Miller lay huddled up in a corner. Even a cursory examination told a man of Horan's experience all he needed to know. Despite the dog's desperate search for extra warmth his nose was already dry and red-hot. The brown eyes, normally so quick and inquisitive, were lifeless. Mick was shivering and shirked the touch he otherwise loved. Horan offered him a dish of milk. No reaction. Dull and listless, running a temperature and off his feed. The symptoms hammered out the worse possible diagnosis: distemper.

Distemper is a viral fever affecting the mucous membranes, mainly those of the respiratory tract. The intense inflammation paves the way for other infections, such as pneumonia. In 1928 there were no inoculations to prevent the disease and no serum to treat the disease. What remedies there were verged on quackery, with vets concocting their own individual potions.

The prognosis was grim: the mortality rate was 25 per cent, rising to 75 per cent should the victim contract the more virulent form. The young Mick the Miller would need all the famed resilience of his courageous grandsire Let 'im Out if he was going to combat this killer disease.

Distemper is only contracted by direct or indirect contact with a dog suffering or recovering from distemper. Racing kennels, therefore, were prime breeding grounds for the disease. Mick could quite easily have picked up the virus from the urine or faeces of an infected dog; even the sole of a careless shoe could have been the culprit.

Horan's first priority was to isolate his sick dog. Beyond that, his principal job was to keep him warm in order to ward-off any possibility of pneumonia. He wrapped the dog in an old sheepskin to keep his chest warm and put some long woollen socks on his legs to do likewise for his extremities. Trying to get some goodness inside the dog – milk mixed with honey; beaten eggs, spiced with a tot of brandy; or a drop of beef tea and port wine – was going to be a thankless task, but it was essential to compensate for the loss of condition brought on by the immediate onset of vomiting and diarrhoea. Beyond that, regular bathing to keep the patient clean and a flow of soothing words as a means of comfort was all any sympathetic nurse could offer.

There are several types of distemper, which are more or less indistinguishable in their early stages. Recovery rates from comparatively milder forms offered Horan some encouragement. If the inflammation affected the entire chest contents and resulted in pleurisy or pneumonia, however, all hopes of an athletic career for Mick the Miller could be forgotten.

It could be worse still. If the disease attacked the nervous system Mick was as good as dead. This lethal variety of the disease – eventually called hard-pad owing to a resultant inflammation and thickening of the pads – tended to afflict saplings and puppies more than adults. The critical period in any dog's recovery came after two or three weeks when the benefits of intensive care were seemingly beginning to take effect. After regaining its appetite and beginning to put on weight, proof that the brain and/or nervous system had been attacked may suddenly be provided by the onset of fits and convulsions.

The early signs were not good. Mick's condition deteriorated, and a discharge from both eyes and nose was followed by a cough. Father Brophy was on the verge of conceding defeat. It looked as if Mick the Miller would have to be put down.

Luckily for Mick the Miller, the vet at Shelbourne Park kennels was Arthur Callanan, described by the *Cork Examiner* as 'One of the most popular and able figures in the greyhound world.' If anyone could work the oracle it was Doc Callanan.

A native of Cork, where his father was Secretary to the County

Council, he was born with a rheumatic heart complaint which effectively ruled out any of the more ferocious athletic pursuits favoured by eager young bucks in the 1920s. A man of considerable charm and generosity, he was, for instance, of a much milder disposition than the most notorious of the five Callanan boys, his brother Eugene, who earned the soubriquet 'Nudge' as a result of his fierce proclivities on the hurling fields of University College. Nudge Callanan also risked life and limb by taking a year's sabbatical from medical school to go 'on the run' with a flying column of General Tom Barry's Third West Cork Brigade in the dangerous capacity of medical officer.

Eugene Callanan senior had no interest in greyhounds or coursing, but Arthur's passion for the sport was fanned once he left Cork's Christian Brothers School for Dublin's Veterinary College, and he quickly became a well-known figure in the coursing world prior to replacing Louis Magee as Shelbourne's veterinary surgeon in 1928. For three nights running Callanan stayed at Mick the Miller's side, nursing him through the crisis. We will never know what medicines Callanan used: quinine for the fever, perhaps; possibly arsenic or strychnine in small doses to stimulate the animal's vital organs. But whatever potions Doc Callanan administered, they worked. Mick was going to pull through.

Callanan was clearly blessed with the gift. It was he who had operated on Macoma's broken hock and he also successfully pieced together Wily Attorney's split hock with a three-inch bone graft. Even greater miracles were worked on Maiden Show and Creamery Border. Any untoward movement while removing numerous bone fragments during an operation to repair the former's fractured skull would have resulted in death, yet six weeks later she was back winning over hurdles. He was also said to have rescued Creamery Border from the jaws of death, a dog he himself later trained to win the 1933 Scurry Gold Cup after he had taken up an appointment at Wembley in February 1931. The successes of Altamatzin (often a thorn in Mick the Miller's side) in the 1931 Welsh Derby and Kitshine in the 1935 Oaks likewise testified to Callanan's skill as a trainer, while once back at Harold's Cross (where to this day the Arthur Callanan Memorial Cup is still run) it was he who owned and prepared the remarkable little black bitch Nannie

Goosegog. Some claim she was beaten only once in a sequence of 37 races in the early 1940s – 31 of them in a row which, if true, would have given her sole possession of the world record until equalled by America's Joe Dump in 1979. Unfortunately, Nannie Goosegog's career record has proved terribly difficult to authenticate.

Doc Callanan's chronic ill-health caught up with him at a tragically early age. He died at the Gresham Hotel in Dublin on 16 October 1945 in his 51st year. Every major Irish newspaper carried his obituary. His hometown newspaper, the *Cork Examiner* was typical. 'His death will be a distinct loss to the greyhound world,' it said beneath a bold headline. The headline read: 'The Man Who Saved Mick the Miller.'

There is an intriguing postscript attached to the story of Mick the Miller's illness. The Horan family is adamant that the input of a second vet was instrumental in curing the dog. On many an occasion when the subject of Mick the Miller came up at the Horan dinner table, Michael and Adrian Horan listened to their father's tale of how Mick the Miller's recovery resulted in part from the intervention of PA 'Paddy' McGeady. Doc Callanan's medicine, they heard, eventually went down the sink and McGeady's went down the dog. In later life, McGeady was president of the Irish Veterinary Association and Professor of Veterinary Surgery at University College Dublin, but in 1928 he was just 22-years-old and had only recently completed his studies in Ballsbridge. However unlikely it seems for McGeady to have had the temerity (or been so unprofessional) as to have interfered in a case under the aegis of a vet of Callanan's standing (it is a less disputed fact that McGeady did successfully treat Abbeylara for distemper before that dog went on to win the Irish Derby of 1938), the Horan boys are unequivocal in the veracity of their father's knowledge in the matter.

The faint possibility also exists, however, that Mick wasn't struck down by distemper at all. During a period when veterinary science was still very much in its infancy, diagnosis of the disease was far from definitive. Any gravely ill dog showing the appropriate range of symptoms was frequently talked of as having distemper when it may have been suffering from nothing more than a bad bout of canine influenza.

One thing was certain. Any dog that miraculously survived what patently had been a severe case of distemper would be in no condition to subsequently embark on a racing career of any description – let alone one of the lengthy and arduous magnitude completed by Mick the Miller. That fact alone unequivocally states Mick the Miller to have been suffering, at worst, from a mild dose of distemper.

Whatever it was that ailed Mick the Miller, and whoever it was that cured him (and, bizarre as it sounds, a dog might survive of its own accord, irrespective of any medicines), one can state with utter conviction that he revealed infinite reserves of courage and character to emerge in one piece from the darkest tunnel a young dog can enter. Whether the canine athlete in him had come through the ordeal totally unscathed, however, could not be ascertained until he resumed action. Father Brophy was not about to take any chances. For the second time in his life Mick the Miller was put up for sale. And there was no telling how successfully Macoma would recover from his broken hock, so he'd better go as well.

The two brothers were offered up for sale in August at one of Shelbourne Park's regular auctions. As was to be expected, the stadium was thick with English buyers eager to secure the newest Irish talent. Father Brophy was one Irishman certainly disinclined to sit back and risk watching the English depart empty-handed and unhappy. He possessed the dogs – they had the money. He'd already sold two more of the Na Boc Lei litter to English buyers in recent weeks: the bitch Mitella was acquired by Philip Simpson of Waltham Green; while two gentlemen from Pershore bought Cluain Na Ngall (a white and fawn dog originally registered in 1926 to Killeigh neighbour Aidan Kennedy) who, renamed Pershore Pride, eventually showed winning form over hurdles.

Once again Father Brophy sought to line his pockets. Although the average price of an Irish export to England was a measly £9, Mick the Miller and Macoma were right at the premium end of the market. Thanks to their exploits in the spring, Na Boc Lei's sons had to be two of the choicest lots in the catalogue. Accordingly, Father Brophy placed a reserve of 200 guineas on each of them.

One man determined to take the brothers across the Irish Sea was William Washbourne, a builder from Wolverhampton who had already purchased seven Irish dogs in the past year. A man with the widest sporting interests for whom the term Corinthian could have been coined, Washbourne had spent several years in South Africa where he'd bred champion bulldogs while amassing a considerable fortune. As far as he was concerned Irish greyhounds were the best money could buy – and Mick the Miller and Macoma were the best of the best.

Mick came onto the podium first. 'Gentlemen, here we have a brindle dog, a June 1926 whelp, by the outstanding Glorious Event out of Na Boc Lei,' intoned the auctioneer. 'The dam earned winning brackets in the coursing field, and this dog has divided stakes to his credit at Roscrea and Kilbeggan. More to the point, gentlemen, he has won four of his five races on the track and has clocked 28.80 for 500 yards at Shelbourne. Gentlemen, what am I bid for this outstanding prospect?'

The bids came in thick and fast to begin with, quickly soaring above 100 guineas. At 150 guineas the flurry stilled. The nod was with Washbourne. 'Gentlemen, do I see 160 anywhere?' The auctioneer's plea fell on deaf ears. Father Brophy was stunned.

This setback made Washbourne even more determined to buy Macoma, broken leg or no broken leg. He wanted him for stud purposes not racing. But he still had to go to 290 guineas to get him. With that singularly extravagant gesture, Father Brophy sensed all might not be lost. At the conclusion of the sale he approached Washbourne and offered him Mick the Miller at 200 guineas. Washbourne demurred. A bid of 150 guineas had won the day in his book. He wasn't going to pay an additional 50. Washbourne had acquired one gem in Macoma but to a dog-lover of his magnitude, the moment he declined to add Mick the Miller to his string of greyhounds would haunt him to the grave.

Father Brophy was now displaying all the signs of a man desperate for cash. After another Horan-trained dog called Bodyke found a buyer at £100 he made the purchaser aware just how inferior his new acquisition was in comparison to Mick the Miller. A deal was struck at £150 for Mick the Miller if he demonstrated this superiority in a private match round Shelbourne. Somehow Bodyke prevailed by a length! The client, Samuel Garcia, offered £120. Father Brophy was dumbstruck. There was nothing for it. He would have to retain Mick the Miller.

Thus, after more than two years of living virtually cheek by jowl, the brothers Macoma and Mick the Miller were finally separated. While Macoma headed for the ferry and a new home in a new country, Mick the Miller returned to Millbrook House and the devoted attentions of Michael Greene.

CHAPTER SEVEN
A CHAMPION IN THE MAKING

In the short term, Mick the Miller would have to earn his living back in the coursing domain. Assuming, that is, the distemper had not robbed him of his innate ability.

Callanan's parting instructions to Father Brophy back in the summer were to be in no hurry. On no account rush Mick the Miller back into action before he'd been given a lengthy period of convalescence: afford Doctor Time and Nurse Sunshine the opportunity to work their magic. Three outings at old stamping grounds during November suggested they and Michael Greene had indeed worked the oracle.

On the first day of the month, Mick went to Maryborough for the 16-dog two-course maiden Portlaoighhise Stakes, once won by his mother. He got the decision in his first two courses (taking the scalp of a future divider in Collegian) before going down in his semi-final to the bitch Bashful Kitty – who eventually divided. A fortnight later it was off to Roscrea for a similar event, the Inane Stakes. After dispatching Old Burgos in his first course, he got the better of a good second-round scrap with a black dog called Foy's Farm (who would later win a decent stake at Cappawhite and run-up in two more), but he again fell to an eventual divider at the semi-final stage in the form of another bitch, Madge's Worry. Finally, on Tuesday the 27th, he visited Castletowngeoghegan in County Westmeath for the Rathdrishogue Stakes, another 'Duffer' event.

The Irish midlands had yet again been lashed by gales, leaving Mick and Musty Miller (his companion throughout the month) as two of just 21 dogs who turned out for the day's three events. Even in the three-dog Castletown Stakes, Musty Miller still found one to good for him. All hopes now rested with Mick the Miller.

Mick's first obstacle was to overcome Rose of Cullion, a bitch coming back from whelping. She hardly stretched him. Weirs Folly posed no more of a problem in the second round. Then a stroke of luck. Mick's allotted semi-final opponent was withdrawn, giving him a bye into the final. The rules of coursing, however, insisted all byes were to be run out (solo or in the company of an approved sparring partner) and judged to be sufficiently strenuous to ensure no dog carried an unfair advantage into the next round. After fulfilling his obligation, Mick retired for one last short rest before the final in which he was to meet Ard De Hille.

Michael Greene went through the routine he had practised between the preceding rounds one last time. Walking his dog slowly back to the car, he hitched Mick's leash to the door handle before going to the boot and extracting a bottle of water, with which he proceeded to gently wash Mick's feet. Then he drew the half-bottle of Tullamore Dew from his pocket, poured some of the precious golden liquid into his hands and began administering a brisk massage, starting at Mick's shoulders, travelling down his back and ending at his haunches and back thighs. After successfully easing away the lactic acid that had accumulated in the muscles and towelling him dry, all that remained was to give Mick a drink.

Between earlier rounds this had taken the form of cold tea. But this was Mick's first final. Now was the moment to treat Mick to a 'moment of darkness', that time-honoured pick-me-up tailor-made for an occasion like this one. Greene flipped the cap off a bottle of Guinness and filled the bottom of Mick's bowl. The dog lapped up the foaming black elixir with all the gusto of a character straight from the pages of a James Joyce novel. Greene looked at his watch. Just enough time for some shut-eye. He unhitched Mick's leash, opened the door and motioned toward the jumble of coats and blankets heaped along the back seat. The dog sprang obediently onto the pile and began nuzzling out a comfy bed for a well-earned nap.

While Mick snuggled down to enjoy his forty-winks, Greene clambered into the front seat to escape the elements and attempt something similar, but only found himself consumed by thoughts of Mick's final opponent. Ard De Hille was a brindle bitch belonging to John Scally of Mullingar. Although the same age as Mick, she had shown nothing approaching his ability on the running ground or the racetrack. Mick, he assured himself, could take care of this bitch all right.

Half an hour before Mick was due back in slips, Greene roused both himself and his dog. A loosening stroll was in order before the slip steward called them. Away up the field Father Brophy was behaving like a man on hot coals. His money was 'down'. Not that a man of the cloth would dream of executing such a brazen act as approaching a bookmaker in person, of course. Fortunately, there were plenty of willing agents in close attendance whose investments disguised his own.

Mick's nose began twitching in anticipation. He was an old hand at this now. He was a second-season dog after all. Neither Father Brophy nor Michael Greene need have worried. Mick vanquished Ard De Hille with minimum fuss and maximum efficiency. He had lived up to his heritage, going one better than his gifted brother Macoma. He was a winner in the coursing field.

Even more importantly, that squally Tuesday at Castletowngeoghan demonstrated Mick had lost none of his ability as a result of his brush with distemper. He would visit the running grounds again. In fact, he was actually slipped by Mick Horan himself when he contested the 32-dog Shelbourne Park Cup (confined to dogs who had run at the Dublin track) at Newbridge on the following 4 February, beating Lady Delage in his opening course before succumbing to Five Speed (who ultimately ran-up) in his second. Newbridge was one of the few Irish venues to indulge in 'open' coursing. Mick was not asked to brave this more gruelling branch of the sport again. His destiny lay back on the racetrack.

Mick resumed track action at Shelbourne Park on 25 March 1929, and during the ensuing 3 1/2 months up to 6 July he raced more or less once a week. Of those 15 races he won 11. To be more specific, he lost three of the first four but won 10 of the last 11 – and that single loss came in the most suspicious circumstances – by which time he was being lauded in the pages of the *Irish Independent* as 'the best dog that has ever stretched a leg on a track'.

After winning his comeback race at Shelbourne by three lengths (getting badly away but coming with a rare bat in the straight) Mick lost three in a row at the Dublin oval. However, on each occasion it required no mean performer to lower his colours and he lost no caste in defeat.

On the first day of April, Mick contested heat three of the Easter Cup, a richly endowed event at Shelbourne Park over 525 yards for which a silver cup and a cheque for £60 awaited the eventual winner at the conclusion of the final a fortnight later. Despite entering the traps a warm favourite at 5/4, Mick could not cope with the sustained pace of his closest market rival, Care Free, who had two coursing successes to his name from the recent season, and went down by two lengths.

Care Free would encounter Mick on a further four occasions during the following weeks – but he would never again get within hailing distance. One of those four occasions was their semi-final of the Easter Cup on 8 April. Mick, running from the outside trap six for the first time in his life, had Care Free's measure but failed to recover from some early scrimmaging and could not peg back the even-money favourite Entomb who held him at bay by half a length. Entomb was to cross Mick's path throughout 1929. But the fawn son of Spalding Bishop would likewise never again finish in front of Mick.

Mick still qualified for the final six of the Easter Cup (from an entry of 54) and drew trap three, inside Entomb and a regular Shelbourne crowd-pleaser in the shape of Odd Blade. Tim O'Brien's brindle was another animal who had converted his acknowledged prowess 'up the field' into impressive form on the track, most notably when collecting the inaugural Easter Cup of 1928. Even so, Odd Blade was only a 4/1 shot to achieve the double because the third semi-final had fallen in the most spectacular fashion to the Limerick City Challenge Cup victor, Captured Half. The Kerry visitor was all the rage and backed as if unbeatable at 6/4 on.

The punters quickly knew their fate, however, for the favourite became a victim of track racing's greatest blight, crowding on the first bend. While Odd Blade opened up a useful lead, the remainder were dusting themselves off after a right shemozzle. By now the Shelbourne faithful had grown accustomed to seeing Mick the Miller make up ground hand over fist toward the end of his races, so the sight of the white jacket spearing down the home stretch was not entirely unexpected. Mick failed by half a length to get up.

In two successive races Mick had paid dearly for becoming embroiled in an argy-bargy at the first bend. Something in that brain of his began to tell him that a modicum of restraint at this critical juncture of a race might be both prudent and, ultimately, rewarding. A form of canine intelligence was being slowly activated that would see the emergence of a distinct racing brain totally absent in his fellows. If he did not fly the box it was clearly not in his interest to try and retrieve the situation at the first bend. This was a veritable minefield. Best to hold back, take a considered look, weigh up the situation and then make a move. As if to prove the point, in future even the mighty Odd Blade – just like Care Free and Entomb – would finish their encounters seeing nothing but the white tip of Mick the Miller's tail.

Mick's rapid elevation to Dublin superstar coincided with his initial appearances at the city's other venue, Harold's Cross. Of similar circumference to its sister track (though it boasted only one covered stand to Shelbourne's two), Harold's Cross had been in business for a full year when Mick stepped onto its grass for the Leinster Plate to be run over 600 yards on 23 April 1929.

This was the furthest trip he'd thus far been asked to negotiate. He handled the distance well enough to win, but some observers noted the unlucky run suffered by the runner-up Real Rustic. The possibility that the extra distance might uncover Mick's Achilles heel was seemingly confounded when he notched facile victories (by four lengths and a distance) in the first two rounds of the Stayers' Sweepstakes. But the final suggested otherwise.

Mick had a very tough nut to crack in Ukelele Lad. This grandson of Mick's own sire Glorious Event had advertised his coursing lineage with two victories and a division in the last 12 months. He was not going to fall short of stamina. Drawn next to each other in traps one and two, both dogs broke smartly and with the length of the straight to complete before the first bend they soon left the other two finalists for dead. Unfortunately Mick's enthusiasm seemed to get the better of him and he careered way wide on the first bend to find himself in last place as the back straight opened up before him. So fast did Mick then set off in pursuit that the rest of the race devolved upon the answer to one question... Had he sufficient time to recover all the lost ground? First he overhauled Marcus. Then he caught Lord Melksham. Up in the judge's box Father Brophy was roaring on his dog. Mick put in an awesome late surge to close on Ukelele Lad as the line neared.

'He's beat! Mick's beat!' the owner blurted out in dismay as the pair flashed across the finish line. Father Brophy had subsequent cause to rue that exclamation, for there was no photo-finish camera in action. It's not impossible that the judge was influenced by the priest's involuntary outcry because he gave the verdict to Ukelele Lad by a head. The time of 34.42 was a new track record. Many present trackside that night were adamant Mick the Miller had succeeded in snatching victory from the jaws of defeat and vented their spleen by hurling bookmakers' stools onto the track.

Mick Horan was more intrigued by what had happened to Mick the Miller rounding the first bend than crossing the finish line.

'Did you see that?' he had enquired matter-of-factly to nobody in particular. 'The hare stopped on him! What's going on here? That hare was shortened! I don't like the look of this, I don't like it one bit.'

Horan detected foul play. The hare – an outside hare at Harold's Cross – had slowed dramatically, too dramatically for his liking. This had the effect of firstly encouraging Mick to falter and then, since he was on the outside, enticing him to run across to the hare-rail in the hope of actually grabbing the bunny. Ukelele Lad was, thus, left with a clear path and a clear opportunity to steal a valuable march up the inside. It bore the stench of a neatly executed coup. Mick the Miller was the 5/2 on favourite; Ukelele Lad was the second favourite at the generous odds of 5/1 in a four-dog field. Horan reckoned the hare-driver had been 'bought'.

Horan bided his time. One evening, he and the said hare-driver fell to drinking in one another's company. Horan plied the official with stout and Powers whiskey, waiting for the alcohol to kick in and defences to lower before seizing his chance to pop the incriminating question: 'Who told you to stop the hare on Mick the Miller that night at Harold's Cross?' There had indeed been a sting, came the slurred reply, organised by one of the track directors. It had been simplicity itself, a classic of its kind: stop the favourite and collect on the second favourite. Records show that Mick Horan was reluctant to race a dog at Harold's Cross ever again.

In between these rounds of the Harold's Cross 600-yards endurance test Mick the Miller had been sweeping all before him over the classic distance of 525 yards to win the Spring Cup at the track and progress to the semi-final of the National Cup at Shelbourne Park, both events being worth £100 to the winning owner. Furthermore, in the course of this winning spree over the shorter distance, Mick twice thrashed Ukelele Lad.

The two preliminary rounds of the Spring Cup amounted to little more than exercise gallops for him. Mick was now grabbing the headlines every time he stepped onto the track. With the final, on 21 May, appearing to be a one-dog race, Mick injected a spot of melodrama. During the parade, the correspondent of the *Irish Independent* thought he detected a limp in the favourite's gait. He passed on the observation to those closest to him, and the kind of wonderful demonstration of Chinese Whispers that only finds expression on racetracks rapidly did the rest. The message infected the betting ring with the speed of an August heat rash. As Mick was loaded last into the outside box, his price had drifted out to 5/1 with only one of his five rivals less fancied.

It's not known whether the journalist in question invested any of his salary on Mick the Miller, but he could not have engineered a potential coup better if he'd tried. The bookies were well and truly scalped. 'Mick the Miller never showed with a winning chance until close to the final bend,' he wrote in the following day's paper. 'Here he took up the running from Una's Cutlet and putting in a great burst in the straight he won easily in the end by four lengths from Real Rustic in a time of 30.79.'

The National Cup would be a much more severe examination. For a start, reaching the final meant the successful negotiation of three rounds not just the two of the Abercorn, Easter or Spring Cups. And every dog worth its salt would enter the lists against him. Mick was given a two-week break after lifting the Spring Cup, resuming winning ways in his heat of the Stayers' Sweepstakes on 7 June, prior to commencing his tilt at the National Cup only 24 hours later.

Mick proceeded to blaze a trail to the final that left opponents reeling and both spectators and headline writers drooling. He won his three rounds by an aggregate of 14 lengths with awesome exhibitions of raw power. First, he trounced old rival Care Free by four lengths and then he humiliated Carrodotia Boy by six. Both dogs re-opposed in the first semi-final on 26 June. Now Mick would surely face his moment of truth because Odd Blade was also drawn in this line-up. Mick dethroned the old champion by four lengths as easy as winking.

The clock added substance to the naked eye. Despite a series of summer thunderstorms, which left the going consistently on the heavy side, Mick had mounted a concerted assault on Shelbourne's track record. He warmed to the task when beating Care Free in 30.18 and then tied the record with a time of 30 seconds dead in round two. Thirty seconds for 525 yards was quickly becoming the holy grail of track racing, and he peppered that elusive mark once more in his semi with a time of 30.06. None of the other finalists – who numbered Entomb beside Odd Blade – had posted a time anywhere near his, a fact reflected in the ante-post market framed by local bookmaker Richard Duggan: 6/4 on Mick the Miller; 3/1 Odd Blade; 4/1 Entomb, so far unbeaten in the competition; and 6/1 the bitch Loughadian, the joint holder of the track record, who'd likewise progressed to the final unbeaten. The two complete outsiders, Marcus and Lounge Lizard could be backed at 10s and 33s respectively.

Despite further heavy thunderstorms, Saturday, 6 July saw Shelbourne Park packed to the rafters with over 10,000 people eagerly anticipating the final of the National Cup. Each and every one of them, it seemed, wanted to be 'on' Mick the Miller. The bookies strove manfully to stem the tide of money and restrict their obligations: while the rest drifted in the market, Mick's odds hardened to 2/1 on. But the public mood was unequivocal. Why should one bother about the proven strength of the opposition? Why worry about the inherent perils of that hazardous dash around the first bend which corresponds to a booby trap in every dog race? With due deference to his owner's calling, the public merely insisted: 'Mick's a certainty! Why, hasn't he God on his side!'

Mick entered trap two with Odd Blade on his inner and Entomb on his outer. There would be no hiding place when the lids sprang, no quarter given as they ran the opening gauntlet. The red and the blue jackets left the traps as one, with neither Odd Blade nor Mick prepared to concede right of passage to the first turn. The champion of Raheny was not about to tip his lance to the champion of Offaly without a battle royal. Odd Blade unleashed all the accumulated guile of the courser and street fighter he undoubtedly was to shoulder Mick aside as they met the bend in unison.

A precious three-length gap opened up while Mick found his feet and steadied himself for a response down the back straight. The bay of the crowd, briefly muted at the sight of its money going down the drain, rose again in approval at the sight of Mick the Miller hurtling after Odd Blade like a javelin. Mick caught the old champion halfway down the straight, ran past him as if he was a back-number – which subsequent victories in both the Belsize and Cork Cups proved he was not – and pulled further and further away rounding the final parabola to win by four long lengths in a time only 1/100th of a second outside his track record.

Horan led Mick back toward the grandstand amid a tumultuous ovation. Waiting to greet the greyhound now hailed by the press as 'a real champion' were Father Brophy and Michael Greene. The master of Millbrook House was beaming from ear to ear. He had good reason. This was Mick the Miller's 15th win from 20 starts on the Irish tracks, which in total had netted him the tidy sum of £332 in prize money and goodness knows how much in winning bets.

Greene was, as usual, more subdued. He gave Mick the Miller a pat and a surreptitious hug. Greene may have tarried longer had he appreciated he was in effect bidding his surrogate child farewell. After the semi-final of the National Cup on 26 June, Horan had suggested Mick be entered for the English Derby. Father Brophy warmed to the plan. The entry and £10 fee was duly dispatched to London before the 4 July deadline. Springing his champion on unsuspecting English bookmakers bore the hallmarks of an almighty coup in the making.

So it was that while Father Brophy and Michael Greene drove back to Killeigh, Mick Horan and Mick the Miller prepared to leave Ireland for an assault on the English Derby. Two days later, on the morning of Monday, 8 July 1929, Mick the Miller bade Ireland and Killeigh farewell, never again to place a paw in the verdant heartlands of the O'Connor Faly that had forged him.

CHAPTER EIGHT
THE ENTERPRISE OF ENGLAND

The well-dressed man entering Mick Horan's compartment on the 12.18 boat-train out of Holyhead bound for Euston was no Black and Tan, but his countenance and demeanour shrieked ex-British army and told Horan he was liable to be just as mean spirited.

'I'm not travelling in the same compartment as that flea-bitten, scruffy looking hound of an animal there,' said the newcomer with a disdainful cock of his head in the direction of Mick the Miller who was curled up happily at Horan's feet. 'And neither is my daughter!'

Horan eyed the young girl his inquisitor had in tow and lent back in his seat. The journey from Dublin to London was arduous enough without this additional aggravation. And there was a long way to go yet.

The two Micks had checked out of the North Star Hotel early that morning in order to catch the 8.25 train from Westland Row station that delivered them to Kingstown Pier (the modern Dun Laoghaire) ready for the 8.50 sailing of the steamship *Hibernia*. The unfortunate Mick the Miller was then incarcerated in a special crate (the size and shape of a single trap) and stowed in the hold, water lapping round his feet, for the duration of the three-hour voyage across the Irish Sea, while his trainer fretted away the time on deck. Ahead of them still lay the unappetising prospect of a further 5½ hours by rail for 'The Irish Mail' was not due into Euston until 5.50 that evening – that is, if they were lucky. Then, as now, railway timetables seldom lived up to the paper they were written on and the journey would as likely be closer to six hours.

Consequently, Horan was not in forelock-tugging mood and, irked by his fellow passenger's attitude, he gave as good as he got. 'I think more of my dog,' he fired back through gritted teeth, 'than you do of your daughter there. If you find me alternative accommodation, I don't mind moving. It's entirely up to you.'

A truce was ultimately declared, with trainer and dog retiring to the mail van, where they made themselves comfortable on the numerous sacks and caught up on some sleep. Aside from this unwelcome intervention, Horan had come prepared for most eventualities the train journey might throw up. When Mick the Miller grew hungry, he unwrapped the mince he had brought along and put it in a dish on the floor; once Mick had scoffed the lot, he then refilled the dish with water from a bottle. The brown paper had one further usage. When Mick duly emptied himself, Horan used the paper to pick up the evidence and throw it out of the carriage window. But if Mick wished to 'cock a leg' he was forced to wait until the train halted at the likes of Crewe, Rugby or Bletchley.

On a hot July afternoon the final few miles seemed to take an eternity, and it was a heartily relieved pair who finally leapt into the comparative fresh air of Euston station. So astonished were the platform staff at the sight of man and dog leaping from the mail van that they initially presumed Horan must be in the act of making a getaway after a mail robbery!

The country that Mick the Miller was sniffing for the first time was in the doldrums, enduring troubles every bit as destructive as Ireland's own. However, whereas the shattering of Ireland's peace and tranquillity involved lost lives and violent civil strife, Britain's hard times sprang from lost jobs and (relatively) peaceful civil strife.

In the year of Mick the Miller's birth, Britain's total unemployed was one million and rising, and on 4 May the country woke to the first general strike in its history after the general council of the Trades Union Congress voted to back the miners following the breakdown of their 'not a penny off the pay, not a minute on the day' negotiations with the employers. While the BBC broadcast prime minister Stanley Baldwin's message (read out by the managing director John Reith) asking the nation to 'Keep Steady! Remember that peace on earth comes to all men of goodwill,' a state of emergency was declared with troops being deployed in key trouble spots such as South Wales, Yorkshire and Central Scotland.

The situation in London typified the situation nationwide with the middle classes rising to the occasion in an effort to minimise disruption to daily life and maintain the flow of essential goods and services. 'Ladies who lunch' volunteered to deliver the post; the likes of students and solicitors jumped at the chance of realising boyhood fantasies by occupying the footplates of strikebound trains or the cabs of buses and lorries. The establishment was not going to give an inch. 'As far as we can see, we have no intention to allow cricket to be interrupted,' harrumphed the secretary of the MCC as the Australians arrived to defend the Ashes and, in the absence of ordinary newspapers, the Chancellor of the Exchequer, Winston Churchill, himself edited the first issue of *The British Gazette* which provided officially approved news. Churchill didn't mince words. He called for the unconditional surrender of the strikers, whom he referred to as the 'enemy'.

The enemy (bar the miners who heal out until November) caved-in after nine days but the repercussions were much longer lasting. The strike cost the coal industry alone in the region of £300 million, and one million unemployed was just the beginning. The figure spiralled onwards and upwards. In January 1927 it reached 1.4 million and the ramifications of the Wall Street Crash on 24 October 1929 would eventually drive it up to 2.7 million by July 1931. The economy lurched toward the precipice of national bankruptcy. Shares prices dropped like a stone; there was a run on gold as confidence in sterling ebbed away; Britain came off the gold standard, leading to a 30 per cent devaluation of the pound; £60 million was borrowed from New York bankers to stem the tide. Poverty became endemic, triggering a 10 per cent rise in the crime rate, principally theft; public disharmony was reflected in hunger marches to London from the provinces that resulted in demonstrations and riots in Whitehall; and the 10 per cent pay cuts in the public sector announced in the government's austerity programme went so far as to instigate a two-day mutiny involving 15 warships and 12,000 ratings on the fleet at anchor off Invergordon. Britain's prestige as a bastion of economic and military power had reached rock bottom.

How was the urban working man to survive this unremitting misery? Seeking pleasure where he may, had always been the surest antidote in the past. The old adage that the quickest way to get out of London (or any other industrial conurbation) was 'to go into the nearest pub and let booze do the trick' was easier said than practised under prevailing fiscal circumstances. An unskilled worker would be lucky to take home £2 a week. Once life's essentials had been taken care of, there was little going spare to finance jolly nights down the boozer with beer at sixpence a pint and cigarettes costing a shilling for a packet of 20. And vast numbers, of course, were not fortunate enough to be on even that lowly rung of the employment ladder.

In any case, the man in the street was forever being warned about the evils of drink. Now there was increasing concern about the health threats posed by his beloved 'fags'. Although a leading surgeon has assured an International Tobacco Exhibition that there is 'no risk of cancer from tobacco', the government announced that deaths from cancer had increased alarmingly in the past 20 years, despite a fall in the general death rate. Even cigarette firms themselves had begun sparing a thought for the welfare of their customers. 'Made specially to prevent sore throats,' ran an advertisement for Craven A; 'Consider your Adam's Apple – Kensitas are always kind to your throat,' promised a competitor. All such warnings fell on deaf ears. Britain was officially declared to be the greatest nation of cigarette smokers in the world with a yearly consumption of almost 31.2lbs of tobacco per head of the population.

So, smoking could kill you and drinking was the work of the devil. Thus, for the vast majority of working-class men in Britain's cities, bright spots amid the weekly grind were few and far between as the Roaring Twenties stuttered to an end. Music hall was a thing of the past, finally killed off by the wireless which stole its capacity to purvey the latest songs and jokes while reaching a far wider audience. Some 3 million homes now owned a wireless set. There was some talk of a new-fangled gimmick called television, but that was beyond the wildest dreams of Mr

Average. The cinema offered the most viable escape from daily drudgery. Perhaps an occasional outing to the local 'flea-pit' or 'bug-hutch', as they were irreverently dubbed, to catch the latest Tom Mix cowboy picture or Douglas Fairbanks swashbuckler. On the other hand, travelling further afield to one of London's new Astorias equipped with sound in order to let the wife shed a tear at Al Jolson warbling 'Sonny Boy' in his latest 'talkie' amounted to the kind of special treat he could ill afford. Now, if she fancied sitting beside him as he drooled over the vampish charms of 'It Girl' Clara Bow in *Wild Party*, something might conceivably be arranged. What with the pub out of bounds, there seemed nothing for it but to seek solace in his favourite armchair, switch on the wireless and turn to the amusing antics of 'Pip, Squeak and Wilfred' in his copy of the *Daily Mirror*.

Yet, there was one other elixir. Sport could ease the working man's burden like nothing else on earth. Reading about it, listening to it on the wireless (both the Grand National and the Derby were first broadcast in 1927), but preferably watching it in the flesh. There was Dixie Dean popping in goals left, right and centre for Everton; 46-year-old Jack Hobbs continuing to knock the cover off a cricket ball; while young middleweight slugger Len Harvey was knocking spots off his opponents; and six-figure crowds congregated on Epsom Downs for Derby day. The Derby held one priceless advantage over the others; you could have a bet. Yes, wages were low but when did that ever stop a man from having a flutter? Unfortunately, many of the country's racecourses were out of town and out of reach to the urban working man on a regular basis. He longed for excitement and betting opportunities closer to hand. What he craved was a racetrack just down the road from his factory or his terrace. What he needed was a greyhound track.

The answer to Joe Public's prayer had materialised on 24 July 1926 – just a matter of weeks after Mick the Miller saw the light of day. Jimmy Walsh's catchy ditty entitled 'Everybody's Going to the Dogs' tapped into the public consciousness, and the embryonic urban sport, soon dubbed 'gracing' or 'greycing', took the country by storm – whilst ironically condemning its rural cousin, which was providing the raw material, to eventual obscurity. Coursing never really recovered.

Track attendances grew from around 5½ million in the first full year of 1927 to over 13½ million in 1928 as ovals sprouted from Brighton to Edinburgh and Ramsgate to Cardiff. In London alone the number of spectators clicking through the turnstiles at its six tracks had reached 6,451,417. The capital's insatiable appetite for the sport was met by meetings every day of the week bar the Sabbath: Monday saw Wembley in the west, West Ham in the east and Harringay Park in the north; Tuesday meant White City in the west and Clapton in the east; on Wednesday, Wembley and West Ham were joined by Wimbledon in the south; Thursday was White City and Clapton; Friday spelt Harringay and Wimbledon; while Saturday brought the week to a close with a bang via meetings at all six venues. All the burgeoning sport needed was a hero, a greyhound who was more than a trap number, a dog with the 'It' factor to match Clara Bow.

Not every section of society was so enamoured with this new pastime, denigrated by Winston Churchill, for example, as 'animated roulette'. Thousands of poor people who toiled all day for a pittance, argued those with less need for a release, then went and lost it in the evening. Said a Church spokesman gravely, 'It is so popular that it threatens to become a social evil and should be discouraged.' The Churches' Committee on Gambling set about so doing by publishing a pamphlet entitled *Dog Racing* highlighting its inherent dangers. There were similar publications on the perils of dabbling on the football pools or even in the murky world of stocks and shares. Describing all forms of gambling as 'an emotional deficiency disease', this polemic went on to aver that, 'only dog-racing has assumed such enormous dimensions that it is already becoming a social problem of considerable magnitude.' Primary poverty resulting from inadequate income is understandable, ran the argument, but secondary poverty resulting from an adequate income being wasted in the main on 'drink, dogs and tobacco' was quite inexcusable.

The pamphlet's findings derived from a series of 400 interviews, 'combining the method of the mass observer with the trained mind of an economist', identified four distinct types of dog fancier: the professional gambler; the semi-professional; the sporting type; and the unhappy type.

The first two categories merely attracted the Church's moral outrage. The professional gambler, or 'fiddler' as he was known, tended to be of 'above average intelligence' and was eager to capitalise on his 'mathematical calculation' of all relevant factors in a dog-race (plus insider information from trainers). He would frequent as many meetings as possible (often using a taxi to get from one to another on the same night) in order to place hefty wagers. The typical 'fiddler' was an unsocial, single man making a profit of £2 per dog-meeting. Apparently, he lived modestly, though a select few managed to live a life of luxury which involved smoking 60-80 cigarettes a day and spending £5 a week on drink without ever being fully appreciative of how the 'morally dubious life' they led brought them close to the 'criminal type'. However, the pamphlet was pleased to record that one such interviewee, when pressed, did confess: 'I suppose you regard my position as immoral because I get something for nothing and contribute nothing to the community.' In contrast to these parasites, the semi-professional tended to be the family man who followed a trade and, with less time for study, became much more of a risk-taker at the racetrack as a result.

The last two categories were the Church's principal targets. These unfortunates comprised two-thirds of the total dog-racing fraternity and could be saved from their weakness. The 'sporting type' could be distinguished by 'their joviality, smart dress and quiet behaviour...they stick to their limits and do not chase their losses...they do not attend primarily to win but to have fun and they are not too disappointed when they lose, because they can afford to lose.' Yet, whatever they might say in their defence, continued the pamphlet, it's the gambling that attracts these people, not some higher sporting or recreational motive.

But at least they were staying out of the pubs. 'This is better than a pub,' said one, 'because I am in the fresh air, I have something for my outlay and I make money from time to time. Racing kills drinking – if I gave up dog-racing I should have to go to the pub and I would be worse off.' The Church's main objection to these men was that they occasionally brought their wives and young children into this den of iniquity that was the dog-track.

The picture painted of the 'unhappy type' seems as relevant today as it was in 1929:

'People in ragged clothes, on a cold winter night shivering without an overcoat or a pullover, who go short, or let their families go short, of basic essentials, who are desperate gamblers. They attend whenever they can get hold of some money, and they spend it as quickly as it comes. They often behave like small children, complaining bitterly about their bad luck. They hold wistful illusions. They keep hoping all the time that their great hour will strike at any moment. Very often they enjoy more moments of agony than joy. People of this type are frequently of inferior physique and emotionally unbalanced. Among them you can see the crippled, the deformed or otherwise physically handicapped, who cannot do a hard day's work. It is they who generally shout loudest and most desperately – "Come on, number two!" – in a spasm of excitement, even though they know it looks foolish to shout at a dog by number. But their feelings are so intense that they feel a release by so doing. "Gambling is my greatest weakness, but I can't help it," said a hysterical 37-year-old. "I don't know what to do next; I must get some money, by whatever means." These are the recruits of secondary poverty.'

The Church's conclusions were damning. On average, five people out of six, it insisted, headed homeward from a dog-meeting beset by feelings of disappointment and dissatisfaction. In addition, it was morally and socially repugnant to discover how 'the distribution of losses and dividends had an anti-social character because the poorest, the most unhappy, the physically and emotionally handicapped, are made to pay for the professionals and semi-professionals who get hold of intimate knowledge.'

The greyhound (the Church never once mentioned the breed by name in its diatribe) racing world was quick to respond with a pamphlet of its own. *Actual Facts About Greyhound Racing* proceeded to

13 May 1931: the only known picture of Mick in full flight, during a solo trial at the White City

October 1933: hitting the traps (left) during the filming of Wild Boy

*July 1926: Michael Greene (centre) unveils Na Boc Lei's newest litter to visitors –
Mick the Miller is the tiny bundle resting on Greene's knees*

*June 1927: Father Brophy holds Macoma and Michael Greene his beloved
Mick the Miller in front of the coach-house in the yard at Millbrook*

June 1927: Greene's right hand keeps a keen grip of Macoma and Mick as visitor Leonard Mathews enjoys an easier task

Mick Horan hand-slips Mick in a London park for the benefit of the English press

25 July 1929: Father Brophy conveniently uses the Derby trophy just presented by the Duchess of Sutherland to obscure his face and calling: Mick Horan (far right) looks like a man knowing he is leaving without his dog

January 1930: Sidney Orton and Arundel Kempton get to know their new acquisition

FIRST & FOREMOST! THE PIONEER OF GREYHOUND RACING NEWSPAPERS.

THE GREYHOUND EVENING MIRROR

FORMERLY "THE GRAHOUND EVENING MIRROR."

WEMBLEY, WHITE CITY, HARRINGAY, CLAPTON AND WEST HAM.

ALL YOU WANT TO KNOW ABOUT THE 'DOGS.'

OUR POLICY: ONLY ONE SELECTION FOR EACH RACE.

The Only Dog Paper That Matters.

No. 288 (Registered at the G.P.O. as a Newspaper.)   Monday, June 30th, 1930.   **ONE PENNY**

AT WHITE CITY ON SATURDAY.

How Mick Won His Second Derby: Full Story.

50,000 PEOPLE SHOUT HOME WORLD'S FASTEST—AND MOST POPULAR—GREYHOUND.

Amazing Scenes Mark A Glorious Night.

KING ALFONZO'S ENTHUSIASM.

(Special Description By Isidore Green.)

The greatest night in the history of greyhound racing occurred at White City on Saturday when Mick the Miller, amid a tornado of cheers, raced round the track always ahead of his rivals, to lead first on the winning line and duplicate his Derby triumph of last year.

H.M. The King of Spain was present at this great sporting event and his enthusiasm was shared by a crowd which numbered 50,000.

The race itself requires very little space to describe. It was won undoubtedly by the best dog and Mick the Miller simply repeated a performance which every greyhound race-goer associates him with. Cunning and speed of a kind which was markedly superior to that possessed by any of his rivals, made itself emphatically proved yells of admiration and as the favourite passed the winning line two lengths in front of his nearest rival, Bradshaw Fold, the ecstasy of the crowd developed into a terrific crescendo of cheers. One of the most delighted spectators was the King of Spain who vociferously applauded the wonderful performance.

THE TRIUMPH OF TRIUMPHS.

Mr. Orton (holding Cup), trainer of Mick the Miller, that won the Greyhound Derby, with Mr. and Mrs. Kempton, owners, and the head lad holding the winner. This is Mick's second Derby and the success was a most popular one.

Block by Courtesy of The Daily Mirror.

nounced a moment after the start of the great dog classic, and apart from a slight hemming in at the first bend, the favourite was never in serious trouble.

The manner in which Mick drew away from his opponents at the first and the amazingly clever way in which he hugged the rails and took the bends

Mick McGee sorely pressed the favourite all down the back straight and fully deserves the highest recognition for his valiant attempt but he just failed to capture second place. Bradshaw Fold in a tremendous effort beating him by a head for this position. So Green, Dresden and Jack Bob

(Contd on page 2)

30 June 1930: the press are in raptures after Mick's second Derby victory

*28 June 1930: Sidney Orton, the Kemptons and Joe Ollis
on the victory podium after the Derby*

*4 October 1931: Primrose Ann
Kempton cuddles her favourite pet*

9 August 1930: Welsh Derby, receiving the trophy at the hands of Lady Hughes-Morgan

Spring 1931: Mick enjoys his daily massage from Mick Horan

refute 'this propaganda' by responding to all those who had 'recently conspired to give "the dogs" a bad name' with an eloquent series of testimonials from all walks of life as to the sport's social benefits. Alongside this testimony came a detailed factual rebuttal of the general charge that greyhound racing had caused, 'an increase of betting of such devastating proportions as to have "demoralised" the working classes, caused widespread "misery and want" and "imperilled Sunday dinners".'

No magistrate in the country, began the defence, could say definitely that there had been a single case brought before him of misery or want due to excessive betting on greyhounds; pawnbrokers repudiated the claim that homes were being pledged to fund betting on greyhounds; and figures from the National Savings Association showed an increase in deposits and new accounts rather than a flood of withdrawals and closures to cover any betting losses. Nor had the police reported any increase in public disorder or drunkenness as a result of greyhound racing – in fact, the exact reverse had been the truth of the matter.

Some members of the Church of England and Roman Catholic clergy even broke ranks to give the sport ringing endorsements. 'I regard the programme you present as being something which even a Bishop could see without being provoked to gamble,' said one vicar from London's East End; while a priest in Leeds testified: 'The Catholic clergy are very much in favour of dog racing. It is not for bookmakers and backers only, as we hear so often mentioned, but a clean sport for the public – equally as interesting as horse racing, if not more so – as it caters for the general public, the working class as well as the rich.'

Thus, Lord Askwith, President of the National Greyhound Racing Society, was acting on solid evidence and not from mere bias when he volunteered the opinion in a 1928 speech: 'There can be no doubt that greyhound racing meets the wishes of tens of thousands of people who have, almost by themselves, taken in hand and started it. Greyhound racing comes as a novel answer to an obvious need, and has been taken hold of by the people themselves. It will ensure open places, open air, and evening entertainment, especially in the summer; it can have added to it other amusements, and affords an opportunity for developing more and more plans for meeting an urgent social need. Moreover, greyhound racing pays around £200,000 per annum in entertainment tax and contributes approximately £15,000 per annum to charities.'

Lord Askwith found allies in both the likeliest and the unlikeliest quarters. *The Sporting Life* referred to 'a great new democratic sport owing to its intrinsic sporting and spectator appeal', while King Alfonso of Spain commented (somewhat patronisingly) after a trip to the White City that, 'greyhound racing is a wonderful sport as it provides workers with congenial recreation in the evenings after their day's work is done and brightens up their drab lives.' One can readily appreciate why Alfonso was deposed a few years later.

Accordingly, the mood of Britain in the summer of 1929 left much to be desired. Although the popular song on everyone's lips may have been 'I can't give you anything but love, baby', the innate melancholy of 'Ol' Man River' from the hit musical *Show Boat* with its haunting line 'tired of livin, scared of dyin' struck a public chord that ran much truer. The country remained uneasy in the aftermath of the General Strike and was presently reeling from the June General Election, which had endorsed this disquiet by yielding a Labour Government under Ramsay McDonald that lacked a Commons majority, instead relying upon the goodwill of Lloyd George's Liberals for its survival. The good ship Britain was drifting, rudderless, uncertain and apprehensive of what lay ahead.

Even the tired body language of the newspaper vendor outside Euston station had betrayed this national torpor. And with good reason. The pages of the *Daily Mirror* ('The Daily Picture Newspaper') Mick Horan thumbed through as he stood in the taxi rank seemed to carry nothing but bad tidings: the King's chest had been cut open to remove an abscess 1½ inches in diameter; the death toll on the roads had reached record levels of 14 a day thanks to the increase in the number of private cars (now one to every 26 people); the current heat wave had killed 21 people and threatened to cause a water shortage; and a dying man was discovered in a railway carriage, bloodstained razor beside him, muttering 'I am an outcast and in disgrace.' Even the most innocent of activities seemed to be doomed. Horan's eyes came to rest on the horrific account of a stunt at a

Fire Brigade fete in Gillingham that had gone tragically wrong. The staged spectacle of 'a house fire and thrilling rescue' ended in tears as 14 of the participants (ten of them young boys) perished in the flames.

Horan cast the paper aside on entering his taxi and instructed the cabbie to ferry him and Mick the Miller across London to the kennels of Wimbledon trainer Paddy McEllistrum at Burhill, in Hersham, near Walton-on-Thames. The Tralee-born McEllistrum, 'Happy Mac' as he was dubbed, had brought over a consignment of greyhounds from Ireland for trainer Harry Leader only the previous year. He grew attached to some of them (throughout his long and successful career he never was one to dispense with a dog unnecessarily) and liked the scene so much he elected to stay put and apply for a licence. In that first year of 1928, McEllistrum immediately showed his mettle by winning Wimbledon's Scurry Gold Cup with Cruiseline Boy; while at the end of 1929 Loughnagare would win him another Classic, the St Leger, a race he was to win again 41 years later with Spotted Rory when he was well into his 70s. McEllistrum's range was just one section of the wooden block shaped into a square that constituted the kennels at Burhill. Two of his neighbours soon began to show a keen interest in his temporary resident. Their names were Stanley Biss and Sidney Orton.

Horan readied Mick the Miller for his trial round the White City track, the home of the Derby, which was due to take place at the end of the week, Friday the 12th. The White City was the first London track to embrace greyhound racing, on 20 June 1927. Built to stage the 1908 Olympic Games, its name derived from the dazzling whiteness of its ferro-concrete structure, which had been latterly augmented by the construction of a new restaurant and the addition of covered terracing. The White City track itself was also in a league of its own. With a circumference of just under 500 yards, its 120-yard straights and wide, sweeping turns invited fair contests and fast times, all of which conspired to make it the logical venue for the new sport's version of the Derby. Greyhound racing's premier Classic was held for the first time in 1927 over 500 yards and won by the home dog Entry Badge, trained by Joe Harmon. A year later the Scottish-trained Boher Ash took the first Derby to be run over 525 yards in a time of 30.48 seconds.

While Boher Ash was due to be tuned up for the defence of his title at Edinburgh's Powderhall stadium, his principal rivals were scheduled to run solo 'trials' over the course and distance at the White City. Sidney Orton's candidate Hidden Jew – Mick's conqueror on his coursing debut at Maryborough – clocked 30.89 seconds; Back Isle, the leading Welsh challenger from Cardiff, posted 30.60; then Palatinus, a full brother to the previous year's Oaks winner Moselle and notorious for catching the hare on Wembley's opening night, stopped the clock at 30.22 – well inside the winning Derby time of Boher Ash 12 months earlier. On Friday the 12th, *The Grahound Daily Mirror* printed as a matter of course that the 'Paddy Noran-trained Mick the Millar [sic] from Dublin' would be among today's contenders running solo trials.

The following 24 hours heralded some drastic changes at *The Grahound Daily Mirror*. Firstly, it metamorphosed into *The Grahound Evening Mirror*. Secondly, it managed to unscramble its spellings. And thirdly, its front page was obliged to acknowledge 'a sensational trial by the Dublin champion' and pose the question, 'Will the Derby Cup go to Ireland?'

Like every other onlooker at the White City, the paper's reporter could scarcely believe what he saw. Mick completed his solo 525 yards in 30.03 seconds, 0.03 seconds inside the existing track record standing to Dick's Son, his old rival from Celtic Park, and, more significantly, nearly one-fifth of a second faster than Palatinus's benchmark from other Derby entrants. In half a minute Mick had made himself the talk of the track, 'the Dublin crack – a real smasher'. With competition, nothing was going to stop Mick ducking beneath the magical 30-seconds mark for 525 yards. However, anyone scurrying off to avail themselves of the 25/1 on offer for the Derby had another thing coming because Mick's odds were slashed to 12s within moments of him crossing the White City finish line.

Father Brophy arrived from Ireland to watch Mick contest his first round heat the following Tuesday. He was unconcerned about his dog's tumbling odds. He had taken the 25s!

The events surrounding Round 1: Heat 12 of the 1929 Derby were to pass into dog-racing folklore. Mick the Miller was badly away and met trouble at the first bend, yet unleashed staggering speed down the back stretch to thrash the Biss representative, Captured Half, by eight lengths and smash through the half-minute barrier in a world record of 29.82 seconds.

That much is true. It is the events of the subsequent 15 minutes that fed conjecture and led to decades of wayward repetition. While it is true Mick the Miller changed hands in the immediate aftermath of his heat for a sum staggering enough to see the story barnstorm that evening's papers, he was not auctioned on the White City terraces in quite the Runyonesque manner routinely depicted in the sport's literature.

Watching heat 12 with less detachment than most of those around him – who included Paddy McEllistrum, Sidney Orton and Stanley Biss – was a thick-set, snappily dressed 41-year-old man sporting slicked down and fashionably parted hair who could easily have passed muster as a 'heavy' in one of Hollywood's latest gangster movies. However, he was no mobster. He was, in fact, deputy chairman of South London Greyhound Racecourses Limited, the company that managed Wimbledon Stadium, and his dog Yellow Bead (trained by Orton) had just finished third to Mick the Miller. His name was Arundel Hugh Kempton, and he determined to buy Mick the Miller as a present for his 23-year-old wife Phyllis, who had recently given birth to their first child.

Kempton empowered McEllistrum to make Father Brophy an offer of £700. The priest was taken completely by surprise. Greyhounds had recently changed hands for greater amounts – future Grand National winner Cormorant for £1,000 and his litter brother Carpio for £1,250 – but this was a tidy sum (around £22,500 in today's money), easily enough, for instance, to buy a house in the surrounding suburbs of Shepherds Bush. Upon introductions being effected by McEllistrum and Con Stevens, Wimbledon's racing manager, Father Brophy and Arundel Kempton quickly fell to talking terms.

'Well, that's a very fine offer but you must consider my position, Mr Kempton,' said the priest cagily. 'If I accept, I'll have given away another £700 once Mick – as he surely will – wins the Final, so at the moment £700 is only half what he's worth to me.'

'Father, you may keep all the prize money,' countered Kempton unhesitatingly.

'Now, that would be most agreeable. But I must first allow Mr Biss the option of matching your offer since he has already expressed an interest in purchasing the dog.'

Stanley Biss was standing nearby with Albert Williams, a prominent Wimbledon bookmaker, the pair of them eavesdropping every word of the negotiations. Biss had indeed made an offer for Mick the Miller: £500 plus 25% of the Derby prize money should the dog finish first or second. But there was also a third prize of £100. Father Brophy insisted on driving a hard bargain: he informed Biss any sale agreement must incorporate third place. Biss demurred: if Mick the Miller was not first or second in the Derby he was not worth the £500. There seemed no way round this impasse. Father Brophy had yet again talked himself out of a deal by succumbing to the god of greed.

Biss now joined the group, and got straight down to business. 'All right, Father. Acting on behalf of Mr Williams, here, I can offer you £800 plus all of the Derby prize money – first, second or third.'

A look of consternation passed over Arundel Kempton's face. Con Stevens lent across and whispered something in his friend's ear. Stevens warned him not to become embroiled in a bidding war. Kempton turned his attentions back toward Father Brophy.

'There you are, Father, there's a better offer, you had better take it,' he said with the dignified air of resignation redolent of a true English gentleman.

Father Brophy and Albert Williams shook hands on the deal, with Kempton adding his congratulations by like gesture.

'If ever I part with Mick the Miller,' added Williams, 'I promise, Mr Kempton, you shall have him.'

Kempton turned on his heel and walked away, masking his disappointment as best he could. By his reckoning Mick the Miller should have been his dog. He had not yet abandoned all hope of making a present of him to his wife.

Father Brophy was suddenly brought back to earth by the sight of Michael Horan advancing toward him. Whether or not he cared about

Horan's feelings on the subject of Mick the Miller, he certainly proceeded to show no audible respect for them.

'I've sold the dog!' That's all he said. No explanation was forthcoming, then or later.

Horan was speechless. Yes, the owner was fully entitled to do as he wished with his dog but now, after they had come this far, after he had advised him to bring Mick over for the Derby and after he'd told him to seize the big price, to sell the dog on what seemed to be a whim, without so much as a 'by-your-leave', left Horan seething. To his dying day he neither forgot nor forgave.

Although Father Brophy confided to a *Daily Mirror* reporter at Wimbledon the evening after the sale that he had been 'loath to part with the dog', the balance of fact does not support that contention. Despite his bravado on the subject, he was well aware Mick the Miller had no divine right to victory – let alone a place – in the final, and any failure would see the dog's market value plummet. The projected deal with Arundel Kempton amounted to the sixth occasion that Father Brophy had contemplated selling Mick the Miller. At this point, he may well have wanted to keep his rising star but he also wanted, and quite possibly needed, the money. He could not have both. He took the money while he had the chance. So, at the seventh time of asking, Mick the Miller finally found himself with a new owner.

Whether Father Brophy would even receive a fair shot at pocketing the prize money on offer in the final was a moot point. Once Mick the Miller's sale was announced in the press, attention instantly focused on his new owner's occupation and possible motives in making such an expensive purchase. Albert Williams stood in the five-shillings ring at Wimbledon and was chairman of the track's bookmaking association. With ante post liabilities on Mick the Miller already standing at considerable levels, it was widely expected that Williams would withdraw the dog, thereby averting a potential disaster for the bookmaking fraternity. An immediate attempt to match Mick the Miller with the Wembley 700-yards specialist Naughty Jack Horner, suggesting he might have other objectives in mind for his dog, did little to allay these fears.

In the meantime, Mick the Miller returned to Hersham where his preparation continued under Horan's auspices as well as the watchful eyes of the press, who were eager to snap photographs of him being hand-slipped by his trainer in advance of his second-round heat on Saturday, 20 July. It turned out to be a terribly muggy evening with a thunderstorm patently in the offing. The storm began crashing around the White City shortly before racing was due to commence and 11/2 inches of rain fell inside 40 minutes. Peels of thunder were still ringing out as the dogs left the traps in the first race, causing the leader to be so petrified that he stopped to a walk before wandering off the track in a state of shock. However, nothing fazed Mick the Miller. Starting at 4/1 on, he overcame the usual tardy start and obstruction at the first bend to streak away down the back and ultimately win by eight lengths.

The two semi-finals were three days later. Entomb won the first from Beadsman, who was controversially given the verdict over Buckna Boy for the crucial second spot in the final. With a four-dog final having been announced in an undisguised attempt to reduce the possibility of first-bend mayhem giving rise to hard-luck stories that would undermine the Classic's credibility, this critical decision was not lost on the connections of the five dogs contesting the second semi-final. There could be no margin for error.

The only dog within 10 points of Mick (4/1 on) in the betting was Palatinus, edged into second spot by Buckna Boy in the previous round after repeatedly meeting trouble in running. Palatinus, who had caught the hare at Wembley 18 months earlier, succeeded in holding the lead to the last bend before Mick swamped him for finishing speed and drew clear to win by three lengths. Although Mick's change of ownership had been registered the previous day, he still contested his semi in the name of 'Mr B Murphy'. Thereafter, all legal ties were visibly severed and he lined up for the final in the name of Mr A H Williams.

Nevertheless, it was agreed that 'Mr B Murphy' should receive the Derby Cup at the hands of the Duchess of Sutherland if Mick the Miller prevailed in the final 48 hours later. What could possibly stop him? The time test stated Mick the Miller only had to stand up and avoid bad luck in order to win. His semi-final time was 0.18 seconds faster than Entomb's, that is the equivalent of three lengths. Of course, even in a dog race prudently reduced to four runners, a trouble-free run for the favourite could not be remotely guaranteed. As it turned out, *The Greyhound Evening Mirror*'s headline screaming 'Sensational "No-Race" incident in the Derby' scarcely did justice to the events at the White City on Thursday, 25 July 1929.

The fiddlers, the semi professionals, the sporting types and those unhappy representatives of the 'great unwashed' the Church sought to save, made their various ways to the White City in their thousands. Eighteen-year-old tailoring apprentice Harry Rothbart was a typical example of the sporting type. He, like many others, had got off early from his work near the Old Kent Road so he might head for the nearest tube station at Bank in good time to complete the rattling journey along the Central Line. His imagination had been instantly fired by this new dog from Ireland who seemed to race as if he possessed radar, so cleverly did he weave his way through any troublespots. Young Rothbart would one day have greyhounds of his own – and some decent ones at that – but this evening his sole intention was to invest one of the new ten-shilling notes recently brought into circulation that was burning a hole in his pocket on Mick the Miller. Eventually he joined forces with 40,000 like pilgrims whose journey by tube, by trams 28 and 30, the 93 bus or by that most celebrated and most reliable form of transport, Shanks's Pony, culminated in them snaking up Wood Lane or down Eastway past the forbidding pile of Wormwood Scrubs prison toward the greyhound mecca that was the White City. Most of them shuffled toward the turnstiles of the cheapest enclosure where every 'bob-a-nobber' who constituted the sport's lifeblood was congregating in anticipation of paying homage to their brand new hero.

Mick Horan, on the other hand, went out of his way – quite literally – to smuggle Mick the Miller from Hersham to Shepherds Bush as inconspicuously as possible. The bookmakers were now on a hiding to nothing, and Horan was wary of an attempt to put Mick the Miller out of the race. For this most important taxi-ride of all across London, Horan ordered the cabbie to take a different route to the one they'd usually driven just in case someone had taken note of it and had planned for a little 'accident' to befall the favourite en route.

It had been another sweltering day. By the time the bugle announced the emergence of the four finalists and their white-coated attendants onto the track a little before 8.45, the evening would have done credit to the tropics. Leading the parade in the red jacket of trap one was Beadsman, a red-fawn dog and the outsider at 20/1. Behind him came another red-fawn, Palatinus, a 3/1 chance, wearing the blue. Then Entomb (4s), his shining fawn coat (he was by common consent the best-looking dog in the race) set against the white jacket denoting trap three. Bringing up the rear was Mick Horan and the 7/4 on favourite, the only brindle in the race, sporting the black jacket of trap four. Each dog halted in turn before the steward responsible for checking muzzle and jacket were securely in place before making its way behind the traps, which were positioned down toward the entrance of the home straight.

Into the boxes they go, one by one. Horan slips off the collar and barely needs to lay a hand on Mick the Miller. He is eager to walk into his box, bursting to run. Horan gently pats his rump, whispers the last of numerous 'sweet nuthins' and steps onto the infield. At the signal, the hare controller, high up under the roof of the grandstand, flips the switch that triggers the hare's journey round the outside of the track. As soon as they hear the familiar sound of the machinery hissing into life, the four prisoners begin to howl with excitement and the noise of the crowd changes from a buzz to a threatening roar which detonates the split second the hare scoots past the traps and the lids spring upwards.

Palatinus makes the best of the break. The favourite languishes fourth of four, having made one of his characteristically sluggish exits. Into the first bend and, having weighed up his options, Mick tries to find the rail from his outside berth. Entomb has the same idea. Unfortunately, Beadsman is moving in the opposite direction and, unable to control his speed, he smacks straight into the pair of them, sending all three sprawling. The 'No-Race' klaxon is whining even before Palatinus completes the course in what virtually amounts to regal isolation.

Pandemonium ensues. Panting dogs are retrieved; rules and regulations checked, an official decision delivered and stressed. Had the race been in Ireland, the result would have stood since re-runs were only ordered if the dogs cease chasing the hare. However, this is England. There will be a re-run at 9.15, until which time all dogs must remain in the centre of the track.

Under cover of all this bedlam, Horan spies the handler of Palatinus attempting to escort his dog from the infield, doubtless in search of some cooler spot or even a sip of water. In weather like this a greyhound's temperature could rise to 105° Fahrenheit (40° centigrade) immediately after a race; and heat stroke can kill a greyhound inside 30 minutes.

Horan seldom, if ever, lost his temper. But in the prickly heat of a sultry evening, feelings are now running high.

'Where's he think he's going?' Horan growls at the nearest steward. 'If he's going to bring his dog off, I'm going to bring my dog off too!'

With an outstretched arm, the steward prevents Palatinus from leaving. 'There you are, Horan. No harm done. Everything all right now?'

Never one to forego the chance of stealing a march on the opposition, Horan demonstrated yet again the shrewdness that was his hallmark. Glancing at his dog lying by the side of the track, tongue lolling and flanks heaving, he extricates a large white linen handkerchief from his pocket and politely says to the steward: 'Could you go and soak this in cold water for me, please?'

When the hankie is returned to him, Horan slowly squeezes it over Mick the Miller who licks every cooling droplet as if it was holy water from the chapel font in Trim. Horan looked around him. None of the other three dogs were enjoying such a restorative. He was content.

The re-run initially appeared akin to a case of *déjà vu* because Palatinus again got away by far the quickest of the quartet but, unlike the original, this attempt was not marred by a snarl-up at the first bend and an unhindered Mick the Miller was soon giving hot pursuit. Lowering and lengthening his body with every stride, he made a magnificent sight down the back straight as he cut down the leader way before the third bend. The final 100 yards amounted to a victory parade, with Mick crossing the line holding a three-length advantage over Palatinus with Entomb a further two lengths in arrears. Despite this being his second race in half an hour, Mick's time of 29.96 was a fifth of a second faster than that clocked by Palatinus in the 'No-Race'.

Father Brophy was at one with the world. His wagers and the full prize money of £700 had been landed. 'What do you do with your winnings, Reverend Sir?' asked a cheeky reporter from the *Daily Mail*. 'Most goes to the poor of my parish,' the priest replied in the manner of a saint. Quite possibly he was equally judicious when posing for photographers on the victory dais, since he managed to mysteriously position the Cup right in front of his face, rendering both him and his dog-collar totally undistinguishable. And there were yet more thrills in store for him because the dais was hauled round the track by the White City tractor so that the crowd might salute the victorious connections, although a *Daily Mail* headline referring to this 'genial Irish parson and his two charming black-eyed daughters' was calculated to embarrass the float's female attendants and stupefy the paper's Catholic readers in one fell swoop. The evening concluded with the Derby Ball in the Stadium Club at which the 'genial parson' was surrounded by numerous 'colleens' and showered with congratulations from all sides – from people he did know such as Albert Williams (whose £5,000 in winning bets more than compensated for the conceded prize money) and Arundel Kempton, to those who were complete and utter strangers – while being plied with a seemingly inexhaustible supply of free drinks. This was, indeed, heaven on earth.

Harry Rothbart had not won as much as Father Brophy or Albert Williams but he could not have returned home any happier. However, not everyone's cup runneth over so much as theirs. Mick Horan's elation was muted. He sank the contents of his first celebratory bottle of Guinness in the customary one gulp his drinking partners had grown to know and love, but this particular party was as much a wake as a celebration. Nor were the connections of Palatinus best pleased. The runner-up's owner lodged an objection to the re-run – which was overruled (as was his subsequent appeal). Fortune had certainly not smiled on Palatinus, for he had not played any part whatsoever in the first-bend incident. On the other hand, for Mick the Miller to have been denied a fair crack of the whip would have been a travesty, since no one seriously doubted that he was by far and away the best dog in the final. After all, he was the only dog to clock below 30 seconds in the entire competition, and he did so in three of the four rounds.

When the news of Mick the Miller's victory reached Killeigh, the villagers lost no time in organising their own party. The Irish need little excuse to carouse; after all, this is a country where it is said parties can start in empty rooms. Barrels of beer were rolled out onto the village green, a celebratory bonfire was lit and the dancing and singing commenced.

Father Brophy had now been away from his parishioners for 11 days. He had surely stretched a curate's freedom to breaking point. The idyll of all idylls had to end. On the Friday, he and Mick Horan shook off their hangovers to catch the Irish Mail on the first leg of their journey back to Dublin. It had been a glorious trip, this 'Enterprise of England', hugely more profitable than its Spanish precursor thwarted by Elizabethan sea-dogs back in 1588. The priest's luggage contained silverware while his wallet contained two cheques and plenty of banknotes, somewhere around £2,000 in total. For the man who had masterminded its success, however, nothing compensated for the emptiness in his heart and the void at his feet. Conversation was sparse and forced.

Michael Horan would train other champions: Guideless Joe to win the very first Irish Derby in 1932; Magheragh Soldier to land a hat-trick of Trigo Cups at Celtic Park, to name just two. But he would never know a greyhound like Mick the Miller. Horan loved him like one of his own children and spoke of him to them with as much affection. He would hold his sons spellbound with the stuff of legend. How Mick had the brain of a child: you see, he'd explain, Mick was reared with people and met a lot of people; he was like a little terrier brought up to live on the streets, dodging in and out of traffic; he was streetwise, quick on the uptake. How he never saw such a clever dog going to a bend. How Mick would lift up his head and, if he saw he was likely to be crowded, how he'd ease off, let the others run wide and then cut across to the inside. How he wouldn't come back past the crowd if he'd been beaten, but if he won, he'd come back past them, wagging his tail!

And their father's fond reminiscences always ended with the same telling refrain. 'Make no mistake, most of the time Mick would be wagging his tail!'

CHAPTER NINE
ALL THAT IS CLEANEST AND BEST

Aylsham is a small market town straddling the River Bure, a dozen miles north of Norwich. In the spring of 1928 one of its 2,266 populace was slowly wending his way through the market place. Below a luxuriant mop of dark shiny hair was the open, honest face – dominated by a long fleshy nose – associated with men who earn their livelihood from the land. He appeared to be in no hurry and took every opportunity to gaze in the window of any shop displaying its wares: Keymer's Ironmongery; Miller the bootmaker; Ward & George Outfitters; and especially the assorted temptations of Mrs Dazeley's sweetshop.

Any resemblance to a man without a care in the world, however, was misleading. He was a 37-year-old farmer with a wife and children to support. At his age, and with his responsibilities, scratching a living from the Norfolk soil was proving to be a precarious occupation on the cusp of an economic depression. Any excuse to tarry was gladly seized upon, for he was on his way to a meeting he'd rather not be attending. Sidney John Orton had an appointment to see Bertram Sewell, manager of Barclays Bank.

The prognosis – as Orton suspected – was not good. Bertram Sewell had done his homework. He'd examined the accounts; checked the figures. All that remained was for him to be cruel to be kind.

'Well, Sidney, times are hard – and, to my way of thinking, they're going to get harder and harder for the farming community. Can you not turn your hand to something else? What about the greyhounds? You've been training coursing dogs for years now. Why don't you try this new-fangled track racing that everyone is talking about? It should suit you down to the ground and give you a good living wage.'

Orton strode out of the bank with renewed brio. Sewell's chance remark spawned the germ of an idea at that. He possessed few qualifications for any alternative to farming – other than this suggested avenue for which, quite perversely, he possessed every conceivable qualification.

Sidney Orton was born on 11 July 1890 into a world overflowing with greyhounds. The lullaby which sent the infant Orton to sleep each night was the 'singing' of the numerous coursing dogs kept by his parents, George and Sarah, on their 400-acre Stonegate farm. George Orton also bred hackneys and his eldest son frequently accompanied him to Norfolk's various agricultural shows with the high-steppers. However, it was not these jaunts on balmy summer days that made the biggest impression on young Sidney but outings on those marrow-chilling days during the winter when he joined his father on the running grounds of the Swaffham Coursing Club, the oldest coursing club of them all. The pony and trap bobbing along deserted lanes; his father up front, reins in gloved hands, hunched against a screaming January wind that sucked freezing Russian temperatures straight from the Urals across the featureless Norfolk landscape with a vengeance; while he in search of warmth huddles closer to the couple of dogs who share the blankets and straw heaped in the back. 'That part of the world really was bleak,' Orton later recalled. 'It was a place where two rabbits would watch one blade of grass grow.'

For the most part, local coursing was low-key. Farmers ran their dogs against each others for five shillings a side – though after a few tots from the hip flask over lunch, the shillings tended to become pounds! Sidney Orton warmed to the entire ambience and after George's death in 1909, he assumed his father's mantle in both the running of the farm and the greyhounds. After the First World War (for which he was rejected for national service), he became a licensed trainer and immersed himself fully in the local coursing scene, establishing lifelong friendships with Jack Masters, secretary of the Swaffham club and breeder of the famous 'Toftwood' line of greyhounds at his farm in Dereham, and Harry Cator, prime mover behind the establishment of the Woodbastwick Coursing Club, at whose first meeting Sidney Orton acted as slipper. Orton's most noteworthy greyhound during this period was Stride On, acquired from a butcher friend as the 'weed of a litter', who won the President's Trophy at Woodbastwick in 1924. Stride on should also have won the Club's Gold Bracelet event, however, the judge inadvertently pulled out the wrong flag from his pocket and showed the other dog as the winner!

Sidney Orton's prospects, that had looked so dismal at the onset of 1928, began to perk up dramatically. Hard on the heels of Bertram Sewell's chance remark came a chance meeting with Murray Wilson, an old coursing friend who was now racing director at the new Wimbledon track, which was due to open in May. Wilson urged Orton to act on Sewell's suggestion and advised him to apply to Wimbledon for a position as trainer. It turned out that all such posts were filled, but Orton was offered the position of Paddock Steward and Clerk of the Scales. As it happened, Wimbledon's grand opening – Hollywood actress Tallulah Bankhead, filming at the nearby Teddington studio of Warner Bros, was to cut the ribbon – had to be postponed owing to the River Wandle flooding the track. Disappointment turned to farce – and very nearly tragedy – when the management threw an impromptu consolation party in the clubhouse only accidentally to set fire to it!

Orton never abandoned his hopes of training greyhounds for the track, however, and with that objective in mind he moved out of Aylsham and bought a farm at Kelvedon, in Essex, which brought him closer to the developing London action. His chance was not long in coming. In November, Harry Leader returned to Ireland and Orton was offered his range, complete with 60 dogs. Any reservations Leader's owners may have harboured concerning Orton's ability to cut the mustard were instantly dispelled. On the third of the month Orton won his first race with Hidden Jew, Tom Harte's old dog now owned by Joe Cave, and on New Year's Eve he pulled off a hat-trick of wins in trophy races to bring up an astonishing £1,000-worth of prize money.

One of those trophy winners was Bouncing Hawk, who belonged to another of the delighted owners Orton inherited from Leader, Arundel Kempton.

Arundel Hugh Kempton came from a privileged background. He was born on 1 July 1888 to Charles Henry and Alice Charlotte Victoria Kempton of 18 Bolwell Terrace, Lambeth Walk. Charles Kempton was a prosperous businessman with interests in glass-making whose contacts and connections throughout the many guilds instrumental in the City of London's local government and administration smoothed the way for his third son to be accepted as a 'Liveryman and Freeman' of the Glovers Company. Arundel himself was the director of a company that manufactured 'incandescent gas mantles' – gas lamps by any other name – and operated street lamps. One of his daily chores involved driving into London early in the morning to hire (and of necessity pay in advance) the casual labour who walked round the capital extinguishing the lamps in the morning and re-lighting them in the evening.

Running for public office was also on Kempton's agenda. In 1928 he had put his name forward as a candidate for City of London Sheriff, one rung below – and stepping stone to – the office of Lord Mayor. Kempton even boasted his own coat of arms and motto of *Labore Attingam* (Let me attain through hard work). Prominent atop his crest was a goat, somewhat apt since he had acquired for himself the reputation of being a bit of a ladies' man.

Kempton's love life, however, did not always run smoothly. His first wife Bertha had died shortly after the birth of their son Bertram in 1920. But he had found love again, and on 21 September 1926 he married Phyllis O'Neill, the daughter of a wealthy merchant and some 17 years his junior, at Holy Trinity Church, Kensington Gore. The newly-weds set up home at 19 Arthur Road, one of a row of splendid properties in Wimbledon Park, which they christened 'Deepdene'. In the early summer of 1929 their domestic idyll was completed by the birth of a daughter, Primrose Anne. Unfortunately, his wife's difficult pregnancy had necessitated his withdrawal from the race to become Sheriff.

Apart from this setback to his aspirations in public life, things could scarcely have been sweeter. Rundel and Phiddy, as they were known to fellow socialites, made a handsome, gilded couple. He, urbane and charming, the possessor of a fine singing voice which he proudly used to entertain guests with a touching rendition of his favourite tune, 'Her

Name Was Mary'. His principal indulgence was a penchant for collecting motor cars, particularly the latest American marques. She, a pretty, gold-en-haired 20-year-old 'Bright Young Thing', as *Tatler* magazine was wont to label her ilk, who confessed to a weakness for 'dining and dancing in the West End', where she might sample the very latest cocktails such as a 'Manhattan' or 'White Lady'. Not everyone shared Phiddy's love of the dance floor. 'Dancing Maniacs are for the most part young and frivolous,' wrote one correspondent to the *Daily Mirror*. Another stressed that, 'English dancers have not the lithe gracefulness of the south Europeans nor the infectious vitality of the North Americans,' before signing off with a warning to one and all that 'the Charleston is not suitable for English dancers because of its jerky precipitation.' Collecting cars, however, was not to Phiddy's taste. She preferred ancient Chinese ivories.

The main interest shared by the Kemptons was a passion for grey-hound racing, which they assuaged with a string of a dozen or more dogs. 'I find it so much more interesting than horseracing,' the new Mrs Kempton informed the gentlemen of the press. 'Plenty of other women I know share my opinion on the matter – and, of course, expenses are not nearly so heavy as for the upkeep of a racing stable.'

Thanks to owners like the Kemptons and Joe Cave, Sidney Orton and his wife Gladys expanded their own circle of friends to encompass personalities from the world of show business, such as the actor-impre-sario Tom Walls (who turned to training racehorses and won the 1932 Derby with April the Fifth) and Bud Flanagan and Chesney Allen from the Crazy Gang. Orton was going places.

On 19 December 1929, Arundel Kempton re-affirmed his faith in his new trainer in a big way. Kempton had failed in his bid to buy Mick the Miller for his wife as a maternity present, but he had finally got him as a Christmas present. The gift set Kempton back £2,000 – something like £64,000 in today's terms. And Orton, rather than his other trainer Paddy McEllistrum, was the man chosen to take charge of Mick the Miller from Stan Biss in the New Year.

On his first day at Wimbledon, Orton had only managed to reach the Elephant and Castle from Kelvedon before losing his way. Stopping his car to find his bearings, who should draw up alongside and put him right but Stanley Biss.

If Sidney Orton did have a contemporary of equal training ability, that man was unquestionably Stan Biss. Three years younger than his rival, Biss also brought with him the legacy of a highly successful grounding in the coursing fields of his native Essex and the eastern counties. Yet Biss was no son of the soil. By trade he had been an apprentice engineer before joining the Royal Flying Corps during the First World War and winning the Air Force Medal for conspicuous gallantry through climbing out onto the wing of his damaged plane. After the war he started a bus company, which he still owned at the commencement of his track training career in 1928.

Success followed success. He secured his first Classic in 1932; in the next calendar year he netted the astronomical sum of £10,000 in stakes; and in 1948 he broke the £20,000 barrier. Unlike Orton, he had a nomadic training career, leaving Wimbledon for West Ham in May 1930 and having stints at Catford and Clapton prior to training privately in 1949. He retired two years later and died, aged 59, on 9 March 1952 following a stroke.

Biss played his cards close to his chest. Pressed for his secret, no beans were ever in danger of being spilled. His mantra never amounted to anything more than, 'giving my dogs good food and plenty of exercise.' However, a better illustration of the painstaking lengths Biss was prepared to take in the interest of his dogs came during a distemper outbreak when, in order to kill the virus, he had all of his grass paddocks dug up and replaced with hot ash. He won the English Oaks on a record six occasions, most famously with the dual winner Queen of the Suir, and also handled, later in her career, the marvellous Bradshaw Fold, a black bitch who regularly smashed records and occasionally jousted with Mick the Miller.

Oh, let's hear it for Bradshaw, noble Hammer so fine,
Her battles with the Miller will be remembered through time.
Shout 'hooray' for that glorious West Ham bitch,
That has made every Cockney in pride so rich

Such an uncanny knack did Stan Biss possess with bitches that he, too, was serenaded by the same contemporary balladeer:

Stanley Biss is a trainer of wisdom so bright,
As the maker of bitches he gets it right.
He watches and thinks and sees things ithers would miss,
This is our man, West Ham's Stanley Biss.

Track master, greyhound teacher sublime,
He knows every dog, their form he will prime,
And when the right moment for victory is comw,
A Stanley Biss dog will have the race won.

Given that Stan Biss was never to train an English Derby winner, the loss of Mick the Miller was galling to say the least. More so as he had done nothing wrong with him. Quite the reverse, in fact. Since the Derby he had trained Mick to win 11 times (including three matches) for Albert Williams, with just two losses; and prior to the 1930 handover Biss would send out Mick to add two more successes in the name of Mrs Arundel Kempton.

After romping through the afternoon heat and evening final of West Ham's Grand International (by seven lengths and four lengths) over 600 yards on 5 August, Mick reverted to 525 yards to accept the challenge of home and away matches with the Welsh champion Back Isle, who had recently broken Mick's world record 525 mark with a time of 29.64 in the final of the Welsh Derby. Mick travelled down to South Wales by train for the first leg at Cardiff's Welsh White City on 24 August and was given a private trial 48 hours before the match in which, though no time was announced to the public, it was believed he ran close to Back Isle's record.

This rumour had no impact on the partisan Sloper Road devotees who sent their hero off the 7/4 on favourite – the first time Mick the Miller had not started favourite since the Easter Cup – and they roared him home to victory by 2½ lengths in a time only slightly slower than his world record. The turning point of the match came at the third bend as

Mick made his move and collided with Back Isle's hindquarters, for the Welsh dog had survived the contretemps the better. The following Saturday's eagerly awaited return – 'Tit-Bit at Wimbledon tonight!' – saw Mick exact revenge over the longer trip of 550 yards, edging out the visitor by a neck at the conclusion of an epic struggle completed in a new world record of 31.72 seconds.

With honours even, the Wimbledon executive announced the running of The First International Greyhound Derby Sweepstakes for which the winner of the Scottish Derby, Cleveralitz, would be invited to join Mick the Miller and Back Isle in a conscious effort to resolve the identity of the country's premier racer. Mick settled the debate by extending his superiority over Back Isle to a length, with Cleveralitz trailing by a further six.

Next on Mick's agenda was a White City match on 14 November which amounted to a battle of the bookies. Wimbledon's Albert Williams versus Harringay's Billy Chandler, the owner of Bishop's Dream. Mick won by half a length ('A neck and neck duel sends big crowd into hysterics,' reported *The Greyhound Evening Mirror*) before sailing through the opening two rounds of the London Cup at the same track. The semi-final provided stiffer opposition and he was, in the words of the sport's bible, 'obliged to prove his worth in the sternest battle of his racing career – great victory after bordering on defeat.' Hemmed in 20 yards from the line, he somehow extricated himself from the pocket to stifle the cries of 'Mick's beaten! Mick's beaten!' and nail Melksham Endurance right on the line.

However, the decision went against him at the conclusion of the final on 26 November when Peerless Call pipped him by a head. Although Peerless Call was widely tipped to win (he had clocked a faster time in taking his semi by six lengths from War Cloud, a dog whom Mick had just half a length behind him in an earlier round), public sentiment ensured Mick started favourite but despite 'racing with marvellous grit and uncanny cleverness' he could never quite escape the attentions of his chief rival who made the best use of his trap-one draw to get up in the final few strides.

Mick the Miller's last race in Albert Williams's ownership was a return match with Bishop's Dream over 500 yards at Harringay on 11 December. It proved to be Mick's one and only visit to the north London venue constructed on the site of a former refuse tip. Harringay was just 438 yards in circumference, yet with long 120-yard straights like the White City's, the resultant bends were too sharp for Mick. By contrast, Bishop's Dream, as the home dog, knew every inch of the track, knowledge he proceeded to demonstrate by immediately establishing a five-length advantage. There followed what was described as 'a sight for the gods' as Mick, repeatedly denied the rails-run he hankered for, capped 'one of the most delightful exhibitions of running and canine cleverness ever demonstrated' by passing Bishop's Dream on the outside up the run-in to snatch the spoils by half a length.

The preliminary rounds of the Champion Stakes before and after Christmas provided Rundel and Phiddy Kempton with the first opportunities to bask in the reflected glory of their newly acquired star at their home track. However, the Plough Lane circuit was another not built to suit Mick the Miller. The oval measured just 439 1/2 yards with straights on the short side at 100 yards, and although the turns were slightly banked to aid passage, Wimbledon spelt potential trouble for Mick every time he ran there.

And that's just what occurred on New Year's Day in the final of the Champion Stakes, his first race in the official care of Sidney Orton. Buckna Boy beat him eight lengths. Orton was subsequently given six weeks to get Mick to his liking before the two dogs contested a match over the same course and distance on 19 February. Mick won by a head in a time half a second faster than the Champion Stakes final. Throughout the rest of 1930 Buckna Boy never got closer to Mick the Miller than two lengths, and some of the hammerings Mick handed out to this trusty yardstick – seven lengths and 12 lengths in heats of the Cesarewitch and Welsh Derby respectively – go some way to demonstrating how much Wimbledon incapacitated him. Those subsequent humiliations also serve to demonstrate how Sidney Orton increasingly found the key to Burhill's pre-eminent resident.

The press soon discovered that Sidney Orton was not one of those trainers from whom information had to be prised like the lid off a rusty tin of paint. Nor was he the liverish sort who resented criticism and bore grudges at any perceived slight. No one could recall Sidney Orton saying an unkind word about a living soul – human or greyhound – and to any interviewer who left Burhill giving the slightest impression he might step over the traces in print, his standard farewell, delivered in the Norfolk burr he never lost, always ended with the same *noblesse oblige* '...as long as you spell my name correctly.' And Orton remained such a humble and modest man that despite enough material to fill several volumes, he never kept even one scrapbook.

Orton's open house policy with reporters ensured there was no cloak-and-dagger element to his training methods – with but one exception, which was his trick of educating them 'to leave the trap in the quickest possible manner.' Onto his father's traditional Norfolk coursing lore, Orton merely grafted his own ideas about feeding and preparation in order to achieve, as he phrased it, 'eyes bright, noses wet, coats shining like silk and tails a'waggin.' Back in his formative days he had given his dogs plenty of roadwork, often walking them a good 6 miles from Aylsham along the railway route before bringing them home by train, because abundant stamina was a prerequisite for coursing dogs who might be asked to run for minutes on end. Consequently, certain aspects of Orton's *modus operandi* astounded his new colleagues at Burhill. His dogs were never given a drink other than some cold tea after racing, for example, because he had long ago reached the conclusion that dogs could get all the liquid they needed out of their food. To provide a dog with a completely separate and additional water supply, he reasoned, might just tip its fitness level over the top.

'I took over kennels at Burhill from Harry Leader, regarded as the best trainer of them all,' he explained to one interviewer in November 1931. 'Naturally, I felt very nervous at stepping into such a great man's shoes and when I commenced my duties in my own special way, I am not ashamed to say that other trainers laughed at me. Well, that's ancient history now, for some of them are imitating me at present.'

For the benefit of another guest, Orton described in more detail a typical day for the 60 dogs in his care:

'Routine is everything. Promptly at 7.30am the greyhounds are let out in the nine paddocks attached to my kennels. Each paddock is surrounded with seven-foot chestnut fencing and close boarding nearly four feet high, in order to prevent the dogs chasing their energetic neighbours alongside the partitions. The greyhounds are let out into the paddocks two at a time, when they can enjoy the freedom to gallop or just lie down. A dog will also relieve himself much more comfortably when he's loose than when he's on a lead. During that period their kennels are thoroughly cleaned and fresh beds of straw with sawdust on the floor greets their return. The utmost cleanliness and regularity of habits are essential. A dog hates dirt and the air of the kennel must always be fresh and of a sweet odour. After the dogs have had their run, those considered in need of a gallop are exercised accordingly over various distances. This takes us to almost nine o'clock, the time the greyhounds receive their breakfast.

'My success is largely due to the food I give my dogs. I see that all my dogs are well catered for. Each has its own particular whim and I do my best to please them all. Breakfast consists of a special kind of bread, which is toasted, chopped and soaked with water and milk; some dogs have fresh eggs and cod liver oil. Then they are allowed half an hour's siesta whilst the kennel lads indulge in their breakfast.

'After this brief kennel rest the dogs are taken out for road exercise, along the Burhill and Burwood Roads, each of four lads being in charge of a string of six – muzzled of course. They are walked over a distance suitable to the requirement of their needs, perhaps up to five miles. Whilst this is in progress the greyhounds remaining in the kennels are periodically let out into the paddocks. Each morning eight "teams" of an average of six greyhounds are exercised, and it is usually 12.30 before the last greyhound has returned to his kennel having had its feet washed and inspected for grit and tar.

'From one to two is lunch hour for the staff, and should any-one disturb the dogs, or their trainer, during this period they are by no means popular! After lunch the dogs are again taken into the paddocks, where they are thoroughly groomed and massaged, teeth cleaned, and the innumerable essential details necessary to the health and fitness of a greyhound attended to. A report as to the condition of each dog will already have been passed to our resident Veterinary Surgeon, Mr Alfred Sams, earlier in the morning.

'From the greyhounds' standpoint the most unanimously popular period of the day is 4.15, when they are given their chief meal of the day, consisting of stew made from fresh meat, vegetables and all kinds of edibles, with which is soaked toast-ed brown bread, together with a sprinkling of raw meat given according to the need of each individual dog. After this impor-tant meal has been concluded they are again systematically turned out in the paddocks for a run before being put to bed for the night. By six o'clock everything is closed down.

'The race runners, of course, are not fed at 4.15, but receive their steaming hot meal on their return from the track. The fleet of big vans collect the racing greyhounds at 4.45. Those about to proceed to the track register their joy in no uncertain manner, while those remaining behind do not hesitate to sound their moaning note of disapproval!'

Orton had inherited a diligent team of kennel lads from Harry Leader and it was a mark of the esteem in which he was held by them that, despite the job's long hours, the likes of George and Jim Farrar, Peter Heywood and Joe Ollis remained the backbone of his staff for 30 years. As head kennel-man – and Mick the Miller's closest human companion – Ollis was a key member of the team. He did once venture to Shanghai when a track opened out there, but after leaving his digs one morning to find the body of a man with his throat slit lying on his doorstep he thought it prudent to return.

Completing the backroom team was the formidable figure of Gladys

Orton. 'But for Gladys there wouldn't have been a Sidney Orton. She stood by me, kept me out of trouble, entertained the lady owners for me and was everybody's friend. The only occasion she's given me a tongue-lashing was when *Picture Post* sent down a photographer and I took off my jacket to reveal my braces. He told me to keep the braces on because it made it look as if I was really working. But Gladys tore me off a strip because she thought it didn't present a good image of a greyhound trainer!'

All this undeniably valuable support notwithstanding, it remains impossible to disagree with the view of the Special Commissioner of the *Greyhound Express* who concluded from one of his visits, not without reason, that the smooth operation at Burhill was the direct result of, 'the organisation and directing genius of the Wizard of Wimbledon', a man who lived for his greyhounds and little else. Orton's one concession to leisure was a putting green laid out in the garden of his bungalow. 'You will find Orton always the same, modest in victory, imperturbable in defeat, a conscientious, talented trainer in whom owners have confidence and who carries the respect of the public and the affection of his friends. He stands for all that is cleanest and best in the sport of greyhound racing.'

That the majority of Mick the Miller's English career should be guided by a man such as Sidney Orton suggests a liaison approved and forged by the gods. Only the best would do for Mick the Miller. Not that Orton pampered him above and beyond the norm. 'I must say that Mick the Miller has been one of the easiest of dogs to train,' he confessed to any enquiry. 'He has never received a special preparation for any of his races. A good dog is rarely difficult to manage – it is the moderate animal which requires special patience. He has never receives a special preparation for any of his races – I do not slip a hare for my dogs to chase, for instance.'

The mark of a good trainer or kennel-man is to establish a rapport with their dogs, reaching inside their heads, as it were, to find out what they are thinking. Orton and Ollis quickly discovered Mick the Miller's idiosyncrasies; chiefly that he'd run through a monsoon but couldn't abide the sound of thunder, which scared him to death. Though a few greyhounds possess Jekyll-and-Hyde personalities, they soon found that Mick displayed no vices and didn't snap or bite. In general, he was as docile as most of the breed and occasionally even a shade aloof, choosing to ignore humans altogether.

The same could not always be said about his relationship with fellow canines. Greyhounds are customarily kennelled in pairs and when Mick first arrived at Burhill, Stan Biss housed him with a dog called Brisbane. On the off chance that separating them might cause Mick to fret, Orton subsequently bought Brisbane for £100 to maintain the domestic status quo. The duo lived together quite amicably until three nights before the 1930 Derby final when, in Orton's words, 'they had a hell of a row'. Since parting them at this critical juncture seemed the more upsetting option, Orton elected to leave them together and hope for the best – that plus Joe Ollis keeping a beady eye on them night and day. After the Derby, Brisbane was replaced with Toftwood Misery, a bitch Orton had acquired from Jack Masters for £150 and passed on to the Kemptons. Apart from when she came into season, necessitating temporary isolation, Toftwood Misery was Mick's constant domestic companion. Perhaps some of Mick's magic rubbed off. She eventually did so well on the track herself that Arundel Kempton expressed his appreciation by sending Masters a further £100.

Peace and harmony thus returned to Burhill, that is unless someone thought to put a coat on Mick to keep out the cold of a night. 'Mick would never wear a coat in the kennels, not even in the depth of winter,' said Orton. 'Whenever I tried to put one on he would bite through the securing tapes, and toss the coat into the corner of his box. One evening I put coats on both him and Toftwood Misery and returned the following morning to find that Mick had chewed his way through both sets of tapes. The coats were flung into the corner of the box and the little bitch was curled snugly between his paws!'

When the ante post market for the 1930 Derby opened up on 10 April, Mick the Miller was a 7/1 favourite to retain his crown. He had run five races since beating Buckna Boy in the Wimbledon match on 19 February and won the last four. A defeat at the paws of So Green (one of 1929's star puppies) in the opening round of the Wembley Spring Cup on 17 March (his first appearance at the self-styled 'Ascot of Greyhound Racing') was avenged by four ritual humiliations of the same dog, including the final of the Spring Cup, and culminating in two matches at Wembley and Wimbledon. Mick then further strengthened his market position by lowering the White City 525 track record to 29.76 in the course of administering a seven-length thrashing to Fairy Again in another match. Both he and Orton were flying. The trainer had won 48 races in the last two months. Two more wins in May – the Loafer Trophy at Wimbledon and the Farndon Cup at the White City – brought Mick to the first round heats of the Derby on 7 June in very fine fettle indeed. The bookmakers were offering 16s bar the favourite.

Opposition to the champion appeared thin on the ground. The likes of Buckna Boy and So Green were now exposed types, whose measure Mick had regularly taken. Two former Northern challengers he had never met constituted more serious threats. First of all there was the magnificent black bitch Bradshaw Fold, bred from a dam said to have roamed the streets of Manchester. She was often referred to as the female Mick the Miller because she also tended to start slowly before a combination of guile and guts saw her invariably finish with a mighty rattle – especially over extreme distances. More of a pet to her doting owner than a racing greyhound (she nearly always slept in a chair by the side of his bed when not in training), 'Jewel', as she was known in the kennels, seemed to spend her life on trains and on the back seats of cars en route to open-class events the length and breadth of the country. She was already mistress of the Manchester White City 525 record when she came south to beat Captured Half at West Ham over 600 yards, having been all of ten lengths down on the home turn. Rematched over 550, Bradshaw Fold then broke Mick's world record with a time of 31.58. And, in a 700-yards match with the previous year's St Leger winner Loughnagare at West Ham, she had set a world record 40.04 that would stand for almost 20 years. For her 1930 Derby campaign she was placed in the care of Stanley Biss at West Ham.

Oh sing out for Bradshaw, East London's her home,
She's a runner, a racer and West Ham's very own.
She's brave, she's a champion, she's worth her weight in gold,
Our Coronation Stakes girl, our 'Jewel', our Bradshaw Fold.

Then there was Deemster. This brindled dog had never been led or beaten on the running grounds, collecting the Appleton Cup at Stowmarket and the Grange Farm Stakes at Hockwold. Another Northerner in Johnny Canuck had beaten him on the track at Belle Vue in the spring, but thereafter he improved by leaps and bounds, meeting and beating Bishop's Dream, Fairy Again and the selfsame Johnny Canuck. He also looked good on the clock. A 28.87 Belle Vue 500 during a thunderstorm was matched in its impressiveness by a White City 525 of 30.07, which was two lengths faster than Mick's time in winning the same night's Farndon Cup. As the first of the 26 Derby heats commenced on 7 June, the odds-layers could no longer split Mick the Miller and Deemster as overall favourite to win the competition. 'It will be a battle of wits when Mick the Miller meets Deemster,' promised The Greyhound Evening Mirror.

The first series went strictly according to plan: Buckna Boy wins easily; Bradshaw Fold slightly less so after a typically dozy start; but Mick gallops in by 20 lengths (at his shortest ever odds of 100/8 on) in what amounted to little more than a time trial. Then came Deemster. Left lengths out of the boxes, he proceeds to scorch the grass with a time of 29.90, the fastest of the qualifiers. Watching reporters were beside themselves: 'Mick the Miller certainly has something to be afraid of now,' wrote one; 'A dazzling display – the greatest dog we have yet seen,' gushed another.

Days later the same scribes were talking of 'The Deemster Catastrophe'. Halfway down the back straight during his second-round heat, Deemster was leading Bradshaw Fold by a mile and once more threatening the watch when he suddenly stopped as if he'd been picked off with an air rifle – which is precisely what many in the crowd believed had indeed happened to the 8/1 on favourite. Fortunately for the sport's integrity and good name, Deemster's plight was found to be a crushed bone in a rear hock rather than a pellet in his rump. Whatever, he was out of the Derby – for which the bookies were eternally grateful because he had been backed to win £10,000.

With the demise of the current headline-stealer, Mick would have to come up with something special on his second-round appearance two days later if he was to satisfy the press. He couldn't and didn't. On a wet night, he trapped poorly, wandered unconvincingly mid-race, and hesitated once he finally struck the front instead of imposing his authority. The critics pounced: unimpressive and disappointing were two of the milder words used to describe the champion's performance.

The White City kennels at least provided one ray of sunshine for Mick. A very familiar face was contesting another Derby heat – that of his brother, Macoma. At one point toward the end of 1929 Macoma had actually been placed with Sidney Orton (finishing last of three over hurdles at Wimbledon) but he'd gone back to the Kidderminster kennels of his owner who trained him to win his first round heat in the Derby before going out in the second round behind Buckna Boy and Doumergue. Macoma, however, was proving a revelation over hurdles, thumping the reigning champion Duveneck by 12 lengths at Birmingham's Hall Green venue in a new track record.

More importantly, Macoma was already fulfilling the stud duties for which he had principally been acquired by William Washbourne, and he went on to become a huge success in this sphere. Arthur Callanan trained the bitch Kitshine to capture both The Oaks and The Laurels in 1935, while repeat matings with Bright Emblem produced litters containing Long Hop and Mick's Fancy, and Scapegoat. In 1932 Long Hop not only completed the hurdler's hat-trick of the Grand National, the Empire Stadium Stakes at Wembley and the Wimbledon Challenge Trophy but also notched up 16 consecutive wins; the year younger Scapegoat won the National in 1933 from his elder brother; while Mick's Fancy was destined to humble his illustrious uncle Mick.

Toward the end of Long Hop's triumphant 1932 campaign, Washbourne received a letter from Macoma's breeder. 'I sit down to write to you as some would do about a long-lost love,' said Father Brophy. 'I know as much about greyhounds as most of them. Macoma was not only the best dog I ever owned but the best dog I ever hope to own. I regard him as a dog that might have won the Waterloo Cup in any normal year. They talk of Mick the Miller – wonderful dog without a doubt – but I should know their merits if anyone does, and I have no hesitation in saying that Mick the Miller was a poor second to Macoma at any game known to greyhounds before Macoma got hurt.'

Father Brophy was entitled to his opinion and one might forgive him his need to express it so unequivocally. But a lot had happened since those far-off days at Maryborough, Kilbeggan, and the two Parks of Shelbourne and Celtic when a less precocious Mick the Miller was getting to grips with his trade more slowly than his brother.

Mick the Miller was more like his old self on Derby semi-final night, 21 June. In a battle-royal summed up by *The Greyhound Evening Mirror*'s headline of 'Mick the Miller confounds his critics,' the champ used every brain cell at his disposal to beat the crack hurdler Dresden and Tipperary Hills, the winner of a prototype Irish Derby at Harold's Cross in 1928. Finding himself with nowhere to go from trap four after Tipperary Hills cut across to grab a first-bend lead, Mick gradually weaved his way through to poach a narrow advantage heading toward the finish line. As Dresden and Tipperary Hills desperately tried to mount one last thrust, Mick executed one of his renowned party tricks by deliberately cutting back to the inside rail and instantly brickwalling their progress.

And so to the final a week later, 28 June, a date of some significance. It was the eve of Mick's fourth birthday. It was a six-dog final this year and, on a strict interpretation of the watch, not one of them could be ruled out of contention for the huge prize of £1,480 (and ten shillings) because they had run within just 0.15 seconds of each other in the semis. Bradshaw Fold had won the first by a neck from the 1929 'Irish Derby' winner Jack Bob; and in the third Mick McGee – 'Mick the Second' to the punters – emerged victorious from the clash of the youngsters, beating So Green also by a neck.

The cosmopolitan crowd of 50,000 that crammed into the White City – which included King Alfonso XIII of Spain, middleweight 'king' Len Harvey, the omnipresent Harry Rothbart and a stocky, silver-haired Irish cleric lately transferred from Killeigh to Daingean – was alive with but two topics of conversation. There were understandable mutterings of discontent at the latest news from the Test match at Lord's where a 21-year-old Australian tyro named Donald Bradman had flayed the English attack for 155 undefeated runs by the close of play (he was later out on 254), thereby putting his country well on the road to its then record total of 729 for six declared and a victory that more or less reclaimed The Ashes. Bradman's series aggregate of 974 at an average of 139.14 provoked the adoption of the 'bodyline' tactic during the following series of 1932-33.

And, naturally, there was also fierce debate on far more pressing issues. Could Mick the Miller give two years and a beating to a pair of thrusting up-and-comers like Mick McGee and So Green? Would he come out on top in his first encounter with the redoubtable, habitually late-lunging Bradshaw Fold? Could Mick really celebrate his fourth birthday in the convincing style of a great champion?

As the band of the Irish Guards blew and beat merrily away in the background, many well-versed in racecourse old wives' tales sought out Sidney Orton to gauge his degree of optimism based on the shininess of his oiled-back hair. 'Orton's tonsorial splendour is deemed a barometer of his expectation,' suggested one reporter with tongue firmly lodged in cheek, 'for it is said his successes are in direct proportion to the degree of polish reflected by his hirsute adornment.'

All enquiries were deflected by Orton's customary beaming smile rather than any tonsorial shininess. He had done his job and was content to let Mick do the talking in the only way a racing greyhound can. Mick looked as fit as a flea in the parade and, unlike his rivals, toddled into his box without Joe Ollis having to exert even a finger of pressure. The Kemptons, on the other hand, were finding the tension harder to bear: Phiddy was making her first public appearance after having had an undisclosed problem attended to in a private nursing home. In truth, as her husband well appreciated, her convalescence should not have been cut short but, despite the strain imposed on her fragile nerves, the prospect of foregoing Mick the Miller's greatest night had proved utterly impossible.

Mick had drawn the coveted inside box, and with the bookies' boards showing 7/1 bar the favourite at 9/4 on, he was an even hotter shot than in 1929. And he proceeded to win like a sure thing. Beneath a headline in greyhound racing's daily declaring, 'Amazing Scenes Mark a Glorious Night', Isidore Green reported: 'The race itself requires very little description. Mick the Miller simply repeated a performance which every greyhound racegoer associates with him. Cunning and speed of a kind which was markedly superior to that possessed by any of his rivals, made itself emphatically pronounced a moment after the start.'

For one of the comparatively few occasions in his life, Mick hit the boxes like a dog inspired. Refusing to be shouldered aside in the race to the first bend, he clung to his rail as if it were a piece of prime juicy steak and bounded down the back straight holding a healthy lead over Mick McGee. Surely, nothing could catch him now. Then, for those of acute hearing, amid the Derby hubbub could be faintly discerned cries of 'Where's the bitch? Where's the bitch? Here she comes!'

Off the final bend the dark shape that was Bradshaw Fold began to make its move from the rear of the field. It was too late. She was indubitably better over a longer distance, and had simply got going too late in the day. Although she picked off Mick McGee for second place, there was still a yawning two-length gap between her and Mick at the death.

Joy was unconfined. The fans had got the result they craved. 'The dog's a regular knock-out,' Len Harvey was heard to say, before resorting to boxing parlance: 'He beats 'em all – any weight and any size!'

The Kemptons were rather more circumspect with their comments as they descended the steps to the track for the presentation ceremony. 'Isn't it wonderful?' cooed Phiddy. 'Please don't ask me to say too much – I am overwhelmed.' While King Alfonso waited on the dais for Phiddy to compose herself, he playfully positioned the owner's trophy – a magnificent 15-inch high silver cup and cover modelled on Tudor lines – on Mick's back before duly handing it over. Playing to the crowd like the actor he was to become, Mick dutifully stood there, tongue lolling and tail wagging, so that the cameramen could get the pictures they wanted.

Sidney Orton stepped forward to receive his own cup from Lady Chesham. 'The man in the moon dazzled by Sidney Orton's head withdrew his orb behind a cloud,' recorded the jocular observer of the trainer's pate, 'fully realising that his brilliance was under eclipse by the transcendent brightness that was Sidney John Orton's head and smile.'

There was yet more for Orton and the Kemptons to smile about. News came through that they had bagged not just one but both of the night's major events because, over at Wembley, Toftwood Misery had won the Coronation Stakes, an elite 525 event confined to bitches. She truly had earned the right to share a kennel with Mick the Miller.

Finally, Mick picked out a figure in the throng he knew and missed. Mick's tail suddenly began beating frantically from side to side as he tugged Joe Ollis toward the approaching cleric. For a brief moment Father Brophy and his Mick the Miller were reunited.

Thus it came to pass that Mick the Miller did indeed welcome his fourth birthday in the style of a paragon. Yet he would not rest on his laurels. Even as his followers were reading of his Derby-winning exploits in *The Sporting Life* over their Monday breakfasts ('No more eloquent test of the-sport's-the-thing where Englishmen are concerned'), Mick was preparing to enter the West Ham traps that very evening in round one of the Cesarewitch. He was about to provide both press and public alike with all the evidence they needed to bestow upon him the title of 'World's Wonder Dog'.

CHAPTER TEN
WONDER DOG

One phenomenon that could always be guaranteed to knock the country's economic misery off the front pages and temporarily divert public attention from the grimmer realities of life, was the current fascination with speed. In fact the public was not so much fascinated as obsessed with speed, especially those proponents of it identified by the *Daily Mirror* as 'Greyhounds of Air and Ocean'.

On land the latest exploits of the fastest car vied with news of the fastest locomotive for column space in the print media and on the cinema newsreels. The giant six-cylinder Bentleys hog the headlines from Le Mans, while the duel between gentlemen racers Captain Malcolm Campbell and Major Henry Segrave for possession of the world speed records on land and water is brought to a tragic conclusion in June 1930 when the latter is killed on Lake Windermere while attempting to place a 100-mph mark alongside his land best of 231 mph. On the railways, The Flying Scotsman exceeds speeds of 70 mph during the course of its 392-mile journey between London and Edinburgh, while on the oceans, the German liner *Bremen* deprives the *Mauritania* of the Blue Riband by steaming across the Atlantic in four days and 14½ hours.

Pride of place, however, went to the so-called 'Wizards of the Air'. First there was the phenomenon of the airship. The Graf Zeppelin, which took a little over 21 days to soar majestically around the world with just three stops, was soon joined by British counterparts in the R100 and R101. However, the inherent danger of this mode of aviation manifests itself a full seven years prior to the infamous Hindenberg disaster when leaking gas causes the R101 to explode in a fireball over France in October 1930 with the loss of 44 lives.

Then came 'Those Magnificent Young Men in their Flying Machines.' Any amount of newsprint was devoted to the aviators who followed in the publicity slipstream of Charles Lindbergh's solo flight across the Atlantic in May 1927. Major de Bernardi captured the air speed record for Italy with 296 mph; Costes and Le Brix of France complete a 42,625-mile flight around the world; American Amelia Earhart becomes the first woman to fly the Atlantic; and Britain's Amy Johnson makes it to Australia; two Italians set a new record by flying 5,000 miles non-stop, an achievement soon bettered by a US Army plane that flies 11,000 miles in 150 hours thanks to the innovation of mid-air refuelling. All these endeavours, however, are eclipsed in the public's eyes by the feat of Flying Officer HRD Waghorn's Supermarine Rolls-Royce S6 seaplane (the prototype Spitfire), which flew at a record 350 mph to win the Schneider Trophy for Britain in September 1929. Within two years Waghorn himself would perish in a crash. Like Segrave before him, Waghorn became an early martyr to the message 'Speed Kills'.

Yet these assorted 'Greyhounds of Air and Ocean' were no substitute for the real thing.

There was no substitute for Mick the Miller. And even he was not like other racing greyhounds. In neither appearance nor aptitude did he conform to the breed. He was as much a non-conformist in his sporting sphere as Muhammad Ali and George Best were in theirs.

At the age of four Mick had developed into a fully furnished racing machine, weighing in at around 64-66lb, standing 27½ inches at the shoulder and possessed of a 30-inch girth and a 19½-inch tail. Not too small – a bitch like Bradshaw Fold only tipped the scales at 50lb – but not overly big, either. For instance, Ballyregan Bob and Scurlogue Champ, arguably the two most popular crowd-pleasers of the post-Mick era, usually raced at 70½lb and 73¼lb respectively; and were correspondingly taller at 28 and 29 inches. Master Myles, the champion Irish courser of the late 1970s, was a monster of 95lb.

Like all machines, function superseded looks. Mick was no oil painting, and his appearance was not helped by the unsightly scar on his muzzle below the right eye, a war wound from combat on the running grounds. In the opinion of the noted judge Bert Edwards Clarke, he did not conform to the accepted *beau ideal*: 'There was just the suggestion of coarseness throughout his make-up. The purists, too, could say that he was not as deep through the heart as they would have wished; that, in horsey language, he "showed too much daylight". The muscular development of his shoulders and haunches, however, had to be seen to be believed, and no one could possibly quibble at his superlative length of thigh and gaskin.'

These two last-named points of a greyhound invariably attracted the most attention from experienced dog fanciers who fully appreciated the direct link between the muscular development of Mick the Miller's thigh and gaskin and his source of propulsion. Indeed, Mick was so 'well-breeched', as to plant the idea in some minds that his prominent and highly developed hindquarters were out of proportion with the rest of him.

An equally significant element of Mick's conformation was his length of back, at 29 inches some 4 inches longer than Ballyregan Bob's, for instance, and no less than 8 inches longer than Master McGrath's. Unlike the racehorse at full tilt, the greyhound extends its hind legs a good distance ahead of the prints just left by its forelegs when in full motion, which demands a whip and elasticity from its back that extra inches will tend to exaggerate to advantage.

To the overwhelming mass who regularly flocked to Wimbledon, Wembley and the White City, these aforementioned aspects of Mick the Miller mattered not one iota. What mattered to Joe Public was what he saw once the spotlight picked up Mick the Miller skipping onto the track. When the bob-a-nobbers watched Mick approach the traps they saw a dog savouring every second of his time in the limelight and a dog who could not wait to enjoy himself. There was never any sluggishness in his step, no need for his handler to tug at the leash, his gait was sprightly, his eyes the windows of an eager spirit. He would be on his toes, raring to go. The proximity of the traps, of other dogs sharing a modicum of his own excitement, not to mention the noises and smells attendant to a gathering of human beings, aroused Mick to the verge of ecstasy. It was almost as if the electricity running through the hare hummed through him as well. The racetrack transformed him. This was his kingdom.

As the man at his side throughout the preliminaries, Joe Ollis was better situated than most to sense this metamorphosis. 'I never have to put him in the starting box,' he told a reporter from the *Daily Mail*. 'He runs to it himself, as he loves racing. The secret of Mick's success is his marvellous intelligence. He runs a race as though he had a clever jockey guiding him. He hangs back at the start, watches the other dogs, and cuts in to take the inside position at just the right moment. I love to see him run wide at first. The spectators groan in disappointment. Then Mick cuts in and wins by a head. It is sheer brainwork. He is a nice tractable dog to train, never worries about a race and the most intelligent I have ever come across – see also how he swings his big tail to act as a rudder on the bends and as a brake when he is easing up. It's perhaps difficult for some people to realise the great wind pressure a greyhound encounters at full speed, and how that pressure can be used for curving round bends. During most of a race Mick will keep his tail well down, almost touching the ground when he's at top speed, but see him approach a bend at 40 mph. Down comes his tail, turned to the inside of the bend, and he is steered round.'

Once Mick left the traps everyone knew a performance of canine virtuosity was in the offing. All boxes came alike to him. He won six-dog races from every box; if he was coming out of trap one, however, you could go straight away to the Tote window or bookie's joint ready to collect your winnings, for Mick never lost to a full complement when starting from the inside berth. In truth, all boxes came alike to him because he was not reliant upon any physical advantage, be that his draw or even raw, inherent speed. Mick relied on stealth.

Natural speed has to be allied to a racing brain if a greyhound is to win races on a regular basis. A degree of track craft is essential. The more a dog possesses, the more he proves successful. Pelting down the straights full throttle at speeds approaching 38 mph, for instance, is a complete waste of effort if that speed carries the dog wide on the bends to invite bumping or baulking. Even after making allowances for the constant improvement in racing surfaces throughout the 1930s and 1940s, the time test suggests Mick the Miller was certainly not the fastest greyhound of the pre-war era. But whereas hell-for-leather merchants like Ataxy and Tanist, for example, could not hold their line on the corners, Mick the Miller's more thoughtful, controlled – almost sedate – approach paid immediate dividends because he seemed to go round them faster than he went down the straights. Thus, instead of losing races on the turns, this is where he frequently won them by stealing both position and lengths off his opponents. And, once in front, he seemed to enjoy the luxury of a rear-view mirror, because he would often contrive a tiny swerve that slammed the door in the face of a rival just as it was about to throw down a dangerous looking challenge, causing the unfortunate dog to break stride and forfeit all momentum. By any standards, and in any language, this behaviour amounts to cleverness.

'To attribute craftiness to a greyhound,' added Edwards Clarke, 'is to invite the rebukes of those who argue that such a sense – approaching as it does an ability to reason – is denied to all but humans. Be that as it may, to my mind the ability to exercise muscles in a special way, to control and moderate pace, to preserve perfect balance at all angles of full speed, is surely an ability that at least owes something to mental direction. Certain it is that the phrase "track sense" is the best description of just that "something" that distinguished Mick the Miller from the rest of his contemporaries.'

Sidney Orton was never going to pick holes in this judgment. 'Of the many greyhounds which have passed through my hands, not one had half the intelligence of Mick the Miller. He seemed to understand every word you said to him. Brains helped him to win races as much as his speed. You could see before he was put in the trap that he was sizing up the opposition. He was a wonderful judge of pace and knew just where to make his effort. He never raced more than necessary. As soon as he had crossed the winning line, he would slow up at once.'

Theories could – and frequently did – become unnecessarily technical and esoteric in nature. Mick's weight, some argued, enabled him to exert finer control of his body's kinetic energy (the energy possessed by a moving body by virtue of its motion, which tends to act in a straight line) when it came to altering direction at the bends than might a heavier, larger dog. Another school of thought pondered the explanation for his mid- and late-race charges. The suggestion was that he recovered lost ground so eagerly because he was attempting to re-establish contact with the mesmeric noise of the hare trolley that had momentarily been lost. And, finally, was he not a perfect manifestation of the 'jealous dog' concept? The kind of dog consumed by an inherently selfish urge to outwit its rivals, one impelled into using all the cunning at his disposal in order to claim sole possession of the hare rather than risk affording any other a chance of sharing it with him. All very interesting, if a little far-fetched.

Thanks to his victory in the Derby, Mick had extended his unbeaten sequence to 11 since So Green beat him in a heat of the Wembley Spring Cup on 17 March. Within six weeks he would add a further seven to pass Idle Chief's 1929 total of 16 (all at Slough) by storming through the various rounds of the Cesarewitch and Welsh Derby, during the course of which he set four world records. Having grown tired of using the 'Wonder Dog' headline, sub-editors resorted instead to 'Invincible!'

Record number one arrived in Mick's first round heat of the Cesarewitch just 48 hours after his exertions in the final of the Derby. Monday, 30 June was also a big day in the life of Sidney Orton's son Clare. The 12-year-old was on holiday from his boarding school in Southsea and, as a special treat, he was taken along to West Ham to see Mick the Miller compete. 'Under sixteens were not really allowed to go greyhound racing but I was smuggled into the top deck of the old three-tier grandstand,' recalled Clare Orton. 'There was a very good crowd to see Mick, and he got a tremendous reception both before and after the race. He seemed to know it was for him and not the other dogs because he was the only one wagging his tail and looking around to see what all the fuss was about. I used to see a fair bit of him when I was at home, often going for walks with him – he loved chasing squirrels! – and my father or with Joe Ollis, but I was never allowed to walk him on my own. There was constant publicity about him, a constant stream of visitors to interview father, and photographers were always taking pictures of Mick with my sister Joan, who is ten years younger than me.'

There was scant likelihood of anything spoiling Clare Orton's party. Even though Mick (at 10/1 on) merely played ducks and drakes with his four opponents to come home alone by a dozen lengths, he still managed to slash a full fifth of a second off the 600-yard world record of 34.27 standing to Dick's Son with a time of 34.06. Young Orton also enjoyed the privilege of watching Bradshaw Fold in another heat perform her customary Houdini act and overcome squeezing and baulking to get her nose in front bang on the line.

Mick was proving unstoppable. West Ham could have been constructed with him in mind. 'The Newmarket of Greyhound Racing', as it liked to advertise itself, was the largest track in the country with room for 100,000 spectators, and it boasted a unique surface composed of a wooden foundation akin to a well-sprung dance floor, matted with a special fibrous substance. Moreover, with a galloping circumference measuring 562 yards on the inner rail, its 123-yard straights and scientifically banked sweeping bends ensured lightning quick racing and minimal scope for interference. All-in-all, West Ham was a track built for record breaking and one guaranteed to bring out the best in Mick the Miller. Thus it came as no surprise to the *ognoscenti* when he beat Mick McGee in the next round in a barely slower time, or when he lowered his record to 34.01 in defeating Buckna Boy by seven lengths in his semi-final.

Neither Buckna Boy nor Bradshaw Fold nor any of the others in the final could get in a blow at Mick when it counted. The clock (34.11) once more yielded irrefutable evidence that he was in the form of his life after he'd dodged in front of Buckna Boy to claim the rail and ultimately cross the finish-line three lengths to the good over the long-shot Five of Hearts. Phiddy Kempton chose the post-final celebrations to announce that Mick was now going to be rested 'in order to give other owners a chance to win big events' and would not be contesting the Welsh Derby in two weeks time.

Phiddy's largesse proved premature. In 1930 the Welsh Derby had not yet been accorded full Classic status, and its prize of only £115 and ten shillings was hardly much of a financial carrot, but here was an opportunity for Mick to excel on another of the country's fastest circuits and perhaps recapture his 525 world record.

When the time came, Mick and Joe Ollis duly made their way to Paddington and the first of three quick-fire train journeys to Cardiff. In direct contrast to his initial experience of hospitality aboard British trains a year earlier, on these occasions Mick was a privileged guest given the freedom to roam at will in the guard's van.

A local ship-owner, Mr Grove Williams, had kindly offered to accommodate the two visitors at his home, where he had set aside one bedroom for Ollis and another especially equipped to cater for every need of Mick the Miller. The Welsh White City's springy highland turf harvested from the mountains near Caerphilly was held responsible for the Sloper Road oval gaining a well-deserved reputation as the fastest track in Britain – quicker even than West Ham – and the world-record setting exploits of Back Isle over 525 yards in 1929 had recently been complemented by a world record over hurdles. If past form was any guide, Back Isle's mark of 29.64 was going to be put under immense pressure in the very first heat of round one because the four-dog line-up read like a final, featuring, as it did, the names of Mick the Miller, Back Isle and Buckna Boy. Mick was truly imperious, thrashing Buckna Boy and Back Isle by 12 lengths and eight respectively. Even the partisan Cardiff crowd was reduced to cheering abeyance. There was to be no world record, however. South Walians had to wait until the semifinal four days later to watch Mick steal Back Isle's record, leading from box to line in 29.60. *The Greyhound Evening Mirror*'s headline writer was forced into scaling new heights: 'World's Greatest Racing Genius.'

With both Back Isle and Buckna Boy (last in his semi) now eliminated, all possible stumbling blocks had been removed from Mick's path and in the final he entered trap two an 8/1 on favourite to beat the Slough dog Filon, local representative Barleybree and Sidney Orton's second string Hydrometer. The result – 'A Gift for Mick the Miller' according to the *Western Mail* preview – was a foregone conclusion. The real interest lay in the time Mick the Miller was going to clock.

'On the morning of the final it was pouring with rain when Mr Kempton, Mick and I set off for Cardiff,' Sidney Orton later recounted. 'The weather brightened up later on and I was hopeful of Mick's chances of breaking the world record. He trapped a bit better than usual but then took a bump from Hydrometer.' For Mick to meet interference, of course, was nothing unusual – but what happened afterwards most certainly was.

'Mick was the sort of greyhound who could not stand being hustled,' continued Orton, 'he preferred to be the one doing the hustling. He set off round the track bristling like a scalded cat! I don't think he would have set a new world record of 29.55 if he had not been fired-up by his brush with Hydrometer. And when I went to pick him up he tried to bite me for the only time in his life!'

That bump from Hydrometer on the first bend had knocked Mick broadsides and, incensed or not at the sheer effrontery of his disrespectful kennel-mate, Mick proceeded to demonstrate, in the words of the local correspondent, 'all his wonderful powers' to streak away and win by ten lengths from Barleybree in a time of 29.55, five spots inside his old world record, running at an average speed of 36.34 mph or less than six-hundredths of a second per yard. Put another way, if one takes one length to equal 1½ yards, this equates to Mick travelling at a staggering 12-times his body-length per second.

There was nothing for it. The man at *The Greyhound Evening Mirror* was obliged to resurrect the 'World's Wonder Dog' headline. Nothing less would suffice.

A notable absentee from the Welsh White City was Phiddy Kempton. She was resting in a London nursing home after an unspecified operation, which had been delayed so that she might attend the Greyhound Derby. Rundel was soon on the telephone to relay the good news, however, and once back in London he took Mick round to visit his mistress in her sick-bed.

Orton and the Kemptons had not been having things all their own way on the track. Paddy McEllistrum's range housed a cracking bitch named Faithful Kitty who was posing a thorn in the side of Toftwood Misery, beating her in both the semi-final and final of The Oaks. There was no alternative if the honour of Mick's trusty female consort was to be salvaged. He would have to put Kitty in her place. A match was arranged for 20 August over 550 yards at Wimbledon.

Wimbledon was the obvious venue, even if both camps might have harboured some misgivings at the choice. Two of Mick's rare defeats had come round its tightish curves, although any reservations concerning his ability to handle the track were offset by the fact that Faithful Kitty had never even run at Plough Lane before. On the night, Mick showed Kitty a clean pair of heels in the most unchivalrous manner possible. He unceremoniously barrelled across her at the first bend and then put the tin lid on any late progress she may have mounted inside the last 50 yards by once again making for the rails and sealing off her passage. Mick won by half a length.

This was Mick at his most artful. It seemed as if he knew exactly where the bitch was going to be on the track at every stage in the contest and, in consequence, he deliberately took possession of each one of those precise spots half a second before she had chance to occupy them herself. There was not a single soul present who did not believe that Faithful Kitty, as a result of constantly being made to check and seek alternative openings by Mick's delaying tactics, must have lost at least three or four lengths – and yet she only lost the race by half a length. A potheen of clairvoyance and chicanery had won the day. Mick was becoming more human by the minute.

The winning streak had now reached 19. If Mick was to bring up number 20, he would need to exhibit superhuman qualities because his next appointment with the boxes was for a heat of The Laurels, Wimbledon's very own Classic over 500 yards. If the track constituted enough of a potential booby trap in itself, inserting the race distance into the equation made it doubly so. Mick had run this sharper trip just three times in his life – twice at Shelbourne Park way back in the spring of 1928 and at Harringay nine months previously (and that was a match). Here, he would be coming out of trap five in a six-dog race with a relatively short run to the first of Plough Lane's tight turns.

An accident seemed inevitable, and it was Mick the Miller it happened to. By his own standards, Mick broke well, as did his five rivals. Each wanted that prize spot on the rail – but six into one won't go. As the rail began to curve away to the left, Mick felt the bulk of Never Certain pressing against his haunches in a frantic effort to cut across from his trap six draw in the same split second that Off You Pop was squeezed onto him from the inside as a consequence of the bunching rail-runners.

Mick flew into the air like a spent cartridge. Body skewing sideways, he instinctively threw out his forelegs to regain a secure footing for the rest of the bend but the power of kinetic energy was irresistible and he only succeeded in swivelling his entire mass of 66lb around his front end as it made contact with the grass. The pressure was too much. He felt a hot dagger of pain slice into his shoulder. But he kept on running.

For once, Lady Luck had chosen to shine her light elsewhere, because as the runners emerged from this typical early fracas, the orange jacket could be seen dropping back through the field. Disbelief began to pervade the Wimbledon roar. Mick was clearly in trouble. Something was badly wrong. Eventually there was not one opponent behind him. The streak was over.

Mick struggled to the finish where the ignominy of trailing five dogs for the only time in his career was quickly ended by Joe Ollis who gently cradled him in his arms before tenderly lifting him off the ground. The pair left the track enveloped by a small group that included Sidney Orton, Arundel Kempton and the track vet, Alfred Sams. Up in the grandstand a distraught Phiddy Kempton buried her head in a handkerchief. A hush descended over Plough Lane. Was this the last the bob-a-nobbers would see of their idol?

Sams' initial examination was encouraging. Mick had torn the muscles in his off-side shoulder. In his opinion he would be out of action for up to six weeks. If the injury healed satisfactorily he might be back in early October.

Mick's recovery did not progress as swiftly as Sams hoped. His season was over. Mick the Miller had been luckier than Segrave and Waghorn: speed had not killed. But, the *annus mirabilis* that was Mick the Miller's 1930 campaign, a campaign that took Britain by storm courtesy of the sustained brilliance and scene-stealing character of its instigator, had been brought to a close in the cruellest fashion imaginable.

Mick the Miller in his prime

27 June 1931: entering the traps for the Derby

3 October 1931: Mrs Jean Elvin presents the St Leger trophy to the winning connections

Phiddy and her 'Darling Mick'

Mick with steeplechasing alter ego Golden Miller

4 October 1931: Mick guards his Ledger spoils

11 December 1931: Phiddy bids Mick a tearful farewell
as he leaves Liverpool Street Station to start a new career at stud

15 November 1933: Mick offers his sons, Mick the Moocher, Mick the Miracle and Mick the Matchless, some advice before the final of the Trafalgar Cup

10 July 1934: Mick helps three of the Crazy Gang and assorted showgirls promote their latest revue at the London Palladium

Phiddy shows off all Mick's trophies

16 January 1939: Mick joins his owner and trainer for a final appearance in the ring at a charity boxing tournament prior to the auction of three of his offspring

Mick's name is the only one above the title in the posters for Wild Boy

Before the film cameras at Gainsborough's Shepherd's Bush studio

*Mick enjoys a nap (top) and a boiled egg for breakfast (bottom)
with co-star Sonnie Hale*

The 'real' Mick enjoys a day out at the Derby

Fans may purchase their own replica of 'The Greatest Greyhound Ever'

The wise old head of greyhound racing's one and only icon

CHAPTER ELEVEN
LEFT WITHOUT A PENNY

The sun came up over Liverpool just as normal. But 13 June, 1931 was to be no normal Saturday for Jimmy Brennan. For once in his young life he couldn't wait to jump out of bed. The 18-year-old kennel-lad at the city's Stanley greyhound stadium was taking the 7 o'clock train to London. His boss, Jimmy Shand, was attending the sales at Aldridges, the renowned greyhound mart in Upper St Martin's Lane. Jimmy was to bring home any purchases.

Any day away from kennel routine was welcome but this particular day promised a bonus. This perk was the real cause of Jimmy's excitement. Mr Shand had consented to him delaying the return journey to Liverpool Lime Street. You see, Jimmy was desperate to go to the White City to watch the first round heats of the Greyhound Derby. Jimmy was about to fulfil a dream. He was going to see Mick the Miller.

Jimmy Brennan knew greyhounds. He came from Mick the Miller country, Rathleague near Maryborough. His mother had died when he was seven and he'd been brought up by his uncle, Jimmy Conroy – the same James Conroy who had stood Glorious Event. Once upon a time, Jimmy Brennan had actually taken Mick the Miller's sire for walks. Jimmy's grandfather, Ned Conroy, who had trained Swordfish to run-up to Osprey Hawk in the Irish Cup of 1918 and Boys-oh-boys to win the Cork Cup of 1919, immediately inducted him into the world of coursing. He loved it. At 14 Jimmy was thrown out of school for taking some unauthorised holiday to go potato picking. Six strokes of the strap on each hand and a further six on each wrist was his leaving present from the Christian Brothers. Luckily for Jimmy Brennan, in this summer of 1927 Jimmy Shand was in the district collecting greyhounds for his new track at Southend. Introductions were made and, the following year, Jimmy started work at Stanley, another of Shand's tracks on the Prescot Road out of Liverpool.

Jimmy had read all there was to read about Mick the Miller. This might be his only chance of ever seeing the living legend in action. The odds on offer would be cramped but he was equally determined to capitalise on this singular opportunity by having a bet. He wanted to be able to tell his grandchildren that not only had he seen the greatest greyhound of all time in the flesh but he had also won money on him. Out of his weekly wage of 25 shillings (£1.25) Jimmy had around five shillings (25p) in spending money after settling his weekly dues. That five bob was earmarked for Heat XI and Mick the Miller.

Mick was 7/2 on when the bugle announced his arrival on the track. Jimmy scanned the boards of Hector Macdonald, George Barnett and the rest in a last-ditch effort to find the best value. The bookies were not giving an inch. Jimmy opted for the Celtic connection and walked over to Macdonald's pitch. He looked at the two half-crowns nestling in his palm. What was he, a man or a mouse? Five shillings was no bet for a man! This was no time for pussyfooting around! He reached into his back pocket for a ten shilling note, took a deep breath, and wrapped it around the two coins.

'Fourteen shillings to win four, if you please!' he said, bold as brass.

Best keep a shilling back for emergencies even though he was only loaning Macdonald the money for a couple of minutes.

For the first 20 seconds of the race Jimmy Brennan's dream is played out before his eyes just as he imagined. The five greyhounds break in a line. They hurtle toward the bend and the inevitable tangle of limbs and jackets. The dog in the blue jacket checks and, while the other four are trying to disentangle themselves, this brindle bullet fires directly behind them, aiming for the rail. The roar acknowledging this trademark manoeuvre loses nothing in comparison with those greeting a Dixie Dean goal, a Jack Hobbs boundary or a Len Harvey uppercut. Mick the Miller is putting on a performance, strutting his stuff for Jimmy

Brennan and countless others like him who are only here in expectation of savouring just such a thrill.

Round the last bend. The cheering suddenly stops. The crowd watches in stunned silence as Mick runs wide, toward the hare. Perhaps he has caught the hare-driver unawares. He is devouring the ground so easily that he has got too close to the hare and is sensing a 'kill'. However, the cause doesn't matter: only the effect. Those taking the shortest route are eating into Mick's advantage. The pack is hunting him down.

The terraces jolt back to life. 'Look out, Mick!' yells Jimmy Brennan in concert with thousands of others, 'Look out, Mick! Watch your inside!'

Leading the charge up the rail is a brindle-and-white dog with more than a touch of Macoma about him. And why not? This dog is none other than a son of Macoma called Mick's Fancy.

His 'Uncle Mick' seems to have heard and understood the crowd's warning. Alerted to the presence of a challenger on his inside, he corrects his line off the bend and swings back toward the rail. Uncle and nephew collide, shoulder to shoulder. The younger dog comes off best. The champion can find no more. Mick's Fancy crosses the line 11/2 lengths to the good.

Jimmy Brennan went on to become a highly respected and successful trainer of greyhounds. However, he was obliged to revise the story he had always hankered after telling his future grandchildren, the one about the day he got to see the greatest racing greyhound who ever saw the inside of a box. Instead of impressing them with a tale of how he'd made his fortune from the punter's pal, he confessed to being one of the few 'eejits' ever to lose money on Mick the Miller.

Up until this shock setback, Mick the Miller's comeback campaign during the first half of 1931 had progressed pretty nicely. He had won five of his six outings. The loss came over 550 yards; the wins over 525 included a new track record at Wembley. 'Either Mick is a super dog or last year's crop of dogs was no improvement on previous years,' wrote Leveret in *The Star*. 'I cannot say I welcome the idea of one dog being so supreme so long, as in this way stagnation lies.'

Mick had not resumed competitive action until 16 March, some 6½ months after sustaining his shoulder injury at Wimbledon. In the manner of all celebrity invalids, his recuperation was closely monitored and charted by regular medical bulletins that were carried by every newspaper. If such deference was good enough for the King and the Prime Minister it was good enough for Mick the Miller.

The invalid's progress was alarmingly pedestrian despite an extensive course of electric massage to the injured shoulder. Damage to the joint proved worse than Alfred Sams had initially diagnosed. A bump had developed on the tendon at the point where the shoulder blade meets the upper leg, which led Sams to conclude that Mick had possibly split the sheath covering the membrane. And there was no avoiding the fact that Mick was, in track terms, a veteran now well on the way to his fifth birthday. No one wished to see him struggling vainly to regain his former glory. The sad spectacle of just such a fate befalling the former crack stayer Naughty Jack Horner was still fresh in the mind. And the champion hurdler Carpio never made it back. Was it worth persevering? Indeed, was it fair?

Toward the end of January, Orton was sufficiently confident to announce that Mick would return to the track on the last day of the month with a solo trial over 500 yards at Wimbledon. However, he still expressed caution: 'We cannot be certain if he has recovered until he has been subjected to the test of a gallop at racing pace on a track.'

Within 24 hours Orton was again talking to the press. The trial would have to be put back a week. Mick was lame. He had picked up a small stone in his off-fore pad. No one needed reminding that Mick's off-fore was the troublesome limb. 'I have every reason to hope that Mick will be himself again but one never knows where shoulder trouble is concerned. When the trial does take place, I want it to be such as will satisfy everyone that all ill effects have been dispelled. With this object in view, I naturally want him to be in perfect trim so far as one can gauge before he is called upon for the effort.'

Mick's 'Fateful Trial', as the press was calling it, was rescheduled for 7 February. Not for the first time, however, Wimbledon's perennial enemy, the River Wandle, had something to say for itself. Fog rolled in off the water to wipe out the meeting after just two races. For the benefit of all those who had come to see him, Orton had Mick paraded in front of the stand. Both trainer and fans were pleased to note that Mick had lost none of his competitive juices. Passing the traps, he instantly tugged Joe Ollis toward them, eager to be installed.

Four nights later Mick finally got inside the Wimbledon boxes. The crowd was talking 13 to the dozen as Joe Ollis put him in. How would he take the first bend? Would the shoulder hold up? Could it absorb the pressure? There was no Derby-type roar when the lids rose this night. The hush was palpable as Mick's supporters awaited the answers to those crucial questions. Mick circled Wimbledon as if he was on castors and attached to the rail by a gossamer thread. A tremendous cheer of relief filled the air and continued until he flashed across the finishing line. The clock said 30.69, only 9/100th of a second slower than Orton's Billy Lad had taken to win the last race. Mick was back.

The sublime cocktail of joy and relief was short-lived. As soon as he came to a halt, Mick raised the injured leg off the floor. Standing there motionless on three legs, he cut a pathetic figure. The smile melted away from Orton's face and the tears rolled down Phiddy Kempton's cheeks as she buried her head in Rundel's chest.

Joe Ollis ran toward the stricken dog, fearing the worst every inch of the way. 'Stay still, Mick! Stay Still!' he shouted. Once at his dog's side, Ollis spotted the source of the trouble. 'Thank God, it's only the dew claw. He's torn off the dew claw!'

The dew claw is a rudimentary toe just above the foot on the inside of a dog's foreleg. Mick had injured this particular dew claw at Wembley the previous spring. In the wake of this latest mishap, the usefulness of the dew claw to the racing greyhound now became the subject of newspaper speculation. The *Evening News* printed an erudite piece informing its readers that, 'the back, tail and dew claw keep the greyhound steady, especially the last two ... the tail acts as a medium for steadying the dog and the dew claw acts as a kind of safety point which tells the dog how far he can lean over when racing at speed round bends without falling over.' Indeed, Mick had frequently endorsed this view by finishing races with grass on the offending claw.

The problem was of a minor nature. Mick was soon back on song. The morning of 4 March he clocked 31.12 in a solo trial over 525 on a slow Wembley oval (the next best on the day was 32.08) in preparation for his planned participation in the Spring Cup, which commenced on Monday the 16th. He was as fresh as a pup. Onlookers swore he was two lengths clear of the box before the lid had stopped rising. On the Saturday beforehand, Orton brought him back in the afternoon for his final blow-out. Mick zoomed round in 30.21, a time neither Toftwood Misery nor St Leger winner – and current Derby second favourite – Maiden's Boy could match in their respective trials. The ante post market for the Derby that had been in utter disarray owing to the doubts surrounding Mick's fitness, was suddenly put on a secure footing. Before his comeback trial at Wimbledon, certain unnamed punters had stolen the 20/1 on offer, but after this latest Wembley trial Mick was a firm favourite at a best-priced 6/1. After the forthcoming Spring Cup, punters could get no better than a measly 7/2.

Mick was majestic in each of the three rounds. He thrashed the 1930 Irish Derby winner Prince Fern by four lengths in round one, and recovered from a terrible buffeting in his semi-final to win by three lengths after seizing, in the words of Leveret, 'what seemed only inches of space to positively hurl himself through the gap to the rails and be off in the lead before anyone could say knife.'

The final was another *tour de force*. Mick equalled the three-year-old track record of the bitch Moselle with a time of 30.04. 'Mick the Miller in greater form than ever – world's finest dog!' declared *The Greyhound Mirror and Gazette*. 'I think it highly unlikely that we shall ever see the sport so dominated by one dog again,' mused Leveret in his own column. 'There may be faster dogs but I doubt if we shall ever have a dog with such personality – if one can use that word in connection with dogs.'

Sidney Orton's strategy appeared to be paying dividends. 'I've endeavoured to time his training to comply with his special qualities and temperament,' he told reporters clamouring to know why all entreaties for mouth-watering match-races had been declined. So, what was Mick's schedule? As ever, the trainer was co-operation personified. 'On 13 May he will run a solo trial over 525 at White City, and on

Saturday next on the same track he'll run in the sweepstake; the following Saturday he'll run in the Revenge Stakes over 550 at West Ham; the Saturday after that, the 30th, he'll go for the 525 Gladstone Cup at Wembley. He may run again before the opening Derby heats, and he may possibly run another solo at White City after the Wembley event.' Wimbledon was conspicuous by its absence. Mick would never be asked to race there again.

The following Wednesday Mick continued to amaze. At the conclusion of his latest White City trial, astounded clock-holders stared down at stopwatches showing a time of 29.95, a full half-second faster than the year's best under proper race conditions. And Mick had stumbled twice on the way round. On the Saturday, Mick overcame a rain-soaked track to collect the sweepstake just as routinely. So far, so good.

The papers were unanimous. 'Still nothing to beat Mick!' That is, apart from the unspoken factor: bad luck. West Ham on 23 May was to be one of those nights. Try as he might, Mick could not find a route through the pack and was beaten into third by Passing Fair and Altamatzin. Orton was never a trainer to make excuses, but he pointed out that Mick had been particularly upset by a violent thunderstorm in the hours before the race. He was also mindful of the fact that a gastric disorder had been sweeping through his kennels. But that was not all. There may have been another mitigating factor. At some stage Mick had aggravated the injured shoulder. Orton immediately withdrew him from the Gladstone Cup.

Mick endured 48 hours of considerable pain in the immediate aftermath of the Revenge Stakes and Orton could ill-afford to take any risks if a feasible assault on a third Derby was to be mounted. Even so, he was anxious to get a proper race into Mick before his first-round heat on 13 June. He declined the tempting invitation to participate in the White City novelty race designed as an attempt on Entry Badge's 500-yards track record and chose instead to accept the challenge of a match over 525 at the same venue on 6 June against the former Manchester star, Doumergue, currently kennelled at the White City.

Trainer Harry Woolner had grounds for thinking he had discovered a worthy successor to Deemster. After taking the previous year's

Northern Flat Championship over Belle Vue's 500 yards, two more fine performances over course and distance this season had resulted in Doumergue being elevated to third favourite for the Derby. He beat a second leading Derby contender in Brunswick Bill with one outstanding time and went on to set a hand-timed world record in the other. He had also humbled Brunswick Bill on his home patch at Harringay where he was well-nigh unbeatable. In his current humour Doumergue would be no soft touch.

Orton primed Mick with a couple of stiff gallops, over 640 yards and 500 yards. Significantly, both trials were straight. He chose to avoid subjecting that shoulder to the rigours of a bend for as long as possible. Mick pulled up sound on each occasion. He was ready to play his part in one of the greatest match-races ever seen on a British greyhound track.

Mick (13/8 on) trapped the better of the pair but Doumergue quickly drew level and, profiting from his inside box, had pulled clear going round the first turn. Down the back and round the final two bends, Mick repeatedly probed for an opening on the rail. Doumergue would not budge. There was nowhere for Mick to go except down the centre of the track. With time and distance slipping away, Mick took the outside tack and lowered his head for one final charge. Bit by bit he ate into Doumergue's advantage. First, he reached Doumergue's quarters. Then his shoulders. One last desperate lunge. The two dogs broke the finishing beam side by side. Mick had won by a short head.

The stadium rocked to the sound of the champion's jubilant supporters. 'Mick waited a little too long to get an opening,' *The Mirror and Gazette* would observe with considerable understatement, 'but like the good dog he is, came all out when he saw that was the only way to win.' Leveret waxed more lyrically: 'Had both dogs had jockeys on their backs, the duel could not have been fought out in better style.'

Victory was welcome. But there was a more important issue. How had the shoulder responded to such a gruelling encounter? The news was good. Mick was as right as rain. No apparent after-effects. Mick was deemed A1 for the first-round heats of the Derby, which was now just seven days away.

Mick's surprise defeat in Heat XI at the paws of Mick's Fancy destroyed his air of invincibility. Suddenly he became as vulnerable as the next dog. Although the *Sunday Sportsman*, for one, declared Mick to have been 'bumped, bored and generally unfortunate', other papers reckoned he'd been beaten 'fair and square...the other Mick creates a sensation', and grabbed the chance to advance the claims of younger rivals. Even Sidney Orton was obliged to concede the possibility that *Anno Domini* was finally catching up with his ageing star. 'He does not seem able to pull out that final burst of speed which has been so characteristic of him and which always enabled him to extricate himself from any trouble and go on and win,' he confessed to the *Daily Mirror*. Shrewd players in the Derby market began to seek an alternative to the dual-champion.

The previous year's St Leger winner Maiden's Boy became a popular choice, but he failed to get beyond round one. It was subsequently revealed that three days beforehand he had been found 'tottering on his feet' and had only entered the traps because of the ante post money wagered on him to win the competition outright. If there was villainy in the air, Sidney Orton was not about to take any chances. Mick the Miller was placed under guard 24 hours a day.

Doumergue was another obvious choice. Promoted to favourite on the strength of his first-round victory, he was promptly 'bumped out' in the second round behind the Irishman Lion's Share. The quest continued. As ever, Ireland yielded more than its fair share of 'dark horses'. One live candidate, Future Cutlet, was foiled by red tape, having been sent over too late for completion of the necessary formalities. However, two others had made it to England. Lion's Share came fresh from success in the Easter Cup at Shelbourne to win both of his two opening-rounds. The second dog was certainly 'dark' in one respect, if not exactly in the vernacular. A big black monster weighing 80lb – a full stone heavier than Mick the Miller – yet still only 27-months-old, he had been burning up Harold's Cross and had won the Spring Cup in a new track record. After changing hands for £900, the 'Mystery Derby candidate', as the papers dubbed him, was sent across in late May to Wembley (along with his own supply of food and water) where he was placed in the care (like Lion's Share) of a recently installed trainer. The newcomer's name was Arthur Callanan. The black monster's name was Ryland R.

'The Man Who Saved Mick the Miller' had only arrived at Wembley a few months before Ryland R. However, unlike his trainer's lofty standing, Ryland R's equally tall reputation was to receive two instant knocks. He could only finish third in his Wembley trial and then lost the Gladstone Cup on the same track by a short head to Rory of the Hill. On each occasion the story was the same. Ryland R went off like the wind before slowing up once he'd established a commanding lead. There was more than a hint of quirkiness in his make-up. On his first race at the White City, however, Ryland R unfurled his true colours. Thirty minutes before Mick's demise in his first-round heat, he won Heat IX in a far sharper time. A sterner examination awaited Ryland R three days later in the second round. Drawn against him was Mick the Miller.

Naturally, this also constituted a tall order for Mick. Could the wily strategist peg back the lightningly quick starter? And Ryland R was not the only danger. Callanan also fielded Altamatzin, who had already finished in front of Mick once this year and would go on to demonstrate his worth by winning the Welsh Derby. And then there was Brunswick Bill. While others – including Mick – ducked the White City's challenge to break Entry Badge's 500-yards track record, the Harringay dog had not only picked up the gauntlet but also equalled the world record in so doing. And as if to prove a point, Brunswick Bill came into this Derby heat with the fastest qualifying time of 30 seconds dead.

Thirty seconds would be under attack and no mistake. Mick was made favourite to duck below the magical mark from trap three, but only at 7/4 – the first time in 25 races that he had not been odds-on. Ryland R (3/1) would emerge from the outside box.

What happened next stunned the White City. Ryland R left his box like a rocket and on this occasion completed the entire distance like a rocket. He clocked 29.69 to smash Deemster's track record by 0.21 seconds. Mick trailed him by five full lengths, having been impeded at the first bend and baulked along the back straight.

Ryland R immediately became all the rage to win the competition outright. 'Electrifying exhibition by Ryland R,' said *The Mirror and Gazette* which then went on to commit the ultimate heresy by trumpeting: 'The most wonderful greyhound the sport has so far produced.' Had the paper forgotten so easily what it had written after the Wembley Spring Cup not three months earlier? Someone at the paper had either lost their memory or their mind.

Before Ryland R brought about any successful Derby denouement, however, fate decreed he and Mick should meet once more in their semi-final. The public had seen enough to make up its mind. The old champion was no more: bring on the new champion. On Tuesday, 20 June Mick entered his box for the first time in 41 races, minus the public accolade of favouritism. It was a sequence that stretched back for almost two years. In fact, the single occasion he had not been burdened with favouritism in 48 races since leaving Ireland was his match with Back Isle in Wales in August 1929. No English punters had dared replicate their Welsh counterparts until now.

Mick was inspired. Dogs have no powers of reasoning, no powers of deduction. Since we are assured of that fact, one must assume the race Mick the Miller proceeded to run was the product of pure inspiration. Fifth coming off the first turn, he was bumped and carried so wide that he was all of 15 lengths behind his black nemesis at one stage. But one after the other he reeled-in Lion's Share, Curious Mickey and, on the inside of the last bend, Brunswick Boy, until just the leader remained. If Mick could pull this race out of the fire it would surely be his finest achievement. He just failed. Ryland R held on by half a length. 'Mick has never run a better race,' opined the *Evening News* Nobody demurred.

Mick had made the final and gone part way to redeeming his reputation. Nevertheless, no one could recall him losing three consecutive races before. The 'fiddlers' scurried away to consult the formbooks. It had happened just the once. Way back in Dublin over two years ago. Was this present lapse a sign of deterioration on Mick's part? After all was said and done, he was now soldiering through his fifth year of competition and would be celebrating his fifth birthday two days after the Derby final. In fact, he would be at least two years senior to any of his rivals. Or was the answer somewhat simpler. Perhaps Mick was facing better dogs nowadays.

The five dogs waiting to test him at the White City would surely settle the issue. This number in itself had raised a few eyebrows. 'Is the Greyhound Derby a real test of merit?' asked the *Evening News*. 'A six-dog race is a lottery. All the followers of the sport wish to see the very best greyhound entered win and if only four were allowed to race together, there could be nothing to cavil at.' It's never clever to be wise after the event but, given subsequent events, a four-dog final may well have altered the course of greyhound racing history.

One contention brooked no argument. Should Mick win this final, at his venerable age and coming off severe injury, it would be his finest hour. And Sidney Orton's also. The master of Burhill was being his usual acme of helpfulness to members of the press. But his upbeat mood was distinctly unusual.

'I am very, very hopeful,' Orton informed *The Mirror and Gazette* 24 hours before the final. 'Mick has given me every satisfaction and I have him as fit as he was when he won his first Derby. His shoulder injury is completely cured and there is no sign of it returning. Mick will win if he escapes bumping and boring and I am not much scared of the opposition. I am exceedingly confident.'

Orton was quoted in similar mode by the *Daily Mirror* on the day of the final: 'Mick the Miller will win if he meets with no bad luck. He was never better, gamer nor fitter than I have him now and I am quite content to leave it at that.'

Saturday, 27 June turned out to be a typically oppressive English summer day. Temperatures had hovered round the eighties all day and humidity levels were unbearably high. Staying cool, calm and collected might become a problem to anyone put under stress inside that steamy cauldron otherwise known as the White City on Greyhound Derby night.

Inside the stadium the Pipe Band of the Irish Guards once more earned its fee, puffing and sweating away in a valiant effort to entertain early-comers. Outside the stadium, however, the scenes were chaotic. The public transport network in the vicinity was nearing overload thanks to the confluence of 70,000 people – an increase of 20,000 on 1930. Every bus, tram and tube train was jam-packed. They were bumper to bumper and buffer to buffer. The system was on the brink of meltdown. And all because of one dog.

How ever unfair it seemed to the connections of the remaining contenders, the story of this final was already as good as set on the presses back in Fleet Street. 'Mick Wins!' or 'Mick Fails!' Anything else was superfluous. Owners and trainers were too cognisant of Mick's hold on public affection, too grateful for the reflected attention in which they basked, to take offence at this slight to their own individual pride and joy.

Yet 'Doc' Callanan, for one, had a right to feel aggrieved. He had the fastest dog in the final in Ryland R on whom he had just performed another of his minor veterinary miracles to cure a sprung toe sustained in the semi-final with the application of violet-ray treatment. And there was no logical reason why Mick (or Brunswick Bill) should reverse semi-final form with his 'Black Express'.

Nor did the qualifiers from the second semi-final give Callanan cause for undue anxiety. They were Golden Hammer, Seldom Led and Mick's Fancy. Golden Hammer had once changed hands for £2. He was a decent performer but fully exposed. Seldom Led had sprung from even humbler beginnings to win the 1930 Trafalgar Cup for puppies and then break 30 seconds for 525 yards at West Ham – he had been sold by his breeder for all of five shillings (25p) after being reared on a diet of pig swill. 'I just hope the weather conditions allow the final to be run in daylight,' said his trainer Walter Green, 'for he does not run so well when the electric light is affixed to the hare. Very likely Seldom Led will live up to his name!' One had to admire Green's optimism. Seldom Led had not 'led' his rivals across the line in any of his three Derby rounds.

If the heart pleaded for Mick, the head spoke for Ryland R. The hard-bitten newspaper tipsters said as much. To a man, they concluded: 'Mick eager but will not beat Ryland R.'

The White City faithful, however, clung on to its belief in the old warrior. As the Derby fanfare commenced shortly before 9 o'clock, the market could not separate Mick and Ryland R at 13/8.

Rundel and Phiddy Kempton were safely ensconced in their seats. Phiddy's mother had come along to lend her daughter emotional support – of which she gave every sign of being in grave need. Phiddy could not bear to watch. She sat bolt upright, head bowed with her eyes locked onto the hands firmly clasped in her lap. She was near to tears. Rundel placed a soothing hand on her shoulder. Its only effect was to nudge her even closer to the edge.

Phiddy did not have to watch in order to appreciate the scenes unfurling beneath her on the track. She knew her darling Mick would be revelling in the cheers of his fan club, his tail wagging like a demented white-tipped metronome. She knew her darling Mick would be prancing out of Joe Ollis's hands, eager to savour the momentary solitude of the box that ushered in those exhilarating 30 seconds his life revolved around. She knew her darling Mick would walk sprightly into that darkness where others demanded a push and a shove. She knew her darling Mick would run his heart out for her. She knew her darling Mick would win. But she could not bring herself to watch.

In they go. Golden Hammer into trap one. Ryland R into two. Mick's Fancy into three. Seldom Led into four. Brunswick Bill into five. And, finally, Mick trots into the outside box. The hare starter gives the signal to the hare controller. The hare starts its run. The Derby roar begins to swell. The hare flies past the traps. The lids bang. Thirty sensational seconds have begun.

Ryland R is out and off like the train he has been nicknamed. He puts daylight between himself and the rest way before the first bend. Mick is stone last. Nothing changes down the far straight. Mick is still trailing. Ryland R is still scorching the grass. The head is clearly going to overrule the heart.

Into the final turn. One dog is closing on the leader. It's an orange jacket. It's Seldom Led. The 'Black Express' is stopping. Whether he's feeling that toe injury or whether it's just his old foible of starting quick and finishing slow that's beginning to manifest itself is of no consequence at this precise moment. The two dogs swing wide and appear to make contact.

One man among 70,000 thinks he has spotted something. He is the steward specially appointed to monitor proceedings on this bend. He believes Ryland R has turned his head to snap at Seldom Led. The chief steward is instantly informed and before the dogs have even crossed the finish line the klaxon denoting 'No-Race' is blaring.

No one can hear it. The main reason no one can hear this most raspingly distinctive of noises is because another equally distinctive sound has been building. It's an old hymn. A deafening chant. 'Mick's coming through! Mick's coming! Mick's done it again! Come on, Mick!'

Rundel Kempton was on his feet. 'He's coming through!' he assured Phiddy. 'Here he comes! Look! Look!' Still Phiddy could not break the chains pinioning her emotions. But, yes, she knew deep down, her darling Mick would win the day.

Mick had stealthily made up most of the lost ground. Although cannoned into by the recoiling Seldom Led, he had slipped through on the inside rail and now fixed his sights on the one opponent still ahead of him. It was Golden Hammer. Mick had beaten him in the past and he would beat him now. The crowd knew it. Perhaps Mick himself knew it. He threw himself at Golden Hammer up the straight. The black-and-white jacket began to merge with the red. One last sinew-stretching dive for the line. A moment of held breath. Yes, he'd got him. Mick had won by a head. The White City is engulfed by a tide of delirium.

The spell is broken at last. Phiddy Kempton hugs her mother and then her husband. She is weeping with joy. 'Mick has won! My darling Mick has won!' She does not see the red light shining out from the results board. The red light signifying that all is not well. The red light announcing 'No-Race'.

The buoyant mood is rudely shattered. Instead of Mick's number six going into the frame, the 'No-Race' board is dropped. It is immediately followed by the news that Ryland R was deemed to have been guilty of 'nosing and impeding' another dog who was in a challenging position – which under the Rules of Racing warranted disqualification and automatically rendered the race void.

The stewards found themselves on the horns of a dilemma. Heart versus head again. And they would not be popular whatever they did. Deep in their hearts, Lieutenant-Colonel Denison (Wembley), Captain

Fawcett (West Ham) and Captain Dane (West Ham) – all outside officials appointed by the National Greyhound Racing Club – might like to have courted popularity by giving sentiment full rein. But a spate of lax stewarding, particularly a *laissez faire* attitude toward fighting, had lately given rise to considerable discontent. The stewards could hardly turn a blind eye to this incident just because it was the Derby and Mick the Miller was the beneficiary. As totally impartial stewards they had no choice but to uphold the rules. The head stated there had to be a re-run. It was just as well the three men were professional soldiers. War was about to break out.

As the grim message of hooter and red light gradually sank in, communal numbness turned to shock. People resorted to emotive phrases like 'death-like silence', 'bombshell' and 'thunderclap' to describe the impact of the announcement. It was all too much for Phiddy Kempton whose emotions had been as tense as piano wire all evening. She broke down and wept uncontrollably.

'Mick has won!' she sobbed. 'My darling Mick has won! I don't care what happened! Mick has won!' A dumbfounded Rundel Kempton was unable to console her. 'Scandalous!' he mumbled. 'Disgraceful!'

Down in the public enclosures the decision was greeted with open hostility. Fists began to fly between those patrons ruled by the heart and those ruled by the head. The main beneficiaries – as ever – were the bookmakers. They had good reason to smile. All money placed on the first race had to be returned and a new market formed for the re-run. But one of the biggest 'losers' in their ante post ledgers was safely out of the way. They stood to pay out £25,000 had Ryland R won. If Mick the Miller got beat they'd save a further £30,000. And the old boy couldn't handle two Derbies inside an hour, could he?

The re-run was ordered for 9.55. Ryland R would not be involved. Would Mick the Miller?

Phiddy Kempton dug in her heels. She was adamant. Her darling Mick had won his third Derby. That was it. He was not having anything to do with this bogus re-run. The powers-that-be had their work cut out if the 1931 Derby was not to be clouded further by a second sensation greater than the first. Refusing to start Mick the Miller might just tip the atmosphere on the terraces irrevocably the wrong side of respectability. Greyhound racing could do without such negative publicity. The Church would have an 'I-told-you-so' field day.

The directors of the Greyhound Racing Association, who controlled the White City, swung into action. Major-General Lord Loch, Brigadier-General Critchley, Lieutenant-Colonel Moore Brabazon and Lieutenant-Colonel Cameron had fought many a battle and between them had three DSOs (Distinguished Service Orders) and a pair of MCs (Military Crosses) to show for it. Now they had another on their hands. They had barely half an hour to persuade Phiddy Kempton to change her mind.

Phiddy Kempton did not stand alone. Neither her husband nor her trainer were conducive to the idea of subjecting Mick to a re-run. It was inconceivable that a dog of his age could reproduce his best running twice inside an hour. Together they fought their corner. The GRA spokesmen alternately begged and cajoled. They stressed that the veterinary surgeon reported Mick was perfectly fit to run again. They reminded her of all the money riding on Mick's back, placed there by his legions of supporters who loved him almost as much as she. They told her the good name of the sport, its very integrity in the eyes of the public, was at stake.

Eventually Phiddy caved-in. Mick would enter the traps for what was in effect his fifth Greyhound Derby.

Blissfully unaware of the drama being played out high in the grandstand, the layers had made Mick a shade of odds-on for the re-run but, as the preliminaries were being re-enacted a second time, they eased him to even-money. With Seldom Led's brave display uppermost in the mind, the young West Ham dog came in for plenty of support at 7/2.

The money spoke. At 10.09 the lids rose on the most miserable 30 seconds in Mick's career. After slipping at the first bend in an unavailing bid for the inside, he never showed as Seldom Led overhauled Golden Hammer coming out of the second bend to race clear and win unchallenged by an easy four lengths in the respectable time for a re-run of 30.04. Clearly, Walter Green's concern about his dog's distaste for chasing an illuminated hare was unfounded.

Now, all thought Mick had won it with poise and grace,
But the Irish dog Ryland R made it a 'no-race',
And after the re-run, such an exciting thriller,
We saw that Green's dog had defeated the Miller.

Mick was nearly six lengths back in fourth place. In winning the void race he had been clocked at 29.89 by one independent watch-holder. But now, after giving so much, he was left without a penny. Denied even the £150 for finishing third. He had been asked to achieve the impossible, and in consequence had been cruelly exposed to the kind of humiliation he above all dogs did not merit. Questions would now be asked of others.

Even as Lady Portal was presenting the Cup to Seldom Led's owners amid a welter of boos, thinly veiled recriminations were manifesting themselves elsewhere in the stadium. 'We feel he deserved the race when he came up to beat the leaders in his usual generous style and we were surprised at the voiding of the race,' Arundel Kempton told reporters, 'but evidently the stewards were doing their job with the best interests at heart.' Sidney Orton concurred, though not before extending a congratulatory handshake in the direction of Walter Green: 'Mick deserved to win but it was asking too much of him to come out a second time and beat much younger dogs than himself.'

The press had been gifted a very juicy bone and seized the opportunity to gnaw on it enthusiastically. Greyhound racing has rarely received such publicity as it did in the immediate aftermath of the 1931 Derby.

'Derby Fiasco...Mick the Miller Wins – And Loses.' – *Sunday Sportsman*

'Dog Derby Crowd Goes Wild...the most amazing scene in the history of greyhound racing ... 70,000 people booed and shouted with anger.' – *The Star*

'Seldom Led wins Derby after a Fiasco.' – *Daily Express*

'Sensation in Dog Derby – Mick the Miller Fails.' – *Daily Herald*

'Derby Final Thrills: Bold Decision by Stewards.' – *Daily Mail*

'Surprise at Dog Derby ... considerable hostility at re-run decision ... Mick a gallant stout-hearted winner despite the trouble with which he met.' – *Daily Mirror*

'Amazing Derby Scene ... the crowd roared its anger at the action of the stewards in robbing Mick of the race ... free fights broke out.' – *Daily Sketch*

'Shock for Great Crowd: Dog Disqualified: Amazing Scenes.' – *The Sporting Life*

'Sensation in Derby Final ... Mick the Miller the victim of ill-luck.' – *Irish Independent*

It was in the interest of the specialist greyhound-racing press to adopt a more level-headed approach to the controversy. *The Greyhound Mirror and Gazette*, for instance, led its extensive coverage with the headline 'Mick Fails To Stay Re-Run of Derby Final' and played down the sensational aspects of the night in favour of playing up the fact that, '70,000 Watch Amazing Finish To Great Dog Classic.' It went on piously: 'Those spectators – and it is pleasing to record that they were in the minority – who first of all booed at the "no-race" announcement and then, when Seldom Led had fairly and squarely beaten his field, again booed as the cup was being presented to the winning owners, not only showed complete ignorance of the rules of the sport but acted in a decidedly un-British manner.'

The paper's lead writer Isidore Green concluded his lengthy piece by saying: 'The bend stewards and all concerned in handling the big race had the courage of their convictions. The race, as they saw it, was not truly run and that, in fairness to each finalist, it would have to be re-run. Under the circumstances, one cannot blame them for their decision – on the contrary, they are entitled to congratulation on their determination to see "fair play" carried out to the nth degree. Very few saw the offending incident...and if the atmosphere was charged with some disappointment at the unsatisfactory conclusion to the world's greatest greyhound Classic, no real sportsman will deny that its termination was in keeping with all the principles of clean sport.'

The Sporting Life leapt to the defence of both the stewards and the crowd. 'There were two outstanding incidents which in my opinion showed the sound, honest basis on which the sport, in a few years, has built up its immense popularity,' wrote King Cob. 'One was the courageous and unhesitating manner in which the stewards made their momentous decision to void the first race, and the other the sportsmanship of the huge crowd, who despite a fever of excitement, accepted the decision, involving the loss of many thousands of pounds, without undue anger.'

That the stewards had acted within the letter of the law was not in question, however. The race had to be re-run and – despite one or two writers having raised the possibility of a re-run the following week – the rules stated it had to be run at the conclusion of the meeting. Whether the directors of the GRA overstepped the mark and abused their powers in order to ensure Mick the Miller's participation in that re-run was another matter altogether. Had Phiddy Kempton been railroaded? Did the GRA's rhetoric cross the line from persuasion to downright intimidation?

The *Daily Express* reckoned it had unearthed a scoop. As the dust was just beginning to settle 72 hours after a race whose outcome, the paper said, 'almost anywhere else would have provoked a riot', it ran a follow-up story headlined: 'The Truth About Saturday Night's Dog Derby: Violent Protest By Famous Dog's Owner.'

In the finest traditions of a Fleet Street exposé, the piece began: 'The *Daily Express* is able to unfold this morning the real drama behind the sensational running of the Greyhound Derby on Saturday night at the White City. That which the huge crowd saw was thrilling enough but the struggle between a pretty, broken-hearted young woman who owns Mick the Miller and the directors of the Greyhound Racing Association eclipsed in tenseness any Lyceum thriller. The directors argued, pleaded, threatened. They kept their tempers but put it to Mrs Kempton that a withdrawal of her dog from a race of such importance might jeopardise the prospect of its being allowed to run in future events on licensed tracks. The owner sadly and tearfully gave in. But as the most orderly crowd in the world went sadly home, a sad-faced, pretty woman went to bestow a last good-night pat on the head of the gallant little dog that had won and lost.'

The notion that Phiddy Kempton was, indeed, railroaded against her will into running Mick a second time amounted to an embryonic *cause celebre* potentially more damaging to the sport than the controversial decision that had sparked the contretemps in the first place. The *Greyhound Outlook* was quick to point out that Rule 14 states the owner has 'the absolute right of decision in the case of a re-run'. Nevertheless, the existence of such a rule had no direct bearing on the stated accusation. Of course she had the right to withdraw Mick but what manner of pressure was she put under not to do so? Since the GRA did not resort to threats of litigation to counter this slur on the integrity of its directors, one might infer that there was some foundation to the story after all.

Or could there have been an intervention of more distinguished origin? The plot has been thickened by the possible embroilment of no less a personage than the Prince of Wales, the future King Edward VIII. Clare Orton remembers being told by his father that Mick only participated in the re-run at the express wish of the Prince. Impeccable as this source seems to be, the claim unfortunately cannot be substantiated. The facts suggest otherwise.

On the Saturday in question the Prince was in Scotland, having just completed an official visit as president of the Highland Show. That afternoon he motored from Beaufort Castle to unwind with a round of golf at Nairn. After winning his 'fourball' 6 and 4, he dined with his three playing companions in the clubhouse before piloting his Gypsy Moth aircraft (flying and golf being his twin passions) to Himley Hall, in Staffordshire, the home of his old university chum Viscount Ednam. His Royal Highness was a close friend of the family, and Ednam was still mourning the death of his young wife. Not only was he the godfather of Ednam's son (the present Lord Dudley), he had, by all accounts, once carried a torch for the lad's mother, the noted beauty Rosemary Leveson-Gower, before she married Ednam. In addition, another of his *inamoratas* was Freda Dudley Ward, the wife of a distant cousin to Ednam. Since the Prince stayed at Himley Hall until returning to his Fort Belvedere home on the Monday, there is no logical way in which he could have played an active part in the White City drama.

There were weightier issues to consider back in July 1931 than the veracity of these future footnotes to history. Mick the Miller had served his sport too honourably to be consigned to the role of also-ran. The very possibility of him being reduced to playing bit-parts was anathema to his adoring public. This was one idol unworthy of being dashed to the ground. It was high time to consider Mick's immediate future.

CHAPTER 12
'THERE'LL NEVER BE ANOTHER'

Mick the Miller had been dethroned. He had also lost four races in a row for the first time in his life. Yet the attendant circumstances ensured few thought any the less of him. If truth be told, Mick the Miller, racing greyhound, had long gone. In his place was Mick, public icon.

Mick *was* greyhound racing. The sport had got the icon it had needed to root itself firmly into the sporting consciousness. Furthermore, it had thrown up a personality with the charisma to cross over into the public mainstream. You had to be a non newspaper-reading, non wireless-listening recluse to be unaware of Mick the Miller by the summer of 1931. Mick was extra special. Why, he even gave his own interviews.

The *Daily Herald* landed an exclusive 'interview' in which Mick outlined a typical day at Burhill: 'I get up at six, have a stretch in my paddock followed by a gallop before enjoying bread and milk for my breakfast. Then I have a rest for an hour. After that more exercise in my paddock and a nice long walk of up to seven miles on the roads. Back home for grooming and a massage before my late tea of stewed steak or chicken with vegetables and toast.'

Not to be out-done, the *Daily Express* sent a reporter down to Walton-on-Thames to quiz Mick about his Derby loss to Seldom Led. 'That son of a Pekinese! Heh, listen. I won that Derby. I thought the second time out was just a practice run. He's in training a few hundred yards up the road. We pass each other almost daily at exercise. And next time I pass that son of a half-bred dachshund...I'll..! As a matter of fact, reporter man, I wouldn't be a bit surprised if he had a bit of Airedale in him! G'rrrr, for two bones I'd fetch him one!'

Mick's anthropomorphism continued unabated. In another edition of the *Express* even one of its top columnists, Trevor Wignall, fell into the trap: 'Mick is as nearly human as a dog can be. One night he was a jockey and a dog and a racehorse combined. He helped destroy the common theory that greyhounds are natural-born dumb-bells. It's almost laughable to observe him posing for his picture – his mouth wide open and his tongue out as he walks around to receive the cheers of his countless admirers, and that peculiar movement of his head which looks like a bow – and may well be something of the sort.'

Then the *Daily Mail* oined in. 'Never was there a dog more human than Mick the Miller. This extraordinary dog understands that the beating of hands by men and women signifies approval. Ordinarily, dogs are cowed or startled and break into barking when they hear roars of human noise. But Mick knows the meaning of our noises. He wags his tail and fawns from side to side almost as though he were bowing.'

And the *Daily Sketch* : 'If it is possible for a greyhound to have a personality, Mick has got it,' stated LV Manning, 'For him the hare means nothing. He has eyes only for the rival dogs and he times his effort just as shrewdly as any human sprinter.'

Others focused on Mick's symbiotic relationship with the crowds. He drew inspiration from them. Leveret's view was typical: 'I believe that if Mick the Miller were to meet a fourth-rater in the Sahara desert he would be beaten many lengths, for he is a dog which essentially runs his best while being cheered.'

And he brought joy to them. 'Mick the Miller has long been placed on a pedestal by his public,' said the *Evening Standard*, 'His appearance on any track is the signal for an outburst of cheering and he will be remembered when the identities of some of his rivals who have won temporary fame by flashes of speed are long forgotten.'

The *Sunday Dispatch* went further. 'The amazing Mick the Miller has done more than any other dog – or person – to popularise the sport of greyhound racing. The finest judges admit there will never be another dog like him even if the sport lasts for ever.'

Even the voice of reason, the sport's very own trade paper, could not resist the inevitable. 'Greyhound racing is still in its infancy,' declared *The Greyhound Mirror and Gazette*, 'but already it has produced a popular favourite as idolised as any horse, cinema star, footballer or boxer in history. There is no doubt that Mick the Miller is the Brown Jack of greyhound racing. As that grand stayer Brown Jack – a winner at Royal Ascot for the last four years – is the evergreen veteran of the horse-race course, so is Mick the greatest-hearted greyhound, and judging by the cheers of the crowd, it seems that the more they shout the faster Mick goes.'

Only deification remained. It soon arrived. 'The cat-cult of ancient Egypt can have produced no scenes of adoration half so frenzied as that in which Mick the Miller's devotees indulge,' wrote another *Express* columnist on seeing Mick in action for the first time. 'This was a red-letter day in the calendar of that most fervently catholic of all the English religions: dog-worship. Mick the Miller, as befitted a god, was notably calm. His tail waved slowly in benediction, his mouth gaped in what might have been a yawn or a sardonic smile, probably the latter for there was a twinkle in his eye as he looked up toward the stewards' box.'

Mick's fame had also stretched round the globe. In Germany, *Welt im Bild* introduced him as 'Der beruhmteste Windhund der Welt' (the most famous greyhound in the world). Across the Atlantic, *American Weekly* regaled its readers with a double-page spread profiling: 'the greyhound which has cleared the board in England by winning every race of importance in the last two years.' It went on: 'People talk about a "dog's life" but the life of Mick the Miller is as full of real romance as that of most human beings...but then they say that Mick is human, that he does everything but talk...he seems to use his brains in every one of his races in a manner that has placed him in a class by himself...he has two personalities – in the kennels he is as playful and affectionate as any terrier puppy, he will romp and do doggy tricks and loves to chase squirrels when out wandering the country lanes, but when Mick goes to the trap he shows by his bearing he is well aware of his status, he is aloof, forgets his playfulness and will have no petting because business is serious work.'

On the other side of the world *The Melbourne Herald*'s London-based writer Nell Murray conveyed to her fellow Australians the aura surrounding, 'the wonderful Mick the Miller who runs with his brains as well as his feet, looking back over his shoulder with almost human intelligence, and knowing exactly when to increase or slacken his speed.'

Back home in Wimbledon, the Kemptons received a constant stream of letters addressed to Mick. 'People write saying what food he should eat and what races he should run,' Phiddy confided to the *Daily Mail*. 'All sorts of people ask him for photographs and once I received a letter in Spanish suggesting I burn down a certain track.' The occasional envelope contained offers – one as high as £8,000 – that were always refused unreservedly and unhesitatingly. 'I wouldn't accept a million pounds for him. I shall keep him till the day he dies.'

Currently Phiddy and Rundel had a more pressing matter to resolve. Should they opt to take the potentially dangerous step of continuing to race Mick or should they pursue the safer option of retiring him forthwith. The dog obviously had vast earning potential at stud. Yes, Mick's attentions would be directed principally at their own band of broodbitches, but at 50 guineas a nomination, for instance, even a conservative figure of 15-20 outside bitches per year would net a tidy sum. In addition, they could capitalise on his new-found celebrity by relaunching him as a viable commodity on the 'showbiz' circuit. 'If Mick were a man or a woman,' Tom Walls told them, 'he might command almost any figure for appearance money alone.'

Mick's adoring public was not kept in suspense for very long. Not wishing to play second fiddle to the *Express*, the *Daily Mirror* had announced its own scoop before the week was out: 'the most spectacular incident in the greyhound racing world since the sport was introduced into this country brought about by the initiative of this paper. Mrs Arundel H Kempton has challenged the owners of Seldom Led to a match on a neutral track over the Derby distance in which she is prepared to back her dog for any sum between £5 and £500.'

There was no immediate response from Messrs Hammond and

Fleming, the owners of Seldom Led, but the die was cast. The public had not yet seen the last of Mick the Miller. The following day, just one week after the Derby re-run, Mick found himself back on the track for the opening round of the Cesarewitch at West Ham.

Grounds soon emerged for wondering whether the Kemptons had shot themselves in the foot. Mick's mid-summer campaign was, by his standards, a disaster. Of six races, only two were won. And, worse still, his trip to the Welsh White City for the first round of the Welsh Derby on 25 July resulted in a fall.

Yet the month had begun so well. Mick won his Cesarewitch heat from the dog many believed to be his natural successor, and he garnered rave reviews in so doing. Future Cutlet possessed star quality and had been making hay since being denied his run in the Derby owing to red tape. At the halfway mark, the young pretender was six long, long lengths ahead of Mick. Dividing them was Clandown Sweep, who had recently set a new world record for 725 yards. Neither of these two was going to be short of puff during the closing stages.

But rounding the final curve the inevitable, sure-as-God-made-little-green-apples, Mick the Miller charge began to make inroads. Mick clawed his way up the rail toward the duelling leaders. He got to them with less than 20 yards to go. The three dogs raced nose to nose toward the line. Mick's head was stuck out the furthest where it mattered. 'I knew Mick would do it!' exclaimed Sidney Orton to no one in particular. 'I knew it! He's a wonder!'

The Mirror and Gazette went into raptures: 'It seems every racing superlative has been exhausted. Certainly we can find no more to offer this animal. Mick is something more than a racing greyhound. He possesses an almost uncanny intelligence which is impossible to describe. He reminded us of someone deliberately intent on making amends for a blunder which had robbed him of prestige.'

In the wake of events on the next three Saturdays, however, the paper switched to preparing Mick's racing obituary. In his semi-final of the Cesarewitch he could only finish third behind the long-shots Mahers Prospect and Five of Hearts (whom he'd defeated in the previous year's final) after running, in Orton's words, 'a brainless race'.

Five defeats in his last six appearances bore the look of a slippery slope. After Future Cutlet ruthlessly exposed his lack of speed in the final of Cesarewitch – hammering him by five lengths in a time just a couple of pips outside his own track and world record – the evidence looked irrefutable. Age had finally caught up with him.

Sloper Road and the heats of the Welsh Derby now beckoned. The executive dangled the carrot of a £100 bonus for a new track record. Mick's chances of picking up the bonus and retaining his Welsh crown lasted no further than the first bend. Caught in a sandwich, he was flung across the track on his back and slid into the perimeter fencing. Although an undignified exit from the competition, there was some good news. Mick returned comparatively unscathed. Apart from that to his pride, the only blow he suffered was to a toe.

Nevertheless, a month that had opened with a bang departed with a whimper. August offered little by way of encouragement. Mick proceeded to outmanoeuvre Maiden's Boy in a match over 550 yards on heavy going at Birmingham's Perry Barr on the 8th but, a week later in a second match over 525 at the Welsh White City, Arthur Callanan's Welsh Derby winner Altamatzin got back up to steal victory on the line after Mick had taken the lead off the last bend.

The circumstances of this reverse typified the cleft stick increasingly troubling Orton and the Kemptons. Owing to that toe damage, Orton did not have Mick as fit as he would wish, but once the decision had been made to travel down to Cardiff in anticipation of running, the prospect of disappointing the huge local crowd by withdrawing the dog at the last minute was never really a viable option. The price of fame was proving high. Higher still once Orton noticed that Mick had yet again knocked that irksome dew claw.

The press awaited the inevitable news of Mick's retirement. When Sidney Orton finally spoke to reporters they were flabbergasted. The news was not, after all, a formal announcement of greyhound racing's worst-kept secret. Mick was not retiring. Mick was going to run in the St Leger, the Stayer's Classic at Wembley over 700 yards – a distance he had never raced in his life.

Once the initial shock had worn off, the rationale behind the decision began to come into focus. Mick no longer had the pure speed for the blue-riband distance of 525 yards. No amount of cunning and general-ship could compensate for the loss of his youthful pace. Over longer distances, however, Mick's racing brain could yet come into its own. If he really did win his races through guile on the bends, the St Leger offered six of them instead of four. Furthermore, Wembley was a track truly made for him, with its wide, open turns and long galloping straights, and of seven visits Mick had lost only the first. The distance should not trouble him – his coursing heritage would take care of that. And Mick would have won the Cesarewitch over 600 by a clear margin had he not caught a Tartar in Future Cutlet, the one up-and-coming dog to be feared. Future Cutlet's immediate objective was a shorter Classic, The Laurels on 11 September (which he duly won), so with his training geared toward racing round a tight 500 yards at Wimbledon, simultaneously preparing him for the first round of the St Leger over the marathon trip just 48 hours later was out of the question. That left Bradshaw Fold over her optimum trip to worry about – and she was in fine fettle having won the Coronation Stakes at Wembley and the Welsh Marathon in Cardiff. And there was one old score to settle. The Leger was Seldom Led's autumn target. If these two, admittedly tricky, obsta-cles could be surmounted, the road lay open for Mick to claim another Classic and go out in a blaze of glory.

Orton prepared his old soldier for this arduous final campaign with military precision. Obtaining permission from the committee of Burhill Golf Club, he subjected Mick to a series of gallops on a 700-yard stretch of the course. The troublesome toe seemed a thing of the past as Mick sailed through these dress rehearsals without so much as a backward glance. Only the events of Monday, 14 September could prove whether all this time and effort had been worthwhile.

First round heat or not, Mick would enjoy anything other than a cake-walk with world-record holder Clandown Sweep coming out of the trap next to him. Yet he dispelled every fear, thumping his rival by seven lengths. However, Bradshaw Fold finished well inside his time in her heat, and then Seldom Led brought the house down when winning the next heat by 14 lengths, and the best part of 11 lengths faster, in a new track record of 40.72. The bookmakers had seen enough. Seldom Led was promoted to favouritism at 3/1 with Bradshaw Fold on 5s. Anybody foolish souls wanting to throw money away on Mick the Miller could do so at 14/1.

Mick needed a tougher workout before the second round in which he was drawn against Seldom Led. As such a possibility had always been on the cards, a proposed match on the Saturday between rounds with the improving Ross Regatta, recent victor in the Northern Flat Championship, that had been left on the table, was now taken up.

After the success of the Maiden's Boy match the previous month, the Perry Barr executive was mustard keen to get Mick back to Birchfield. Accordingly, the Mick the Miller roadshow headed to Birmingham where, in the view of the *Birmingham Post* Mick was accorded 'a reception like Charlie Chaplin might enjoy'. That was no help to him over the plainly inadequate 525 yards, a distance he had not won at since the titanic match with Doumergue at the White City back in early June.

Ross Regatta won quite comfortably – though Mick ran a trifle wide on this unfamiliar circuit – in a new track record. In so doing, Ross Regatta, like many others whose lives brushed that of Mick the Miller, achieved a tiny slice of reflected immortality. To Ross Regatta, goes the honour of being the last dog to beat the mighty Mick the Miller.

One who still had the Indian sign on Mick was Seldom Led. But not for much longer. The Derby winner was a 3/1 on favourite to beat Mick in their second-round heat but he could not get the job done. Hardly one tipster gave Mick a chance. There was no earthly reason why they should. Seldom Led was three years younger and bound to be stronger. He'd got the time on the board and would surely improve with experience of the longer trip. Mick was not even second-best in the market: Prince Fern, who had only been runner-up in his first heat, was a 9/2 shot. Mick was a whopping 6/1. The only occasion he had been sent off at more generous odds (7/1) was in the final of the 1929 Easter Cup at Shelbourne Park.

But this was a four-dog not a six-dog race. It would be nonsensical to imagine Mick smarting at such indignity, yet he proceeded to run as if he had something he wanted to prove. Slowly whittling away Seldom Led's expected early advantage, he sliced inside him off the final curve to set up a desperate last-ditch tussle. Mick won a humdinger by a head. The Kemptons were beside themselves with joy. It was their fifth wedding anniversary.

Stan Biss and Sidney Orton watched the finish side by side, virtually drained of all emotion. 'Mick's a dog and a half,' gasped Biss. In reply, all a breathless Orton could manage was: 'There'll never be another!'

The greyhound press was forced to eat giant portions of humble pie. 'Mick the Miller's greatest triumph,' admitted its trade paper. 'The majority of critics, including ourselves, have for some time opined that Mick was gradually losing his old form, that he was a light of other days but last night Mick was his old self – the courageous, never-be-beaten racing marvel that has thrilled thousands with his consistent successes for the past three seasons. It seems that age will never overtake Mick the Miller.'

Leveret was equally contrite in *The Star*: 'The supposition that Mick the Miller cannot stay more than 600 yards was given the lie and was killed stone dead. He simply burst his heart to get on terms with Seldom Led and no Derby final could have aroused more enthusiasm. The place simply rocked with cheers. Men waved their hats and even people who had laid the odds on the supposed certainty forgot their troubles and applauded wildly with the rest. Mick the Marvel!'

The two principals were drawn against each other again in the semi-finals. Could lightning strike twice? Undeterred by the events of five days earlier, the punters again sided with the younger dog, albeit in a more restrained way, making him the even-money favourite with Mick at 7/4.

The story had the same ending (the time was as good as identical at 40.86) even if the narrative differed. On this occasion Mick shot out of his favourite inside box to bowl along at the head of affairs and, never in danger of being caught, stretched his margin of superiority over Seldom Led to an authoritative three lengths.

The pendulum was swinging Mick's way. Although neither he nor Seldom Led had run over 700 yards prior to the commencement of the St Leger, it was the younger dog who was feeling the pinch as the competition progressed. His times were getting slower. Would three gruelling efforts over the distance in the space of 12 days prove to be his undoing? Had he shot his bolt? Mick, on the other hand, seemed to be getting stronger and stronger. In the last two rounds he had come within a few spots of Seldom Led's record. Some former harbingers of doom were now backing him to break the record in the final.

'Marvellous Mick ran like a two-year-old: better and brighter than ever' ran the headline which seemed to occupy the sports pages of almost every newspaper following the semi-final. The last chapter of this improbable fairytale would be written on Saturday, 3 October.

The tall man in the trench coat looked familiar. Perhaps it was something about the way he tied his belt. Or how the brim of his trilby was snapped low above his eyes. A number of people inside the Empire Stadium were convinced they had seen him somewhere before, seen his picture in the paper maybe. Was he a steward or an official of some kind? No, on second glance, he had none of the airs and graces associated with that particular breed. An owner or trainer in town from the provinces? Possibly a bookmaker? A reporter or, yes, that's it, one of those 'private-eye' types that are forever cropping up in films and magazines. Whoever he was and whatever he was, this man seemed perfectly at ease with himself and perfectly at one with the environment of a greyhound track.

And so he should, even though this track was new to him. There was very little anyone thronging Wembley could tell him about greyhounds. He had trained more winners than most of them had enjoyed hot dinners. Today would not see him train a winner. He had only this day arrived from Ireland.

It was a journey he knew well. The bumpy crossing of the Irish Sea; the interminable boredom stifling the carriage as the train slowly clickety-clacks its way south-eastwards through Crewe, Rugby and Bletchley until finally crawling into Euston. He'd endured this tedium once before. However, nothing in the whole wide world could have prevented him from making the journey again on this particular day. The prize was too powerful. In company with 40,000 other disciples he was intent upon paying homage to their sport's one and only icon on the occasion of what was almost certainly his competitive swansong.

The tall man in the trench coat had a burning desire to see Mick the Miller race just one more time. His Mick the Miller. The racing machine he had been instrumental in moulding. Mick Horan, a man as tough as a Dublin docker and as hard as a Belfast rivet, was consumed with a crying need to see his beloved Mick just one last time.

Horan caught sight of the Empire Stadium from some way off. Built on top of a hill, it was visible for miles around. Constructed as the fulcrum of the British Empire Exhibition, it had been completed in time to host the 1923 FA Cup final between Bolton Wanderers and West Ham United, but the exhibition itself proved a white elephant, lost money and was closed down two years later with the entire 220-acre site placed in the hands of the official receiver. A chequered period when the whole edifice seemed on the verge of demolition was ended by considerable wheeling and dealing on the part of Arthur Elvin (a £4-a-week assistant in a tobacco kiosk during the exhibition), who not only bought the exhibition buildings and sold them for a hefty profit but also persuaded a number of City financiers to stump-up sufficient capital to stage speedway and greyhound racing in the stadium. On 10 December 1927, Wembley welcomed the dogs.

Horan paused beneath the famous twin towers to buy a programme, a glossy souvenir number, not one of your ordinary common-or-garden jobs. He was lucky. Such was the volume of people congregating on Wembley that the supply was exhausted well before the last of them was through the turnstiles and the stadium announcer was obliged to read out the runners before each race. This was some stadium, he said to himself, certainly living up to its claim of being 'The Ascot of Greyhound Racing.' And some crowd, too. In fact, Wembley had never seen such a multitude for a greyhound meeting in the four years it had been hosting the sport.

The St Leger was the fourth race, at 9 o'clock. Horan had an hour or so to kill. He hunted for the nearest bar, no great hardship since there were nine to choose from. Elsewhere in the stadium Arundel and

Phiddy Kempton were at this moment sitting down with the owners of the other three finalists, partaking of a slap-up meal at the invitation of the Wembley management. Horan contented himself with a sandwich and a bottle of Guinness.

He took a quick bite of the sandwich and then a long swig of his country's number-one pick-me-up. That's more like it! He flicked through the programme until his eyes came to rest on the centre-page spread containing pictures of the four Leger finalists and the trophy for which they were competing. There was no point reading the form. Horan had wiled away most of his temporary imprisonment on the train reading and re-reading all there was to read about the Leger's earlier rounds. Seldom Led, at just two years of age the youngest dog in the race yet clocking progressively slower times; Harringay's Virile Bill was a three-year-old, a dour stayer at his peak, who would finish strongly; as would Bradshaw Fold, of course, whom his chum Stan Biss would have primed to run out of her skin even though she was an old lady of four. Then there was Mick, the only dog coming into the final running faster than the opening round. On semi-final times, he had two to three lengths in hand over the others. And yet he was the veteran of the party, three months past his fifth birthday. Two Irish dogs in Mick and Seldom Led versus two of English lineage. How curious, too, thought Horan, that the quartet should be whelped in successive years.

Horan threaded his way out of the bar and back out into the fresh air. He scanned the bookies' boards. One was actually offering Mick at 5/4 against. That was ridiculous. Horan was not a man to scorn a heaven-sent opportunity like this to steal money from the bookmakers and instinctively dug into his pocket to take some of the 5/4. Pretty soon, the combined weight of public affection and professional confidence forced Mick to evens.

There were still 10 minutes or so before the parade of the St Leger runners began. Obtaining a close-up view of the quartet in the kennel area behind the grandstand had been his priority but a cordon of security men was deployed to stop anyone from coming within 100 yards. A word with Arthur Callanan or Stan Biss probably would have done the trick but he didn't want to cause any trouble.

Best to find a vantage point from which to view the race. At least, being over 6-feet tall was always a boon in such circumstances. All around him stood members of Mick the Miller's congregation. One well-dressed young woman opened her handbag and brought out a snap-shot of Mick, gazing at it as if it were a photograph of Rudolph Valentino, Douglas Fairbanks or the latest heart-throb, Gary Cooper. To her smartly attired male consort she began extolling the virtues of 'Darling Mick'. Suddenly, she leant forward on the tips of her toes and for a fleeting second Horan wondered whether he was about to receive an unsolicited peck on the cheek. No such luck. Her lips were indeed pursed and her eyes were shining in adoration – but not for Michael Horan. The object of her affections was over his shoulder, down there on the track. The bugle announcing the approach of the finalists for the fourth running of the St Leger had sounded. Her vigil was over. At long last she caught sight of 'Darling Mick' in the flesh. Her expression suggested she had seen a saint. Hitherto, Horan had taken much of what he'd heard and read about Mick's iconic status with a pinch of salt. Now the only worthwhile pinch was the one he felt like giving himself. The look on the young woman's face told no lie. Bejaysus, it must be true. Mick must have lapped nectar of the gods that day he drank the holy water from the font in Trim!

Horan had plenty of time to scrutinise each dog on its way to the traps, positioned halfway down the straight on the far side of the circuit. He couldn't fault any of them. Mick was his usual ebullient self, wagging his tail and pulling Joe Ollis along as if he were a recalcitrant school-child. Installing the four contenders goes smoothly. The stadium lights dim, leaving just a garish oval of emerald green. The hare begins its journey and as it whirrs into life the noise level, instead of soaring, uncharacteristically drops to that of a cathedral close. Forty-thousand tongues suddenly become stilled. Even the bookies have stopped shouting, 'I lay even money on Mick!' The expression on the face of the well-dressed young woman has crumpled into one of barely controlled tension and she clings to her escort's arm with the white-knuckles of someone barely able to stand. She is not alone.

The eerie silence is punctured only by some faint yelping from the distant traps. Finally, the spell is broken by a loud 'ker-chunk' and a monumental groan as the white jacket worn by Mick is noticed exiting trap three at least six lengths behind the blue and the black of Virile Bill and Seldom Led on either side of him. Only supporters of Bradshaw Fold are more glum-faced because 'Jewel' is even worse away, some three lengths behind Mick.

A form of mass hysteria akin to religious mania grips the stadium. The release of the four dogs has simultaneously released the pent-up emotions of 40,000 souls eager for a miracle. If they could see themselves they would not believe their eyes. Everyone is giving a wonderful impression of going quite mad. Agonised shrieks of 'Come on, Mick!' roll round the arena like peels of thunder.

Mick is trying his best to comply but continues to lag behind Seldom Led, who in turn trails Virile Bill down the home straight on the first circuit. 'Poor old Mick's finished!' cries the young woman. 'He's finished! He can't win from there! Oh, come on Mick!'

And Mick does. From somewhere he finds a powerful spurt that takes him whizzing past Seldom Led and right up onto the outside shoulder of Virile Bill. Once he'd worked himself into this challenging position, what followed came as no surprise to Mick Horan or any other keen student of the greyhound game. As Virile Bill decelerates slightly entering the third bend, Mick spears across him to snatch the rail and forge into the lead. The stadium erupts. 'Mick's got him! He's going to do it!'

Down the far straight again. Passing their point of departure, Mick veers out toward the centre of the track. Horan senses what this great dog is up to. Anything trying to pass on his outside will have to come the long way round; any dog daring to try for the inside will be ruthlessly chopped off at the next bend. Horan smiles to himself. Virile Bill is closing but heading for the inside. Horan knows what is going to happen.

Having politely invited Virile Bill into the parlour, Mick proceeds to slam the door in his unsuspecting face. Mick once again whips across to the rail, reducing Virile Bill to one of those hapless cartoon characters who has just been flattened with a giant frying pan.

But in the India-rubber manner of those indomitable celluloid heroes, Virile Bill instantly bounces back. Mick's cunning had bought him a priceless length but Virile Bill begins to eat into it down the finishing stretch. He may even have headed Mick for a second time. Neither are Seldom Led and Bradshaw Fold spent forces. They, too, are mounting last-ditch attacks. With less than 50 yards to run Mick is being harried on all sides. A baby's blanket could as near as dammit cover all four dogs.

Can Mick hold on? He starts to tire. It's as if the accumulated effort of all those races on the track and all those runs up the coursing field has overloaded those old legs of his with a surfeit of muscle-tightening lactic acid.

Mick will have to call on all the combative spirit of Coinn Iotair, Celtic folklore's mighty hound of rage, if he is to come out on top in this battle and avoid being carried out on his shield.

Thus far Horan's voice had not been adding to the din all around him. 'Come on old boy!' he mumbles to himself under his breath. 'Come on, Mick!' he bellows, as his self-control inexorably begins to buckle under the pressure. 'You can do it!'

Any disbeliever in the power of positive thinking ought to have been inside the Empire Stadium at this moment. The crowd is willing Mick to last out those final lung-bursting yards, willing him to cross the line with his nose still in front. The brindle body elongates and the sinews strain in one final supreme effort. He drives for the line flanked by blue, red and black jackets. But it's the white one on his back that the lights illuminating the finish line pick up first. Mick has won by a head from Virile Bill, who is a neck in front of Bradshaw Fold with Seldom Led a further head behind.

A roar capable of rattling window panes fills the night sky. Expensive hats and cheap caps fly into the darkness. Couples, young and old, embrace. Mick Horan was glad he had made the journey, that abominable journey, because like everybody else lucky enough to be inside the Empire Stadium on 3 October 1931, he would always be able to say 'I was there the night Mick the Miller ran into immortality.'

Mick Horan's return trip did not pass so finger-twiddlingly slowly. He had a mountain of newspapers to read. Each paper's take on Mick's St

Leger triumph was pretty much the same. It was difficult to the point of impossibility to find any angle other than the obvious. Horan did not mind. He sat back in his seat to relive the events of the previous night.

He turned first to *The Greyhound Mirror and Gazette*. 'Mick the Miller's Crowning Achievement – Amazing Wembley Scenes' ran the banner headline above a full-page photograph of Mick and Phiddy Kempton. 'This was the most thrilling greyhound St Leger final ever witnessed and the most amazing triumph ever achieved by the one and only "Mick". Never, since the inception of greyhound racing, have such scenes of enthusiasm been evoked. Although Mick could record no better than 41.34, his victory was brilliant – in fact, we shall go so far as to say that it was the most outstanding achievement of his glorious career. His cleverness was more outstanding than usual – his determination seemed to cut through the atmosphere and the huge crowd held its breath at each effort made by the dog to assert its superiority over its rivals. When he reached the line a winner, everybody let themselves go and didn't seem to mind how they behaved. It was a period of memorable deliriousness.'

On the next page, Isidore Green's summary was entitled: 'Mick's Glorious St Leger Triumph – Wonderful Display of Cunning'. Horan's attention was drawn to the paragraphs describing the reaction of the Kemptons and Sidney Orton. They had watched the race, fittingly enough, from the Royal Box and had managed to contain themselves until those last excruciating few yards when Mick was being assailed on all sides. 'Isn't it marvellous!' was as much as Phiddy could say while her husband and her trainer were being subjected to a strenuous session of handshaking and mobbing that reduced Orton to exclaiming 'Gee! But my back is sore and my arms are almost torn off!' After the presentation of the trophy at the hands of Mrs Jean Elvin (wife of the now managing director), Rundel led Mick round the track, taking him wide at every bend so that spectators might obtain a closer view of their idol – who responded to their noisy show of adulation with barks of delight.

What had Leveret to say for himself in *The Star*? 'We shall never have another Mick the Miller. He ran the race of his life to win the St Leger, and if he is retired now "with all his blushing honours thick upon him", he will live in memory as long as the sport exists. Sheer determination and trackcraft won him his race as it has won him many another race, and even when pressed and challenged time and time again he responded with a little extra effort and a smart bit of tactical running that left his rivals at a disadvantage.'

The rest of Fleet Street devoted unprecedented coverage. Horan still had much to read.

The *Daily Express* led with 'Thousands Cheer A Dog – Women Kiss Men During Race Thrill,' a hint of mild approbation for such public displays of emotion that caused Horan to chuckle. 'Mick the Miller, the most amazing dog that has ever been bred, has made his last bow. I have never seen anything to equal his thrilling victory on any track where any kind of race is run. There was not a person present who was not howling to the most popular dog that has ever lived to retain his lead. As he walked off the course – after an ovation that can seldom have been equalled by any famous man or woman – his public saw him as the winner of a Classic for probably the last time. To the thousands of people who are literally devoted to him – and he has a greater following than many a film star – he will remain a cherished memory.'

On this occasion, the *Express* had been outfoxed by both the *Daily Mail* and the *Daily Mirror*. The *Mail* carried a photograph of Mick stretched out on a couch alongside his Leger trophy. Beneath the heading 'Sheer Brain Work of the Greyhound St Leger Winner – Dog That Times Dashes', the paper also printed an interview with the Kemptons. 'My wife and I have not decided about any further racing for Mick yet,' Rundel was quoted as saying. 'Mick is undoubtedly the champion of the world. Experts have told me we shall never see his like again, and we cannot disguise the fact that he is a freak both in build and brain power.'

Although its story was pretty routine ('with almost human intelligence Mick seemed to carry his opponents wide and then cutting across to the rails, kept the inside berth to the end...'), the *Mirror*'s scoop was a picture of Mick being cuddled by the Kempton's cute, curly haired blonde daughter, two-year-old Primrose Ann.

The headlines continued to come thick and fast, staring out at Horan from every newspaper. 'Mick At It Again! (*Daily Sketch*); 'Mick's A

Mint – His Gold Standard Soars' (*Sporting Chronicle*); 'Amazing Mick the Miller – Great Crowd See Crafty Winner' (*Sunday Dispatch*); 'Mick the Miller Scores Greatest Triumph Of Unique Career' (*The Sporting Life*); 'Mick the Miller Wins St Leger After Appearing To Be Beaten' (*The Evening News*); 'Dog St Leger for Mick – Wonder Greyhound Still Winning' (*Sunday Graphic*).

Mick Horan paused for breath and reflection. It was taken as read (although nothing concrete would be announced until 4 December) that Mick had run his last race. What a way to leave the sport he, more than any other individual, canine or human, had put firmly on the map. Whatever the future had in store for Mick, what a way to be remembered.

Amongst all the tributes and accolades, one had registered more than most. Horan kept turning back to the one from his fellow trainer and co-conspirator in the legend of Mick the Miller. Sidney Orton would not utter truer words if he lived to be a hundred. 'There'll never be another!'

CHAPTER THIRTEEN
WILD BOY

On 14 August 1932 the public mourned the passing of a true Hollywood star, the stellar kind pampered by personal valet, chef, chauffeur and dressing room. This celluloid hero of countless movies – a hero who survived Frozen River, overcame The Man from Hell's River and boasted Jaws of Steel – died in the manner befitting any megastar worthy of the title, passing away with his head cradled in the lap of blonde bombshell Jean Harlow. He was only 16-years-old. He had been brought to Hollywood by Captain Lee Duncan, an American soldier who found him cowering with four siblings in an enemy trench during the First World War. He repaid Duncan for this act of kindness to the tune of $5 million. He was a German shepherd dog. His name was Rin-Tin-Tin. 'The dog faced one hazard after another and was grateful to get an extra hamburger for a reward,' said his studio boss Jack Warner. 'He didn't ask for a raise or a new agent or an air-conditioned dressing room or even more close-ups.' Now the word went out. Movie moguls were searching for a new canine superstar.

In due course Hollywood replaced the original 'Rinny' with Rin-Tin-Tin Junior in the same seamless never-destroy-a-winning-formula fashion it would later adopt with any number of Lassie look-alikes in the 1940s. But that was Hollywood. After a slow start, the English film industry was beginning to flex its muscles. Could there be room on the silver screen for an English four-legged hero?

The cinema was one phenomena that outstripped even the rise and popularity of dog racing in the 1930s. Moving pictures had their first British airing at a hall in London's Regent Street on 20 February 1896. Early showings shared music hall premises with variety bills but increasing concerns about audience safety were endorsed in 1909 by the Cinematograph Act which precipitated the construction of purpose-built cinemas, such as the Electric in Portobello Road and the Tower in Peckham. But the cinema age did not dawn without controversy. A dark and dingy ambience at all times of the day quickly gave rise to a disreputable image founded on numerous instances of theft and indecency.

However, the old 'flea-pits' and 'bug-hutches' of the silent era were quickly superseded by magnificent new auditoria, cathedrals to art deco, with the advent of sound in 1927 – the Davis Croydon theatre could seat 3,275 in absolute luxury, for instance. The circuit was dominated by three main chains. The largest, with nearly 300 cinemas, was Gaumont represented by scores of 'Palaces', followed by Associated British Cinema (ABC) and its coterie of 'Regals, Ritzes and Rexes' and, finally, the eponymous collection of 'Odeons'. All these new picture-palaces lived up to their escapist *raison d'etre* by incorporating the latest in art deco design; vistas of starlight skies or underwater kingdoms comprising typically spectacular backdrops on walls and ceilings. Going to the flicks had now become a treat worth sixpence of an afternoon or a shilling in the evening. Sat there in a large, airy theatre reading about your favourite stars in the latest copy of *Film Pictorial* (every Thursday, priced tuppence) or *Picturegoer* (every Saturday, priced tuppence) while the organist tootled away in advance of the main feature, rapidly became a way of life.

Not that the bill of fare up on the screen was remotely compatible with the British cinemagoer's way of life. Escapism not realism was the order of the day. And that meant Hollywood. The British film industry was virtually non-existent until the 1927 Cinematograph Films Act, which introduced a quota system guaranteeing exposure for home-grown productions. In 1926 just 26 British films received a showing (around 5 per cent of the total number exhibited) whereas in the year following the Act some 128 were screened. And the cinema had a voracious appetite. The emphasis, therefore, lay heavily on quantity not quality. Most of these British offerings were 'quota-quickies' made by the major Hollywood companies at satellite studios in Britain at a rock-bottom cost of £1 per foot of film. On the positive side, Errol Flynn got his first chance at the Teddington studio of Warner Bros while James Mason did likewise at the Fox satellite in Wembley.

Gaumont became one of the leading British players. The company dated from 1898 when the brothers AC and RC Bromhead decided to distribute the films of the pioneering Frenchman Leon Gaumont. From 1912 the company began to make a few films of its own at new studios in Shepherd's Bush, but the impetus gained from the Cinematograph Films Act prompted massive expansion. The Gainsborough operation of Michael Balcon (based in Islington) was incorporated into the Gaumont-British Picture Corporation as its production arm in 1928, and then, in 1932, some £500,000 was spent on a lavish rebuilding scheme at the Lime Grove complex in Shepherd's Bush, involving facilities like five production stages, dressing-room accommodation for 600 actors and state-of-the-art laboratories capable of producing 2-million feet of film per week. Gainsborough's output rose accordingly, reaching a peak of 30 films in 1933 and 25 in 1934.

In truth, this surge in production did little for the kudos of the British film industry. British output was dominated by a diet of whodunits, comedies – principally romantic and/or eccentric in type – and the occasional adaptation of a musical stage show. Few of these routine offerings held a candle to Hollywood classics featuring screen icons like Edward G Robinson as *Little Caesar* (1930), James Cagney in *The Public Enemy* (1931) or Greta Garbo in *Grand Hotel* (1932) – not to mention the sheer majesty of *All Quiet on the Western Front* (1928) or *King Kong* (1933). Films of the stature of Alfred Hitchcock's *Blackmail* (the first British 'talkie' in 1929) and *The Private Life of Henry VIII* (1933) were a decidedly rare species. While the Marx Brothers sent everyone into hysterics with their 1933 vehicle *Duck Soup*, the best comedic hat Britain could throw into the ring was *A Cuckoo in the Nest*, the latest stage re-tread from the Aldwych team led by Tom Walls.

By 1933, therefore, going to the cinema and going to the dogs were two of Britain's most popular leisure activities. Thus, there had to be every chance that some marriage would be effected between the demand for cheap and cheerful British films to feed an increasingly hungry British audience and the British fascination with the new-found sport. On the negative side of the equation, sport had never sat easily on the movie screen for it is notoriously difficult to blend contrived footage with genuine footage and come up with an authentic feel – a drawback still in evidence decades later despite vast technical improvements. Throw in animals for good measure and one can appreciate the size of the problem facing early film-makers.

The omens were hardly propitious if the half-hearted stabs at horseracing themes was any guide. The Hollywood musical *Little Johnny Jones* (1929) told the story of an American horse's entry in the Derby, ridden by the said Johnny Jones who gets to sing the famous 'Yankee Doodle Dandy'; while *Sporting Blood* (1931) relates the rise, fall and rise again of the horse Tommy Boy, who eventually wins the Kentucky Derby after his owner cuts the reins so that his jockey can't fulfil an agreement to throw the race by pulling the horse. Neither effort cut much ice. Gainsborough had also tentatively stuck its toe in the water. In 1926, it released a series of four 'two-reelers' starring champion jockey Steve Donoghue, which combined romance with a dash of racing skulduggery. In one of the best received, Donoghue is kidnapped prior to the Derby but rescued by the obligatory gorgeous blonde in the nick of time to eventually win the race and foil the villains. Five years later came a talkie in the form of *The Calendar*, the plot of which revolves around an owner attempting to pull-off a betting coup to salvage his ailing finances. Horseracing had to wait until *National Velvet* (1944) before the big-screen breakthrough was made.

What hope, then, for greyhound racing? With Rin-Tin-Tin dead, Warner Brothers decided to replace him with a champion greyhound called War Cry in a movie entitled *Dark Hazard*, which starred no less a personage than Edward G Robinson. So, why couldn't Britain follow suit? With Tom Walls acting as a go-between, and with its chain of 287 cinemas assuring widespread distribution, and thus the foundation of some success at the box office, Gaumont-British decided to take the plunge. The film would be called *Wild Boy* after its canine leading character. The story was effectively a re-working of Donoghue's Derby caper. All the film needed was the right name above the title, a name in lights that would pull in the crowds. There could only be one choice.

Mick had already demonstrated a natural ease in front of the cameras. Shortly after his St Leger victory in October 1931, a Pathe News crew visited Burhill to film him standing obediently on a bench as Phiddy Kempton pointed out all his various trophies that were displayed on an adjacent table. 'Meet Mick the Miller, whose uncanny skill has literally endeared himself to thousands and whom no money can buy – at home after winning every greyhound racing trophy honour.' The feature lasted 87 seconds and was one of a series incorporated into Pathe Newsreels as a 'Super Sound Gazette'.

Eighteen months later Mick also took centre stage in an early television broadcast. On Tuesday, 11 April 1933 (some two years before a regular public service was established) Brigadier-General Alfred Critchley gave a talk from BBC House called 'Love of an Englishman for a Dog', which acted as a brief introduction to greyhound racing. In essence, it was a reprise of a talk he had given on the wireless the previous October. The General brought along four dogs as visual aids: Fret Not, the 1932 St Leger winner (who thus became the first dog seen on British television); Macoma's son Long Hop; the 1932 Derby winner Wild Woolley; and, finally, the star of the show. 'Now we come to the grand old man of all greyhounds,' intoned the disembodied voice of the General as Mick's instantly recognisable outline flickered onto the screen. 'Here is the dog that made greyhound racing, and I can say without fear of contradiction, the most popular dog in the world.' Mick stood to attention as the General proceeded to outline his 'romantic story...great triumphs and records...a superiority not due so much to speed as his almost human intelligence, you would swear Gordon Richards was up on his back whispering in his ear what to do and when to do it...a moving last victory in the St Leger which left us all near to tears.'

The audience for Mick's television debut was severely limited. Only 35,000 people owned televisions, all of them in the London area. Many thousands more, however, were soon to be granted the opportunity of seeing just how their idol could genuinely strut his stuff before the cameras.

Wild Boy went into production in October 1933 under the banner of Gainsborough Pictures at Lime Grove. No one could cavil at Gainsborough's spirited efforts to capture on film the authentic atmosphere of greyhound racing. Principal exteriors were shot at the Waterloo Cup; at Aldridges (the first occasion the firm had ever granted cameras access); the White City, where a special meeting was staged; and, with the invaluable assistance of trainers such as Joe Harmon and Leslie Reynolds, a camera crew spent a week at the White City's kennels, The Hook in Northaw, near Potter's Bar, to record the necessary peep behind the scenes of a racing greyhound's training regime.

The screenplay was written by Albert de Courville and Stafford Dickens (frequent collaborators for Gainsborough) based on a story by JES. Bradford. De Courville was also to direct the film. Born in London of French parents, Albert Pierre de Courville possessed the pallid skin and heavy-lidded eyes of the quintessential 'tortured artiste' – indeed, he had at one time suffered a nervous breakdown. Gainsborough boss Michael Balcon thought him: 'one of the most capricious men I have ever met, though with extraordinary, if erratic, charm.'

De Courville was essentially a cultured, sweet-tempered man, but his sharp profile (invariably accentuated by a cigar clenched between his teeth) hinted at the utterly ruthless character he became when directing. During the filming of *The Midshipmaid* in 1932 he hectored his leading lady, Jessie Matthews, so viciously she accused him of being crazy. 'I'm not mad and I've got the certificate to prove it,' retorted de Courville, fishing a crumpled scrap of paper out of his wallet. 'It's here in black and white! I'm sane, d'you hear! I'm sane!'

De Courville's eight-film curriculum vitae began with 1930's *Wolves* and was dominated by musicals such as *77 Park Lane* and *There Goes the Bride*, which were derived from stage plays. If truth be told, de Courville was a West End showman of the old school, more at home in the theatre than behind a camera. He'd cut his teeth producing brassy, fast-moving revues full of quick-fire gags and songs catering for the popular taste of former music hall audiences. 'His directing was theatrical,' observed Oscar-nominated producer/director Michael Powell, 'he was an onlooker not a participator, and when he directed action it was from the eighth row of the stalls instead of getting his camera in the line of fire.'

None of this augured well for a film depending for its success on an authentic portrayal of a dynamic sport like greyhound racing. And what kind of omen would de Courville's feud with Jessie Matthews turn out to be? Matthews was married to Sonnie Hale – who just happened to be de Courville's leading man in *Wild Boy*. The set might just turn out to be a powder keg waiting to self-combust.

That the leading role of Billy Grosvenor should be played by 31-year-old 'Sonnie' Hale was highly appropriate, since one day at Wimbledon Mick the Miller had actually beaten the greyhound christened Sonnie Hale in honour of the actor. Even more coincidentally, the feature race at the White City meeting specially staged for the film fell to a dog called Shy Pal that was sired by this namesake. Hale was currently a hot property. He had just completed his sixth film in six years (*Friday the Thirteenth* with his wife) and *Wild Boy* was one of five films released in 1934 in which he starred. Once *Wild Boy* was 'in the can' he and Matthews were to team up again in the film version of the musical *Evergreen*, in which they had starred at the Adelphi in the Strand.

John Robert Hale-Monro, to give him his proper name, had made a seamless transition from stage to screen – from the chorus line in *Fun of the Fayre* at the London Pavilion just after the war to a film debut in *On with the Dance* (1927) – as a song-and-dance-man cum light comedian. Hale's talented theatrical family (his Scots father was a comedian; his Irish mother an actress; and his elder sister Beatrice, 'Binnie', a creditable alternative to Laye and Matthews) left him with a giant inferiority complex. 'I belong to the kind of family where I have to compete,' he confessed to Matthews. 'I can't just be good, I've got to be very good, top their performances ... if I can.'

How he would cope with the threat of being upstaged by a dog was anyone's guess. The noted theatre critic James Agate thought him 'an excellent comedian', but fellow thespian Robert Stephens was less enamoured of him in later life and acerbically called him: 'A gross, unfunny person offstage and someone, on the whole, to avoid.'

When it came to attracting members of the opposite sex, however,

Hale's animal magnetism was staggering. Yet he was no lounge lizard and had no look of the lady-killer about him. He stood barely 5 feet 7 inches in his stocking feet, had a rather pasty moon-face and off stage wore wire-rimmed spectacles which gave him the appearance, according to Matthews, 'of a typical young Englishman who worked on the Stock Exchange or in the City.'

This complete absence of 'knock-em-dead' looks nonetheless proved no barrier to Hale becoming the object of a romantic tug of war between the West End's two prettiest and brightest actresses. Within two years of marrying the glamorous blue-eyed blonde Evelyn Laye in 1926, he had fallen under the spell of the dark-bobbed, gamine charms of the even more vivacious Jessie Matthews. More to the point, although the young star looked, spoke (her rarefied plummy accent belied her lineage as the daughter of a Soho fruit-and-veg trader) and sang like an angel, she did not behave like one. She had the deserved reputation of being something of an incorrigible man-eater. A year after marrying Hale she even attempted to seduce the young John Gielgud who, being homosexual, was one of the few men able to resist her overtures. 'She was an enchanting creature,' said Gielgud, 'but no man was safe in her presence.'

Sonnie Hale certainly appears to have been putty in her hands. 'I'll take your bets on my getting that man off his wife in 14 days,' Matthews had bragged to her friends on first seeing her new co-star in the Noel Coward musical *This Year of Grace*. After a few performances crooning 'We'll bill and we'll coo' to each other as they clasped hands and gazed deep into each other's eyes during the love-duet 'A Room With A View', Matthews lived up to her boast.

Laye fought tooth and nail to hold on to her man but Jessie Matthews was an unstoppable force of nature. The twin divorces that inevitably resulted appalled Hale's staunchly Catholic parents and were the talk of polite London society. In his summing-up of the Hale-Laye proceedings in 1931, the judge observed witheringly: 'It is quite clear that the husband admits himself to be a cad, and nobody will quarrel with that, and that the woman Matthews writes letters which show her to be a person of an odious mind.'

There is little doubt that Matthews could have become a major star (she finished her days famously playing the lead in radio's *Mrs Dale's Diary*) but she resisted every call from Hollywood because she could not bear to be separated from Hale. Gaumont-British wanted him to work behind the camera, and he actually directed his wife in three films before his career faltered upon the abandonment of yet another Matthews vehicle in 1938 owing to financial difficulties. Gainsborough had found itself almost £100,000 in debt, largely as a result of singularly failing to crack the American market. Sonnie and Jessie eventually divorced in 1944 after the biter had been well and truly bitten. Having become embroiled in an affair with their adopted child's nanny (their baby son tragically died a few hours after birth), Hale walked out on Matthews uttering one of his finest exit lines: 'I'm off, dear, to pantomime rehearsals and I shan't be back.' Hale eventually succumbed to the obscure blood disease myelofibrosis in 1959 at the age of 57, his fortunes never having truly recovered from the setback of 1938.

As one might expect, Hale's colleagues in *Wild Boy* were representative of the Gainsborough stock company. The two leading ladies were the personification of 'Bright Young Things' and were dead ringers for Phiddy Kempton. Starring opposite Hale in her third film but first major role was 21-year-old Gwyneth Lloyd. A product of the Gaumont system, she played Marjorie Warren, the kind of 'ridin', shootin' and outdoor gel' she was, apparently, in real life. The part of the *femme fatale*, Gladys Scrivener, went to 26-year-old Leonora Corbett, a statuesque brunette appearing in her fourth Gainsborough film since debuting the previous year. She had appeared in *Friday the Thirteenth* with Hale, and also alongside Lyn Harding in *The Constant Nymph*. David Llewellyn Harding was to be the villain of the piece, Frank Redfern, a part that came easily to him for he had earned a profitable living by portraying heavies and villains in a dozen pictures since the end of the First World War. Harding's previous roles included Henry VIII and Sherlock Holmes's dastardly adversary Professor Moriarty, but his finest hour was yet to come – when he was finally allowed to play the more sympathetic character of Brookfield School's bushy-bearded headmaster Wetherby in the Oscar-nominated 1939 film of *Goodbye, Mister Chips*.

The knockabout elements of the story seemed to rest in capable hands. Former music hall comic Fred Kitchen (himself a successful owner of greyhounds), would essay the role of Mick the Miller's trainer, the intellectually-challenged Joe Plumer. Kitchen had only appeared in a couple of films – and those were 17 years apart – and despite playing Plumer to dim-witted perfection, he did not land another film part for nine years. Further wisecracking and tomfoolery of the seaside-postcard variety came courtesy of Bud Flanagan and Chesney Allen.

Flanagan and Allen were already famous for comprising one-third of the Crazy Gang. They took temporary leave of the Gang to double up as Dick Smith & Partner, a pair of auctioneers cum bookmakers (an occupation they had once actually contemplated). Naturally, they brought the Gang's comic lunacy with them. Their remit was to act the fool at every opportunity by resorting to the silly sight-gags and confusing word-play that had become their trademarks. Few performers could get away with excruciating gags like 'The next lot is Dry Martini, by Johnny Walker out of Out of Order, one of the greatest pullovers in the country – sorry, jumpers in the country!'

The duo could hardly have been more different in background or appearance. Flanagan was born Chaim Reeven Weintrop, a Polish Jew from Hanbury Street in Whitechapel. To say that life in the East End was tough for young Weintrop is an understatement. Hanbury Street was home to any number of brothels and only a few years before he was born the mutilated body of Jack the Ripper's second prostitute victim was discovered in a neighbour's yard. At the age of 13, Weintrop took to the music hall as 'Fargo, the Boy Wizard', and in 1910, still only 14, he travelled unaccompanied across the Atlantic intent on building a new life for himself in America. The land of opportunity failed to live up to its name in 'Bud' Weintrop's case. At one point he was reduced to singing in a brothel for the price of a cup of tea. The outbreak of war provided his salvation. He enlisted in the Royal Field Artillery and, after changing his name to Flanagan (out of disrespect for his bullying sergeant-major of that name), one day in a café he got into conversation with a young officer called Chesney Allen, who was similarly starstruck.

Allen, who was the son of a Brighton builder, had left school to be articled to a solicitor. This calling did not suit Allen, who was soon treading the boards in repertory as a serious actor prior to war service. No doubt owing some debt to an unenviable spell as a hypnotist's stooge, he quickly developed after the war into one of the best 'straight men' in the business. However, while Allen prospered, Flanagan had fallen on hard times. He wrote the duo's future signature tune 'Underneath the Arches' during a fit of depression, for instance, and took to driving a taxi to make ends meet before he and Allen were brought together as a pair in 1924. Six years later they achieved the breakthrough they craved at the Holborn Empire, and in 1931 they became an integral part of the Crazy Gang.

The pair would eventually transform themselves into the perfect comedy partnership, each complementing the other in the manner of all great double acts from Laurel and Hardy to Morecambe and Wise. The lugubrious straight man and the wisecracking comic. Allen provided the quiet touch of refinement that offset Flanagan's frenetic streetwise savvy.

Both men were gamblers and racing nuts, be it horses or greyhounds, who constantly mixed with owners and trainers from both spheres, including Sidney Orton. Their casting in *Wild Boy* was as natural as Mick the Miller's. They were not really required to act at all.

Wild Boy was a routine pot-boiler firmly rooted in the genre of romantic/eccentric comedy. In other words, precisely the kind of film the British Board of Film Censors tended to favour. Balcon's films, it noted with a certain amount of glee and not a little relief, 'were clean and light throughout'.

The film opens at Altcar, where General Stanley Warren's Wild Man of Borneo is about to contest the final of the Waterloo Cup against Frank Redfern's Royal Ranger. The General is a sick man and confined to bed, restricted to listening to the wireless broadcast of the final while his daughter Marjorie and trainer Plumer represent him at the running ground. The excitement of Wild Man of Borneo's victory proves too much for the General's ailing ticker and he promptly expires.

Marjorie subsequently learns that her father had lost all his money on the Stock Exchange and that the house, greyhounds and everything else must be sold-off to pay his debts. Marjorie retires to a small cottage on the estate, taking Plumer and one of Wild Man of Borneo's latest off-spring (Mick is rather too mature to be legitimately described as a pup), called Wild Boy, along with her as a pet.

Wild Boy proceeds to reveal tendencies that suggest he may have inherited some of Wild Man of Borneo's racing instincts, which Plumer attempts to demonstrate to Marjorie by driving up a field with a makeshift hare tied to the rear bumper of his car. Four of the litter give chase but one – Wild Boy – won't budge an inch. That is until a gen-uine wild hare puts in an appearance. Wild Boy pursues the hare until finally plunging into a mill-race in pursuit of his quarry.

The chase has been witnessed by Billy Grosvenor, a racing driver. Realising that Wild Boy is heading toward the mill-wheel and certain death, he drives his Bugatti off the road and hurtles across the coun-tryside in an effort to save the day. Billy ultimately dives into the mill-race and pulls Wild Boy clear of danger. He and Marjorie are instantly smitten with each other.

It transpires that Billy is actually a house guest of Redfern's, as is Gladys Scrivener, an old flame of his who now acts as Redfern's secre-tary and quite probably also his mistress – although that connection is delicately left to the audience's imagination. Redfern's sole ambition in life is to win the Greyhound Derby, for which he has never had a dog good enough to run. Over dinner that evening, he wagers £1,000 to £100 with the Greyhound Racing Association president, Colonel Seymour, that he'll win this year's race: 'When inclined, my efforts will be successful!' Billy is less convinced, and lets slip to Gladys valuable information concerning Wild Boy's ability.

All parties then attend the auction of General Warren's kennels at Aldridges. Redfern buys Black Prince, the most sought-after lot in the sale, for 600 guineas. Lot 24 is the bitch Dainty Girl and her litter – the 20th and last litter sired by Wild Man of Borneo. Plumer decides to bid because Marjorie likes Wild Boy so much but he can only go up to 200 guineas. Billy enters the bidding and is forced up to 500 guineas by

Gladys, acting out of spite for his past treatment of her. Billy presents Wild boy to a delighted Marjorie, and engages Plumer to train the litter at Hook Kennels.

Billy is more interested in Marjorie than his newly acquired dogs. He takes no notice of their progress in training until Wild Boy clocks 28.60 seconds for 500 yards, a phenomenal time that puts him in contention for the Derby. The news reaches the ears of the unscrupulous Redfern who, knowing that his Black Prince will surely lose if the two dogs meet in the Greyhound Derby, offers Billy a bribe to withdraw Wild Boy. Billy refuses.

Billy and Dick Smith trick another bookie, Ed Dorling, into giving them odds of 100/8 about Wild Boy in his preliminary heat. After watching Wild Boy overcome crowding to clock a time only just outside Black Prince's 525-yards track record of 29.58, Redfern knows he must stoop to villainy. He and Gladys conspire to discredit Billy in Marjorie's eyes by suggesting he has, in fact, accepted £5,000 to withdraw Wild Boy from the Derby. Horrified at this disclosure, Marjorie tells Billy she thinks Wild Boy ought to be kennelled with a more experienced trainer and she sends the dog to Redfern's trainer, Patrick Murphy.

Getting wind of their ploy, Billy abducts Wild Boy and sneaks him into his flat, where they share both bed and breakfast. Unfortunately, Gladys has worked out where Wild Boy must be in hiding, and a couple of Redfern's strong-arm men pretending to be plain clothes officers from Scotland Yard arrive at Billy's flat. 'I begged her to do something about that cough!' blurts out Billy as a tell-tale bark from Mick reveals his presence in the boudoir. After roughing-up Billy with knuckledusters, the crooks make a getaway with Wild Boy.

Billy suspects Gladys will know Wild Boy's current hiding place and, playing on their former romantic relationship, he persuades her to reveal the location as evidence of her undying love for him. Wild Boy is incarcerated in the shed behind the garage at Redfern's home. A successful rescue is effected, sealed by a kiss between Billy and Gladys that is witnessed by a heartbroken Marjorie. 'That darn dog must be bewitched,' says Murphy on discovering that Wild Boy has disappeared again.

All seems set for Wild Boy to contest the Derby. However, Billy knows Redfern will not give up easily. Redfern suspects Gladys has betrayed him to Billy and, after throwing her out, takes steps to scupper Wild Boy's chances of winning the final. Wild Boy and Billy set off for the White City in a GRA van ('It's a shame putting him in there with that lot – he's worth a hundred of 'em'), which is deliberately crashed into by a large lorry containing four of Redfern's strong-arm men. During the subsequent Keystone Cops-style brawl, the villains can't find the right dog and Wild Boy runs off across the fields on his own. Billy telephones the AA to organise a search for Wild Boy before jumping in his Bugatti and setting off with Plumer for the White City.

Over at the White City a smug Redfern is congratulating himself on keeping Wild Boy out of the Derby but unbeknown to him Wild Boy, having run over hill and dale, is presently weaving in and out of traffic down the Westway in a sterling bid to catch Billy's Bugatti. He must reach the stadium by 6 o'clock if he to run in the final. Wild Boy seems to have made it to the White City in the nick of time and, after scratching and howling at the gates, he is let in by Plumer and an overjoyed Billy and Marjorie. 'You've used your head,' Billy tells him, 'now use your old legs!'

However, Wild Boy is too late – there is less than 30 minutes to race-time. He may only run if the fair-minded chief steward, Colonel Seymour, who has been appraised of the mitigating circumstances, can persuade two of his colleagues to be equally sympathetic. With Wild Boy seemingly a non-runner, Billy and his ally Dick Smith yet again outwit the hapless Ed Dorling into accepting a bet of £200 to £10 on the off chance of the dog gaining a reprieve. While everyone awaits the stewards' decision there is a parade of past Derby winners that includes Mick playing himself and wearing the famous jacket denoting his two victories of 1929 and 1930.

Wild Boy is allowed to take his place in the final. Coming out of trap six, he lags behind Black Prince (starting with the advantage of trap one) through the early stages of the race but delivers a strong late challenge (filmed in very primitive slow-motion) to edge past his rival and thereby thwart Redfern's evil intentions. As the trophy presentation is made, Billy and Marjorie confirm their togetherness with a lingering kiss. The End.

Few Hollywood movies of the period ever manage to rise above a mediocre mishmash of terrible dialogue and horrendous over-acting, so one cannot sit down to watch a British film like *Wild Boy* and automatically expect to see something approaching *The Private Life of Henry VIII* unfold on the screen. Fortunately, the photography of the experienced New Yorker Phil Tannura (working on his 28th picture) and the art direction of Gainsborough's resident expatriate German Alfred Junge partially offset any shortfalls in de Courville's handling of the action, but the script is banal and the performances amount to prime ham off the acting bone.

Social stereotypes abound: the toffs speak in 'la-di-dah' accents ('the English of the drama schools and South Kensington,' lamented Michael Balcon); the hoi-polloi touch caps and mutter 'Yes, maam' at the slightest provocation; and the villains can be spotted a mile away by their flash clobber. The best one can say – with no condescension intended – is that *Wild Boy* embodied a style of film-making that struck a recognisable chord with audiences in 1930s Britain, a country still riven by class distinction. Consequently, in their own way, these sort of films were depicting Britain's life and times with as much accuracy as the gritty, anti-establishment 'new wave' films like *Room at the Top* and *Saturday Night and Sunday Morning* did to more critical acclaim in the 1960s.

Mick is only on screen for about a third of the film's 87 minutes, but when he is, it is not too far off the mark to suggest that he puts all the real 'actors' to shame. Sonnie Hale, for one, professed to becoming an instant convert to the old maxim 'never act with children or animals.'

Mick hits his mark and takes his cues like a real trouper in a number of key scenes. Chief among these is when he shares a bed and then breakfast with Hale. 'Do you want anything before you go to bed?' asks Hale. 'I'm going to tuck you up in bed because you've got a lot of hard work ahead of you.' The camera then comes in tight on the two heads resting side by side on the pillow, and as Hale stifles a yawn and turns away after bidding his sleeping companion 'Goodnight', Mick lifts his head and yawns back. Then, at the breakfast table, Mick sits quietly on his chair with a napkin tied around his neck, while Billy offers him some boiled egg that Peters the butler has lovingly prepared for him.

Their first big scene together, of course, involved Hale diving into the mill-race to save Mick from drowning. The locale selected was the Castle Mill at Dorking. Given that the scene was shot in the depths of winter but since it was meant to be summer Hale was wearing the thinnest of clothing and the dive measured 17 feet, one might reasonably have expected Hale to 'pass' and hand the job over to a stunt double. However, he didn't flinch – though a coal fire in a brazier was on hand to warm up both he and Mick (who likewise appears to have declined a double) once they'd clambered out of the freezing water.

Hale was also required to live up to his screen persona as a racing driver. During the dash to the White City sequence at the climax of the film, he had to zoom along a dual carriageway in his Bugatti with Fred Kitchen alongside him in the passenger seat, cutting in and out of the traffic. After the scene was safely in the can, Kitchen, who had been reduced to a state of some palpitation, remarked that he'd never seen any driver go so close to other cars at such speed and not collide. Hale apologised profusely for any distress he'd caused but went on to excuse himself by explaining that he couldn't see very well without his glasses, which he was not allowed to wear during filming!

Nor did Hale find the scene where he is accosted in his flat by Redfern's two heavies exactly pleasurable. Having been instructed by de Courville to make the fight totally realistic, the two thugs diligently inflicted such damage on Hale's face that filming was impracticable for the next four days!

Nevertheless, the great joy of *Wild Boy*, especially, of course, for later generations denied sight of the original, is the opportunity to see Mick in full flight. We see him chasing Plumer's dummy hare and he cuts a magnificent figure as he strides out over the fields in the scene which culminates in him jumping into the mill-race. There is also footage of Mick running a solo time-trial on the training track at Northaw, beginning with a wonderful close-up shot of him leaving the traps that highlights his nose-on-the-floor technique of sliding out from under the rising lids.

The most memorable scenes of Mick in action, however, are unquestionably those where he is weaving in and out of traffic on the Westway as he attempts to reach the White City in time for the Derby. At one point he resorts to road drill by looking left and right before negotiating a busy road via a zebra crossing! There was no trick photography, of course, in 1933. Mick actually did run in and out of traffic. And he was a valuable commodity. One wonders what insurance premiums Gainsborough was required to pay, bearing in mind Mick was currently earning 50 guineas a nomination as a stud dog.

Gainsborough Pictures pulled out all the stops to promote *Wild Boy* in advance of general release. 'The cinema is going to the dogs!/ England's popular outdoor sport as the background of an entertaining story/A Real Winner/First Past the Post' were commonly used phrases designed to appeal. 'Dogs are certain in their appeal to the public, an attraction that never misses fire,' Gainsborough declared in its preamble to distributors. 'A dog as hero of a story is always an attraction in a film, and for the first time in screen history, a greyhound plays the leading role – the presence of Mick the Miller provides a distinctive character, a big selling angle to exploit to the general public.'

Indeed it was. On every poster pasted to billboards throughout the country Mick the Miller's name was the only name above the title – usually accompanied by the strap 'That Wonder Dog'. In addition, cinema managers received a fully illustrated brochure containing a nuts-and-bolts guide of how the film might be best promoted:

'...in districts where there is a greyhound racing track, supported by thousands of fans, the film is, to use an American term, "a natural". In every big town and city there are dog owners and dog lovers by the thousands. If the picture is being screened during the greyhound racing season and there is an adjacent track, a tie-up should result in excellent publicity. Offer the proprietors of the track a trophy or cup to be competed for in a special event to be known as the "Wild Boy Trophy". Give leaflets to the crowds entering the stadium, and arrange, if possible, to have a big banner concerning the film carried round the track during intervals and an announcement made through the loud speaker. If possible induce one of the leading players in the film to make a personal appearance to present the special trophy, or alternatively all the prizes won on the evening in question. Theatres in the locality of the White City have a big pull, whether racing is in progress or not, for it was here that Mick the Miller won so many of his successes and at which scenes for *Wild Boy* were filmed.

'...if there should be in the neighbourhood of the cinema a greyhound breeder or trainer, try to arrange for the personal appearance of several greyhounds as a short prologue to the film, with the trainer making a short address on greyhounds with a special reference to Mick the Miller.

'...a big tie-up can probably be effected with Spratts Ltd, the well-known dog biscuit and dog-food manufacturers, in conjunction with local dog food suppliers, who might carry posters on their counters and in their window displays.

'...it might be possible to purchase a greyhound puppy from a local kennel and, if local regulations permit, to offer the puppy as a prize in a guessing competition involving a glass jar filled with Messrs Spratts biscuits.

'...or a street stunt could be worked. Arrange for a number of greyhounds, blanketed, to parade the streets. Each blanket carries particulars of the film. To make this stunt more imposing, have the attendants wearing a uniform similar to those worn by attendants at dog tracks whilst parading the dogs.'

Wild Boy was unveiled in May 1934 and went on general release from 2 July. It was met by enthusiastic reviews, not least for the acting debut of its canine star who was instantly garlanded with the title of England's very own Rin-Tin-Tin – conveniently forgetting that Mick was, in fact, Irish!

'Full starring honours go to Mick the Miller for his most intelligent performance.' – *Empire News*

'Mick the Miller challenges Rin-Tin-Tin!' – *Daily Mail*

'Mick the Miller will become as famous on the screen as he is on the track' – *News Chronicle*

'Mick the Miller in the title role shows positively over-the-average human intelligence and travels like a streak of lightning when necessary.' – *Daily Sketch*

'The appearance of that graceful greyhound Mick the Miller in this picture serves once again to demonstrate that under the skilful direction of producer and cameraman a dog can be just as effective, just as dramatic, just as interesting, and just as full of charisma as any human being.' – *Sunday Times*

'One thing about *Wild Boy* which will make it a sure-fire wrecker of blood pressure among film fans is the presence, in the star part, of the famous Mick the Miller.' – *Sunday Dispatch*

'Just the stuff to give the audiences.' – *News of the World*

'One of the most agreeable surprises to come lately out of the British kennels.' – *Sunday Observer*

'One of the most amusing and satisfactory light pictures ever produced by Gaumont-British.' – *The Star*

'*Wild Boy* has everything one could expect from a greyhound-racing melodrama – and then some, particular praise being due to the fidelity and thrill of the actual racing sequences authentically staged at the White City.' – *The Cinema*

'Ably upholds the flag of British dogdom...those who like their "meller-drammer" hot and strong will find it worth a visit.' – *Film Pictorial*

'Very definitely first-class entertainment...this open-air talkie is going to reap a rich reward at the box office.' – *Daily Mirror*

'A film which is likely to be one of the most popular British films of the year.' – *Evening News*

No box-office records exist to confirm or confound those final assertions. In fact, *Wild Boy* is a film that has sunk seemingly without trace into an obscurity bordering on extinction. Even a manual as exhaustive as *Halliwell's Film Guide* lists no entry for *Wild Boy* (unlike *Dark Hazard*). So, Mick the Miller was not going to follow in the paw prints of Rin-Tin-Tin despite taking to his role like a dog to a lamp-post.

Nor was posterity going to be kind to *Wild Boy*. Apart from special screenings for greyhound racing enthusiasts, *Wild Boy* has seen neither the light of day nor the light of a projector since the 1930s. The six cans containing the 7,808 feet of film remain tucked away in the bowels of the British Film Institute.

CHAPTER 14
TIR NA NOG

Mick the Miller's brief flirtation with the world of film was never likely to constitute anything more than a minor role in his life once he ceased racing.

Mick's principal occupation after 3 October 1931 was to make lots of little Micks. To this end he was dispatched to Mill Farm, the home of Sidney Orton's great friend Jack Masters, at Toftwood, Dereham in Norfolk. Nine days after the formal announcement of his retirement from racing on 4 December, a tearful scene was enacted at Liverpool Street Station as Mick prepared to depart for Norfolk. 'Sad Days For A Dog's Best Pals – Mick Knew It Was "Good-Bye"' reported *The Star*. Both Rundel and Phiddy were in attendance on the platform to wave off Mick and Sidney Orton, who was going to stay with him until he had settled into his new home. Poor Joe Ollis could not hold back the tears as he handed Mick's lead to Orton ready to board the train (first-class section, naturally) and there was sad reciprocation from Mick in the rather feeble way he swished his tail on the floor of the carriage.

'It was worse for Joe,' confided Phiddy Kempton. 'Life will not be the same for him without Mick. He saw to his every meal and slept within reach of the kennel. On the night before a big race he scarcely slept at all and anybody who wanted to "get-at" Mick would have had to do so over Joe's dead body. Mick understands as well as any of us that his racing career is over and what worries us all is that thought that he might be miserable, for he really enjoyed racing and ran with his head as much as his feet. Greyhound racing will hardly be the same for me without the thrills of Mick's amazing success but he has earned his rest and I have many delightful tokens of his brilliant performances. It was terrible to me to make the decision, but my husband and I thought that it would be cruel to let him go on until he was past his best and get graded lower and lower on the track. We thought it better to let him go out while he was in his glory.'

Of that there was no doubt. On the eve of the retirement announcement Mick was still favourite for the 1932 Derby.

The *Sunday Dispatch* best put into words the sentiments of greyhound-racing fans up and down the country: 'The retirement of Mick the Miller will be deplored by a multitude of human admirers. There will be a blank in the world of entertainment, just as there is when an actor takes his last curtain or a sportsman plays his last game. In this country we are not ashamed to make friends of animals. Mick the Miller was not the first, and it is certain he will not be the last, animal hero of the British public but there will be none greater.'

> *We sigh for him, we cry for him,*
> *We had to say goodbye to him,*
> *But Blimey!! What a Dog!!!*

Any breeder requiring Mick's services ('Approved Bitches' only) needed to write out a cheque for 50 guineas – an unprecedented fee, twice that usually set for a Waterloo Cup winner or a dog, for example, like Deemster and five times the amount necessary to secure the services of record-breaking contemporaries such as Naughty Jack Horner, Douro and Tipperary Hills. Such was the aura attached to Mick – and to an extent Macoma – that the services of his undistinguished sibling, Kennel Rex (one of the four pups quickly sold by Father Brophy in 1926), were also valued at 10 guineas: 'Blood will tell – little brother of Mick the Miller!' promised the advertisement.

Mick's first progeny were born to considerable fanfare in March 1932. Pictures of the seven pups (three dogs and four bitches) whelped by Mr W Skerratt's Wallasey Flyer at the GRA's Blythe Bridge breeding centre in Staffordshire were plastered over all the newspapers. A few days later at Blythe Bridge a further litter of six was born to Tempestuous.

Any number of 'approved bitches' queued up for a romantic liaison with Mick – among them Bradshaw Fold – but the most deserving partner had to be Toftwood Misery, for so long his kennel-mate at Burhill. She duly whelped a litter of seven at Mill Farm before March was out. The Kemptons look a leaf out of Father Brophy's book and decided to make a statement with their naming policy. The four dogs were eventually called Mick the Matchless, Mighty, Moocher and Miracle; the three bitches Mick the Maiden, Mick the Mischievous and Mick the Helper.

All Mick's progeny at Toftwood and Blythe Bridge were farmed out within their respective districts and given the freedom to roam. Both Mick the Mischievous and Mick the Milkmaid (out of another Kempton bitch Fond Fashion) owed their names, for instance, to their sly habit of purloining milk during solo rambles around the village. Those belonging to Wallasey Flyer were the first to go into training. In March 1933, a luxurious saloon car pulled into Northaw carrying a cargo estimated to be worth more than £1,000 – lying sedately on cushioned seats were Great Regulation and Genial Rascal (dogs) and a quartet of bitches, Gipsy Rhapsody, Good Review, Glowing Response and Glistening Ripple. The seventh pup, Gay Respondent, was being kept by Skerratt for the coursing field. Two months later, the three bitch puppies out of Toftwood Misery and the five out of Fond Fashion entered Burhill. The pick seemed to be Mick the Maiden, a big imposing bitch of 61lb, and she was given the honour of her mum and dad's old kennel. The slower maturing male saplings would not arrive until June.

The first to run was Mick the Mischievous on Saturday, 17 June at Wimbledon, followed two days later by Mick the Maiden in a heat of the Coronation Stakes at Wembley. Both were beaten – though it was not long before the former opened her account and became the first of Mick's children so to do. However, one race did soon fall to one of Mick's initial progeny – and no wonder. It was a novel contest comprised entirely of his own offspring.

Immediately before the Derby on 24 June, 1933, the six pups ran in an exhibition 'trial' over which Mick himself presided: 'King of the Dogs Holds Court,' declared the Daily Express. It was won by Grim Revenge, in looks a veritable chip off the old block, from the Tempestuous litter.

Mick watched from the White City infield after making every effort to join in the fun – as he invariably did when he attended a big race as the guest of honour. Later in the year, he also chaperoned some of his family at Wembley on the occasion of the final to the Trafalgar Cup, a premier event for dogs not more than 20-months-old. Three of his sons out of Toftwood Misery had made the last six: Mick the Matchless, Mick the Miracle and Mick the Moocher (who had also opened his account on the coursing field). According to Sidney Orton, he had grown particularly fond of his sons when they were all at Toftwood and seemed to understand perfectly when told all three had reached such a prestigious final. It seemed only right and proper to let Mick watch them race. Mick the Miracle came out best – but only back in third place behind the unbeaten Grey Raca (eventually runner-up in the 1934 Derby). After joining the placed dogs in the victory parade, Mick escorted his three sons up to the stadium restaurant for the special end-of-evening cabaret.

Within 18 months of Mick taking up stud duties he had presented the Kemptons with nearly 100 puppies, 'most of them like little lions' in the opinion of Masters. A number were donated to charitable causes. The first to go was Mick the Helper (fondly referred to as 'Ginger'), who was raffled at Wimbledon's charity meeting of 4 June 1932, raising £480. For the price of a one-shilling ticket, Mr George Dean of Blackfriars Road got himself the bargain of the year – whom he rechristened Mick the Charity Ann. Six months later Mick the Primrose Ann was auctioned at the London Palladium in aid of the Charing Cross Hospital Centenary Appeal. Another pup was sold on behalf of the Royal Veterinary College, and at Wimbledon's 1933 charity meeting, one out of Hardwick Surprise was won by John Randall of Tooting. 'My wife has often said she would like a Mick the Miller puppy,' said Mr Randall, 'and she felt I would win it. Some time ago Gipsy Lee, the famous fortune teller, told me I'd be getting something that would give me a start in life.'

Throughout the 1930s a succession of 'Little Micks' endeavoured to bear the family name with pride. They were on a hiding to nothing. Whether discussing the stud careers of exceptional racehorses or exceptional greyhounds, breeding pundits will at some stage invariably point out that the sire in question was only a qualified success because he never reproduced anything approaching his own outstanding ability. This seems at best a spurious yardstick and at worst a fatuous one. The great champions – canine or equine – are such freaks of nature that the chances of them reproducing a champion in their own image is – quite literally – almost inconceivable.

By any other standard than his own, Mick the Miller was a successful sire. From those initial litters, Mick the Moocher, for instance, eventually proved good enough to win the 1935 Wembley Gold Cup and set track records for 650 yards at Wimbledon and 700 yards at Wembley that stood for five years; his litter mate Mick the Miracle set a national record; Mick the Cavalier won for the Kemptons both the British Breeders' Produce Stakes at Catford and the British National Produce Stakes at the White City in 1934; while for other breeders, one of Mick's first daughters was Gallant Ruth who went on to win the 1934 Oaks. His 1936 crop included Glen Ranger, a Derby finalist and a national record holder at 500 yards, and the bitch Greta's Rosary (both out of the 1935 Derby-winning bitch Greta Ranee), who emulated her pop by winning the St Leger in 1938.

Besides the chore of making 'Little Micks', there was also the life of a celebrity to live. Even prior to his official retirement, Mick had begun to make special appearances in aid of charitable causes. On 22 October – barely three weeks after the St Leger – Sidney Orton accompanied him to Belfast to support a gala benefit programme at Dunmore Park devoted to raising funds for the city's Samaritan Hospital that helped sick and ailing mothers.

The return of a prodigal son was the trigger for much celebration. Alerted by a message in the 'Stop Press' of the *Belfast Morning News* to the effect that 'Mick the Miller crossing via Heysham tonight', a crowd of 200 was waiting on the quayside and, numbers swelling with every yard, it provided an honour guard all the way to the Great Northern Hotel. The rest of Mick's day was taken up with photo calls before he finally headed for the track out on Alexandra Park Avenue. Once inside, Orton paraded him round the perimeter, which only prompted hordes of spectators to jump over the barriers. It appeared to be the ambition of everyone present to pat Mick and he wound up getting literally mobbed by his admirers. One of them presented Orton with a shillelagh to hang in Mick's kennel in case he ever needed something with which to ward off intruders.

A record crowd of 12,000 people had gathered for what the *Belfast Telegraph* heralded as 'The Return of Mick – the Good Samaritan' and they were rewarded with a rare treat. Mick ran a solo exhibition over 435 yards and yet, on a strange track and after a hectic day with no preparation, he clocked a time of 24.75 which was comfortably faster than the evening's three proper races over the distance and only 0.25 seconds outside the track record. 'The wonder dog gave away the secret of how he wins races,' went the press report, 'for in his whirlwind dash round the course it was noticeable that he always hugged the corners and kept as close to the inner rails as possible. While they awaited the start many asked themselves the question "Is it Mick the Miller?" It was not long before the air was cleared. Up went the trap, and like a shot from a gun out he came. Faster and faster he moved along the back straight and he rounded the bend closer than any dog had ever ventured, with barely an inch between him and the rail. The crowd cheered with delight. Not only had they seen a dog of great speed but one of great cleverness.'

In return for a mere £100 in expenses, Mick had put thousands on the gate, a fact not lost on either the organisers of the event or its beneficiary. 'Allow us to express our highest appreciation,' James McKee wrote Phiddy Kempton on behalf of Dunmore Park, while at the conclusion of the evening's entertainment itself, WR McKenzie, the Hospital's senior surgeon, proposed a vote of thanks to all concerned, especially to the connections of 'that wonderfully human dog Mick the Miller – all dog lovers realise what it means to send such a precious animal across the Irish Sea.'

It was, however, entirely fitting that the last glimpse of Mick the Miller in full flight on a racetrack should come in the land of his birth.

As the sport's best-known name and favourite son, Mick was much in demand to grace British tracks with his presence throughout the rest of his life. He visited Catford Stadium on the occasion of its opening meeting in July 1932, for instance, and he was still doing the rounds in

January 1938, going up to Wolverhampton to celebrate the tenth anniversary meeting at Monmore Green. Big events that he had won, such as the Derby and the St Leger (he was on hand to personally congratulate his daughter Greta's Rosary after her victory in 1938), seldom passed without Mick's prancing presence. Invariably reunited with Joe Ollis, Mick cut a suitably regal figure kitted out in his crimson jacket with his name picked out in gold braid on the side. Equally invariable was Mick's behaviour because the atmosphere of these big occasions stoked his competitive fires.

Racing was in his blood and the traps acted like a magnet. Ollis would be routinely hauled over to them and obliged to let Mick enjoy a good sniff. The ritual was then concluded by Ollis dragging him away before he tried to enter the boxes along with the runners. 'Mick the Miller tried everything he knew to win yet another Derby,' reported the *Daily Express* one year. 'After parading round the track with former winners, he stopped dead suddenly by the traps, his tail swishing from side to side, and stood expectantly waiting to be put into his box. He was then taken into the middle, and when he saw the hare moving he dashed towards it, pulling his attendant one way and then the other. Eighty-thousand people cheered the old campaigner – and he might have won if they had let him go!'

Furthermore, being the sport's public face, Mick was ever on hand to spread the gospel of greyhound racing as its roving ambassador. After opening the new roof garden at Selfridge's store in London's West End, he was given a guided tour of every department. In return, Mick left his autograph: one of his front claws being used to scratch 'Mick' onto a commemorative window pane.

Meeting millionaires like Gordon Selfridge or posing for publicity shots with the Crazy Gang and his steeplechasing alter ego Golden Miller never caused Mick to turn a hair. Neither did meeting Royalty. On 17 December 1934, Mick attended a charity performance of the play *The Winning Post* at the Adelphi Theatre in aid of King George's Pension Fund for Actor's and Actresses. Mick took it all in his stride. He waited in line beside the American and Belgian ambassadors and when it was his turn to be presented to King George and Queen Mary, greyhound racing's canine ambassador treated them no differently to any other of his human friends and acquaintances. He poked his tongue out and wagged his tail.

However, Father Time is, and never was, a respecter of good deeds. A career at Stud gave way to a life replacing Mutton Pie as the Kempton's house pet. By the beginning of 1939 Mick's public appearances were becoming fewer and fewer and he had returned to his old 'number one' kennel at Burhill to be cared for by Sidney Orton. But if Mick was no longer able to travel far afield to meet his fans, this was no bar to them continuing to arrive unannounced at the door of Orton's bungalow asking to see him. They were invariably accommodated.

The last function Mick attended was on Monday, 16 January 1939 at the Stadium Club in High Holborn, a boxing tournament in aid of the 'Fairplay' Children's Outings Scheme with which Arundel Kempton was associated. Kempton donated three of Mick's last pups – Mick the Conundrum, Mick the Consul and Mick the Courtier – which were auctioned between bouts. Mick dutifully answered the bell one last time and joined his offspring in the ring for a final curtain call.

On Thursday, 4 May 1939 the front pages of the *Greyhound Express* and *The Sporting Life* broke the news those closest to Mick knew was in the offing: 'Mick the Miller – the most famous track greyhound of all time – is Dying!' said the former; 'Great Track Greyhound Mick the Miller is Dying of Old Age' said the latter. Mick was less than two months away from his 13th birthday – a grand age attained by few greyhounds and the equivalent of 90 in human terms. Wimbledon vet Alfred Sams was in constant attendance and had put Mick on a diet of chicken in the hope of lifting his spirits. 'He might fade out at any time,' confided Sidney Orton, 'or hang on for a few weeks.'

The great dog's life moved swiftly and peacefully toward its close. The following morning the once unquenchable force finally began to ebb away and he slipped into a coma. Mick summoned up one last effort and ran toward the bright white light of eternity. And at 6.40 in the evening of Friday, 5 May 1939 he died.

There was little Saturday's newspaper coverage could add to earlier sentiments. *The Greyhound Express*, however, devoted its editorial to Mick's passing.

'If there is such a thing as a greyhound Valhalla, we know full well that our readers will wish the great dog happy hunting,' it began. 'If ever there was a greyhound that gave the sport prominence in the eyes of the man in the street, it was that master of trackcraft, Mick the Miller. We all know that racing men, especially the greyhound patron, is thought by the layman to be lacking in sentiment, but we bet a pound to a penny that there is not one supporter of the sport who can learn of the old star's passing unmoved. It is not silly sentiment to speak of Mick as a great personage, for he delighted the hearts of all who ever saw him run by the inimitable skill with which he won his races. Mick the Miller was the racing greyhound in perfection. It was for the track that he seemed to live. We firmly aver that Mick will never have a peer.'

> *Goodbye old Mick, your life is o'er,*
> *The last parade has called you;*
> *But in our hearts, you're with us still.*
> *No other can foretell you.*

> *O worthy son of Na Boc Lei,*
> *The long-lived fame you've won*
> *Shall never from our memories fade*
> *While champion greyhounds run.*

> *We can't forget the pluck and zest,*
> *With which you made your name,*
> *That Leger! How you stood the test!*
> *A race that crowned your fame.*

> *The delightful thrill of that winning parade*
> *In your little silk coat of glory.*
> *The boisterous wag of a white-tipped tail,*
> *Alone seemed to tell its story.*

To the crowds, dear Mick, who love you so,
You have made your final bow,
But you've left them a name to cherish always.
In Valhalla sleep peacefully now!

Sidney Orton coped valiantly with all the requests for anecdotes and evaluations but he could provide little that he'd not said before. He talked of Mick's 'brains' and his unique place in the annals of the sport. 'I am sure the glamour which surrounded him attracted many people who were seeing greyhound racing for the first time. Mick obviously enjoyed the cheers of the crowd. He would gaze round as if in acknowledgment and wag his tail in delight. I doubt if we shall see his like again.'

Mention of Mick's 'brains' was singularly apt, for a story surfaced that a 'prominent' scientist had allegedly rung Kempton to enquire whether they might be preserved for scientific research. 'We do not know what he hopes to find there,' opined *The Star* sarcastically, 'but we think he is as likely to find something of value as portions of "time-space" in the brain of Dr Einstein, knotted paradoxes in the brain of Mr George Bernard Shaw or an unwritten "Forsyte Saga" in the brain of Mr Galsworthy.'

The exact contribution of Mick's brain to his racing prowess was never – thank goodness – researched and established but his heart was found to weigh 14½ ounces compared with the normal 12-13 ounces. Parallel discoveries of the outsized hearts possessed by Mick's legendary racehorse contemporaries Brown Jack and Phar Lap further endorses the view that a 'great heart' amounts to more than mere hyperbole. There must be some correlation between the extra pumping power provided by larger heart muscles and the exceptional powers of performance associated with Mick, Brown Jack and Phar Lap.

Despite overtures to have Mick's body interred by the winning post at Wimbledon Stadium, Arundel Kempton issued a statement on 24 May saying he had accepted an offer from the Natural History Museum in South Kensington to have Mick's body stuffed and mounted for display in the central hall alongside the skeletons of equine immortals such as Eclipse, St Simon and Brown Jack. The Camden Town firm of Edward Gerrard & Sons took three weeks to complete the taxidermy.

Assessments of Mick's greatness as a racer began even before he was set up in the Natural History Museum and they have been continuing ever since. The question posed by the *Greyhound Express* during the course of two articles in the summer of 1933 was typical: 'Mick – The Incomparable: shall we see his like again?' The paper concluded quite unequivocally that 'We shall NEVER see his like again.'

The paper based its decision on seven criteria that are as relevant today as they were in 1933. As such, they provide a convenient and relevant framework for summarising Mick's career.

1. **Achievement**, particularly in Classic races: Mick won 51 of his 68 races on the track and 10 of his 13 matches, a grand total of 61 from 81 appearances for total prize money of £9,017 and ten shillings. The calibre of races won is indicated by the number of trophies (24), especially those resulting from successes in the acknowledged Classic events of his day, viz two Derbies, the Cesarewitch and the St Leger – the Welsh Derby was not considered a Classic in 1930. The only other Classics open to him were the Scurry Gold Cup and The Laurels, both probably too short for him and run over tracks too tight for him. No dog succeeded in matching his Derby double until Patricia's Hope in 1972-73, followed by Rapid Ranger in 2000-01. His record of winning the Derby and St Leger was not equalled until Dolores Rocket (1971) and Tartan Khan (1975) and his Derby-Cesarewitch-St Leger hat-trick remains unique.

Sadly, the concept of an elite group of Classic races forming the pinnacle of achievement in the sport has been undermined by the relatively recent award of Category One status to upwards of three dozen events. In the minds of purists, however, Mick's Welsh Derby success should be added to his total so that he shares the record of five Classic victories with Local Interprize, who won a Cesarewitch, Scurry Cup, Welsh Derby and two Gold Collars in 1948-49.

2. **Dominance**: Mick was at the top of his game for three whole seasons which he demonstrated by reaching the final of the Derby each year, a feat few dogs have matched. During that English-based period he started favourite in all bar six of his 61 races; in 50 of those 55 he was favourite at odds-on.

Altogether, Mick met 188 different greyhounds. If one excludes those granted a bloodless success when Mick injured himself or fell, Ross Regatta became only the 20th dog to beat him in a fair fight during Mick's four seasons on the track. Ross Regatta boasts another claim to fame; as he was one of just four that Mick never beat – although the only reason Mick did not exact revenge on Moorland Rover and Dick's Son (his Celtic Park conquerors on 11 May 1928) or Ross Regatta and Passing Fair from his last season, was that he was never given the opportunity so to do.

3. **Consistency**: Leaving aside match-races, during the course of his 68 other starts Mick only finished out of the first two on five occasions, that figure inflated by once falling (1931 Welsh Derby), once being knocked over (1930 Laurels) and, of course, being asked to contest the re-run of the 1931 Derby. Mick's consistency was epitomised by the 19-race unbeaten streak during 1930 which began on 19 March and was only curtailed on 23 August by his misfortune in The Laurels. Mick's winning sequence was not bettered until 28 October 1974 when the bitch Westpark Mustard crossed the line at Wembley to win, appropriately, The Mick the Miller Record Stakes.

4. **Versatility**: Mick won at all distances, from 500 yards (three times) to 525 (35), 550 (nine), 600 (ten) and 700 (four); on all types of going; and on every one of the ten tracks he visited.

5. **Time Test**: Mick equalled or set nine track records, six of them world records (four inside 40 days during 1930). He did so on six different tracks and at three distances: 525, 550, and 600 yards. Mick raced exclusively on grass, which meant that, leaving aside any other considerations, improvements in track surfaces would see his name expunged

from the record books sooner or later. His 550-yards time of 31.72 did survive as the Wimbledon track record until the Second World War.

6. **Trackcraft**: Requires little further comment. Unparalleled. Mick could win from any trap and from any position if need be. He possessed as much cunning as a copse full of foxes.

7. **Will-to-Win**: Mick's sheer bloody-mindedness and refusal to quit through the last 50 yards of the St Leger, his fourth race in 19 days over an extreme distance for a dog aged five years and three months, stands as irrefutable testimony.

As the decades rolled by toward the millennium there would be other greyhounds whose exploits drew comparisons with Mick's: from Future Cutlet, Brilliant Bob, Tanist and Ballynennan Moon through Monday's News, Trev's Perfection and Local Interprize to Spanish Battleship, Pigalle Wonder, Scurlogue Champ and Ballyregan Bob. Indeed, thanks to television, the two last-named went some way to outgrowing the sport in the manner of Mick the Miller. Scurlogue Champ won two consecutive runnings of the BBC Television Trophy live on *Sportsnight*, while the BBC's *Nine o'clock News* on 9 December 1986 was interrupted to broadcast live coverage from Hove of Ballyregan Bob's successful attempt to establish a new world record of 32 consecutive victories, an achievement that gained 'Bobby' an invitation to the BBC's annual *Sports Review of the Year* programme.

Magnificent as all these racers were, and popular as 'The Champ' and 'Bobby' were, it is worth bearing in mind that in their racing lifetime less than 4 million people annually attended race-meetings compared to over 17 million during Mick's heyday. Today's winner of the Derby, for instance, performs to 6,000 at Wimbledon compared to Mick's audience of 50-70,000 at the White City. The first greyhound race to be broadcast on the wireless was not until 1940 and the first to be televised was the 1953 St Leger, with the Derby following seven years later. Imagine the colossal size of Mick's profile had it been boosted by television and videotape. As it was, Mick's persona – dependent on newsprint and word of mouth alone – was huge enough and his every exploit held the sporting public in absolute thrall.

The passage of time makes it easy to lose sight of the magnitude of Mick's achievement in bringing a sport – still in its infancy – to the masses in the way he did. But the fact was not lost on objective contemporary chroniclers like Trevor Wignall who, as a sports journalist without portfolio, could be relied upon to exhibit neither fear nor favour in his regular column. 'Mick,' he wrote, 'has done more to make "the dogs" the great sport it has become than any man or combination of men.'

The role of trailblazer is never easy; first up the ladder, an unenviable position. To scale the walls of the broader sporting church required more than a mere champion greyhound. It demanded a truly charismatic figure whose qualities people could readily identify and admire. Thanks to Mick the Miller greyhounds were elevated from numbers to names.

Secondly, and more significantly, Mick's fame transcended sport. At one point, for example, Mick was even adopted by the political cartoonist 'Grime' as a totem of the nation's noble and relentless pursuit of economic solvency (depicted by a hare). Cartoonists could get away with this because there was hardly a household in the land that had not heard of 'Good Old Mick', the dog with a personality, the dog who puts a smile on your face, the dog who brought joy into so many otherwise drab lives.

On those two counts, no greyhound, no matter how successful, will ever deprive Mick of his right to be acclaimed as the greatest greyhound of all time. He remains the sport's one and only undisputed icon.

Death has palpably failed to dent the enduring legend of Mick the Miller. Wimbledon – home to the Derby since the closure of the White City in 1984 – has its Mick the Miller Stand, and when 'virtual' greyhound racing was introduced into betting shops during 2003, the name selected for the mythical track by an overwhelming majority was 'Millersfield'.

Never a year passes or a Derby goes by without the opportunity being taken by some newspaper or other to reminisce about Mick the Miller. Phrases like 'Matchless Mick the Miller'; 'Superdog!'; 'The Greatest Ever!'; 'Miller the Thriller'; and 'The Dog with a Ghost Jockey on his back' are all deployed. Occasionally, just as the mounted hide of Phar Lap is allowed out of the National Museum of Victoria each November to celebrate the running of the Melbourne Cup, Mick has enjoyed an excursion to the Greyhound Derby or exhibitions such as Greyhound 2000 in Newmarket and even one at the Ulster Folk and Transport Museum devoted to the wonders of taxidermy.

Anyone desirous of their very own scale model of Mick had the opportunity to purchase one of the 7,500 limited edition sculptures produced by Royal Doulton in the 1990s. 'The Greatest Greyhound Ever', created by Graham Tongue, stood 9½ inches high and cost £95, though some disputed the manufacturer's claim that 'This work of art perfectly captures Mick the Miller's personality...the realistic manner in which his ears hang and the intelligent look on his face.'

In 1995 the 'real' Mick was transferred to the Walter Rothschild Zoological Museum in Tring, Hertfordshire, as a result of the Natural History Museum's policy decision to no longer display 'personality' animals at South Kensington. Thus, Mick the Miller resides next to Ballyregan Bob and Fullerton in gallery six surrounded by numerous lesser canines and faced by a cabinet full of reptiles. Hardly a suitable resting place for the greatest racing greyhound who ever drew breath.

Yet, in truth, Mick is not there. Mick the Miller long ago returned whence he came. He journeyed far into the West. He had gone to the kingdom of Ossian, the son of Ireland's celebrated 3rd-century hero Finn mac Cool, and entered a fabled land of harmony and eternal youth, the Celtic Valhalla populated by every Irish folk hero from Cahir More to Michael Collins, where the illustrious hounds Coinn Iotair, Doilin and Sceolan gambol at will. He had joined his peers in the timeless land of Tir na nOg.

EPILOGUE

FATHER BROPHY had not long been back in Killeigh after the 1929 'Enterprise of England' when he was transferred to Daingean. Three years later he was given custody of his own parish, Suncroft in County Kildare, a position he held till his death on 29 June 1949, aged 73. Father Brophy's interest in greyhounds had long since waned and in old age he assured one of his three nephews (all priests) that if there was coursing on the other side of the road, he wouldn't cross over to see it. His final request to his nephews was, 'Don't let the cups go for a song at the auction – get them valued and give the proceeds to charity.'

MICHAEL GREENE found intermittent work training coursing greyhounds after Father Brophy left Killeigh, before turning his hand to gardening at the outbreak of the Second World War (when dog-racing was severely restricted) in order to support his wife Philomena and four children. He successfully picked up the coursing thread once again, working for John Dockery of Ballymote, County Sligo, for whom he secured several stakes and cups, notably with the dog Hidden Chops. In his later years he became a familiar figure on the streets of Tullamore selling GAA lottery tickets. He died in 1979.

MICK HORAN left Agher in 1932 to start afresh at Holywood, on the outskirts of Belfast, and enjoyed a successful career as a trainer before a tragically premature death on 28 January 1962. Given the chapter of incidents that befell Horan on trains, it's somewhat perverse to record that it was whilst aboard the train from Belfast to Dublin, en route to slipping at the Old Carton meet, that he suffered what proved to be a fatal heart attack. The train was met in Lurgan by an ambulance but Horan was pronounced dead on arrival at hospital. He was only 63 years old. He is still spoken of in Irish coursing circles as the slipper *nonpareil*.

ARUNDEL KEMPTON died on 26 February 1972 in Cherington, a Bognor Regis nursing home, from cancer of the throat. Pressure of work had seen him resign his position as Vice-Chairman of South London Greyhound Racecourses Limited, his gas-lighting company never recovered from the advent of electricity, and he went bust. He and Phiddy drifted apart and divorced. The high life became a thing of the past. In the months preceding his death he was trying to get his greyhound racing memoirs published in *Reader's Digest* and arranging for the transfer of his family crest to his godson, Arundel Stevens, son of Con Stevens, his lifelong friend and colleague at Wimbledon. Neither bid was successful

SIDNEY ORTON became one of greyhound racing's most successful trainers. By his retirement in January 1959, he had won almost every event worth winning thanks to a succession of star performers, such as Top of the Carlow Road, Brilliant Bob, Ballynennan Moon, Disputed Rattler and Quare Times. On 28 June 1947, at Wimbledon, he also entered the record books as the first trainer to go through a card. He died on 21 November 1978, aged 88, mourned and lauded by everyone in the sport: 'He put the sport on the map in the early 1930s,' said Fred Underhill, secretary of the NGRC; Archie Newhouse, Greyhound Editor of *The Sporting Life*, wrote: 'In its 52 years, greyhound racing has had no finer ambassador'; while Wimbledon chairman John Cearns added: 'He inspired a lot of admiration and respect and it is incredible that even though he retired nearly 20 years ago he remained such a big name in the sport.' His son Clare, who went on to enjoy a successful training career in his own right, delivered perhaps the most eloquently understated tribute of them all: 'I don't think anyone could have wished for a better father.'

RACING RECORD

SUMMARY

IRELAND

Year	Races	Matches	Races Won	Matches Won	Prize Money	Trophies
1928	5	Nil	4	—	£48	Nil
1929	15	Nil	11	—	£284	2

ENGLAND

Year	Races	Matches	Races Won	Matches Won	Prize Money	Trophies
1929	13	4	12	3	£3,342.00/-	5
1930	18	5	15	5	£3,703.10l-	12
1931	17	4	9	2	£1,640.00	5
Grand Totals	68	13	51	10	£9,017.10/-	24

1928

Date	Distance yds	Time	Trap	Fin/SP	Track	Race	Prize Money
18 Apr	500	29.60	4	1 4/1	Shelbourne Park, Dublin	Punchestown Stakes	£10
25 Apr	526.6	30.80	3	1 1/5f	Celtic Park, Belfast	Abercorn Cup, *Round 1*	£5
7 May	526.6	30.60	2	1 5/2f	Celtic Park, Belfast	Abercorn Cup, *Semi-Final*	£10
9 May	500	28.80	3	1 Ev.f	Shelbourne Park, Dublin	Dublin Spring Cup, *Round 1*	£8
11 May	526.6	30.40	1	3 5/1	Celtic Park, Belfast	Abercorn Cup, *Final*	£15

1929

Date	Distance yds	Time	Trap	Fin/SP	Track	Race	Prize Money
25 Mar	525	30.40	2	1 5/4f	Shelbourne Park, Dublin	Shelbourne Stakes	£10
1 Apr	525	30.52	2	2 5/4f	Shelbourne Park, Dublin	Easter Cup, *Round 1*	£2
8 Apr	525	30.44	5	2 5/1	Shelbourne Park, Dublin	Easter Cup, *Semi Final*	£2
15 Apr	525	30.71	3	2 7/1	Shelbourne Park, Dublin	Easter Cup, *Final*	£20
23 Apr	600	35.00	4	1 6/4f	Harold's Cross, Dublin	Leinster Plate	£10
2 May	525	30.83	2	1 4/5f	Harold's Cross, Dublin	Spring Cup, *Round 1*	Nil
10 May	525	30.75	2	1 4/5f	Harold's Cross, Dublin	Spring Cup, *Semi Final*	Nil
21 May	525	30.79	6	1 5/1	Harold's Cross, Dublin	Spring Cup, *Final*	£100
						(Silver Cup)	
7 Jun	600	34.67	3	1 4/6f	Harold's Cross, Dublin	Stayers' Cup, *Round 1*	Nil
8 Jun	525	30.18	6	1 Ev.f	Shelbourne Park, Dublin	National Cup, *Round 1*	£5
13 Jun	600	34.46	4	1 1/2f	Harold's Cross, Dublin	Stayers'Cup, *Semi Final*	Nil
17 Jun	525	30.00ETR	3	1 2/5f	Shelbourne Park, Dublin	National Cup, *Round 2*	£5
18 Jun	600	34.42	1	2 2/5f	Harold's Cross, Dublin	Stayers' Cup, *Final*	£25
26 Jun	525	30.06	1	1 4/6f	Shelbourne Park, Dublin	National Cup, *Semi Final*	£5
6 Jul	525	30.01	2	1 1/2f	Shelbourne Park, Dublin	National Cup, *Final*	£100
						(Silver Cup)	
16 Jul	525	29.82WR	4	1 1/4f	White City, London	Greyhound Derby, Round I	£15
20 Jul	525	30.45	1	1 1/4f	White City, London	Greyhound Derby, Round 2	£15
23 Jul	525	29.98	1	1 1/4f	White City, London	Greyhound Derby, Semi final	£15

Date	Distance yds	Time	Trap	Fin/SP	Track	Race	Prize Money
25 Jul	525	29.96	4	1 4/7f	White City, London	Greyhound Derby,final (Re-run)	£700 (Silver Cup)
5 Aug	600	34.37	3	1 1/5f	West Ham, London	International Sweepstakes, Round 1	£10
5 Aug	600	34.43	5	1 1/4f	West Ham, London	International Sweepstakes, Final	£200 (Silver Cup)
24 Aug	525	29.72	4	2 7/4	Welsh White City, Cardiff	Match vs "Back Isle"	—
31 Aug	550	31.72wr	4	1 4/6f	Wimbledon, London	Match vs "Back Isle"	£200 (Gold Cup £50)
19 Oct	550	32.38	2	1 4/6f	Wimbledon, London	First International Derby Sweepstakes	£250 (Gold Cup £50)
14 Nov	525	29.98	2	1 4/11f	White City, London	Match vs "Bishop's Dream"	£1,100 (Gold Cup)
16 Nov	525	30.66	1	1 1/8f	White City, London	London Cup, Round 1	—
21 Nov	525	30.74	1	1 2/5f	White City, London	London Cup, Round 2	£15
23 Nov	525	30.92	3	1 4/7f	White City, London	London Cup, Semi Final	£15
26 Nov	525	30.69	4	2 4/6f	White City, London	London Cup, Final	£60
11 Dec	500	29.52	2	1 4/5f	Harringay, London	Match vs "Bishop's Dream"	£700
20 Dec	550	33.15	3	1 1/8f	Wimbledon, London	The Champion Stakes, Round 1	£16
26 Dec	550	33.56	3	1 4/9f	Wimbledon, London	The Champion Stakes, Semi Final	£16

1930

Date	Distance yds	Time	Trap	Fin/SP	Track	Race	Prize Money
1 Jan	550	32.99	2	2 8/13f	Wimbledon, London	The Champion Stakes, *Final*	£68
							(Silver Cup)
19 Feb	550	32.40	2	1 2/5f	Wimbledon, London	Match vs "BucknaBoy"	£100
							(Silver Trophy)
17 Mar	525	31.00	3	2 4/7f	Wembley, London	Wembley Spring Cup, *Round 1*	£5
19 Mar	525	30.32	4	1 Ev.f	Wembley, London	Wembley Spring Cup, *Semi Final*	£15
22 Mar	525	30.56	2	1 Ev.f	Wembley, London	Wembley Spring Cup, Final	£230
							(Silver Trophy)
31 Mar	525	30.08	1	1 1/6f	Wembley, London	Match vs "So Green"	£100
							(Silver Trophy)
4 Apr	550	32.93	1	1 1/6f	Wimbledon, London	Match vs "So Green"	£ 100
							(Silver Trophy)
10 Apr	525	29.76TR	1	1 2/5f	WhiteCity, London	Match vs "Fairy Again"	£150
							(Silver Trophy)
9 May	550	32.31	5	1 4/11 f	Wimbledon, London	The "Loafer" Trophy	£40
							(Gold Trophy £15)
17 May	525	30.19	3	1 2/7f	White City, London	The Farndon Cup	£30
							(Silver Cup)
7 June	525	30.14	1	1 8/100f	White City, London	The Greyhound Derby, *Round 1*	£15
17 June	525	30.59	2	1 1/7f	White City, London	The Greyhound Derby, *Round 2*	£15

226

Date	Distance yds	Time	Trap	Fin/SP	Track	Race	Prize Money
21 June	525	30.13	4	1 2/7f	White City, London	The Greyhound Derby, *Semi Final*	£20
28 June	525	30.24	1	1 4/9f	White City, London	The Greyhound Derby, *Final*	£1,480.10/ (Silver Cup)
30 June	600	34.06WR	4	1 1/10f	West Ham, London	The Cesarewitch, *Round 1*	£15
5 July	600	34.09	1	1 1/8f	West Ham, London	The Cesarewitch, *Round 2*	£15
9 July	600	34.01WR	3	1 1/10f	West Ham, London	The Cesarewitch, *Semi Final*	£20
12 July	600	34.11	2	1 1/7f	West Ham, London	The Cesarewitch, *Final*	£1,000 (Gold Cup £50)
29 July	525	29.90	2	1 1/5f	Welsh White City, Cardiff	The Welsh Derby, *Round 1*	£10
2 Aug	525	29.60WR	4	1 1/8f	Welsh White City, Cardiff	The Welsh Derby, *Semi Final*	£10
9 Aug	525	29.55WR	2	1 1/8f	Welsh White City, Cardiff	The Welsh Derby, *Final*	£ 115
20 Aug	550	32.29	2	1 1/3f	Wimbledon, London	Match vs "Faithful Kitty"	£ 150 (Silver Trophy)
23 Aug	500	29.37	5	6 1/6f	Wimbledon, London	The "Laurels", *Round 1* (bumped & injured)	—

1931

Date	Distance yds	Time	Trap	Fin/SP	Track	Race	Prize Money
16 Mar	525	30.44	4	1 1/2f	Wembley, London	The Wembley Spring Cup, *Round 1*	£15
18 Mar	525	30.34	4	1 4/9f	Wembley, London	The Wembley Spring Cup, *Semi Final*	£15
23 Mar	525	30.04ETR	4	1 1/3f	Wembley, London	The Wembley Spring Cup, *Final*	£230
							(Silver Cup £20)
16 May	525	30.51	1	1 1/3f	White City, London	G.R.A. Sweepstakes No. 3	£45
							(Silver Salver)
23 May	550	32.06	5	3 1/3f	West Ham, London	The Revenge Stakes	—
6 June	525	30.10	4	1 8/13f	White City, London	Match vs "Doumergue"	£200
							(Silver Cup)
13 June	525	30.66	2	2 2/7f	White City, London	The Greyhound Derby, *Round 1*	£5
16 June	525	29.69	3	2 7/4f	White City, London	The Greyhound Derby, *Round 2*	£5
20 June	525	30.20	6	2 2/1	White City, London	The Greyhound Derby, *Semi Final*	£10
27 June	525	30.04	6	4 Ev.f	White City, London	The Greyhound Derby, *Final*	
						(Re-run. Won first run)	
4 July	600	34.51	5	1 6/4f	West Ham, London	The Cesarewitch, *Round 2*	£15
11 July	600	34.72	2	3 1/3f	West Ham, London	The Cesarewitch, *Semi Final*	£5
18 July	600	34.03	3	2 5/2	West Ham, London	The Cesarewitch, *Final*	£200

Date	Distance yds	Time	Trap	Fin/SP	Track	Race	Prize Money
28 July	525	30.72	4	5 4/6f	Welsh White City, Cardiff	The Welsh Derby, *Round 1* (Knocked Over)	—
8 Aug	550	32.20	4	1 4/6f	Perry Barr, Birmingham	Match vs "Maidens Boy"	£100 *(Silver Cup)*
15 Aug	525	29.69	1	2 10/11f	Welsh White City, Cardiff	Match vs "Altamatzin"	—
14 Sept	700	41.40	4	1 2/5f	Wembley, London	Greyhound St. Leger, *Round 1*	£15
19 Sept	525	30.19	2	2 11/8	Perry Barr, Birmingham	Match vs "Ross Regatta"	—
21 Sept	700	40.85	3	1 6/1	Wembley, London	Greyhound St Leger, *Round 2*	£15i
26 Sept	700	40.86	1	1 7/4	Wembley, London	Greyhound St. Leger, *Semi Final*	£15
3 Oct	700	41.31	3	1 Ev.f	Wembley, London	GreyhoundSt.Leger, *Final*	£750 *(Gold Cup £50)*

WR World Record   TR Track Record   ETR Equal Track Record

229

PEDIGREE

```
                                                        Mandini
                                        Hillcourt
                                                        Camorra
                        Osprey Hawk,
                        bk, 1915
                                                        Gloomy
                                        Prairie Hawk
                                                        Prairie Flower II
        Glorious Event,
        bd, 1918
                                                        Busaco Boy
                                        Dick the Liar
                                                        Stormy Sea II
                        Merriment IV,
                        bd w, 1917
                                                        Royal Tim
                                        Royal Leily
                                                        Royal Annie
Mick the
Miller,
bd dog,
29 June 1926
                                                        Howtown
                                        Lock and Key
                                                        Lonely Musing
                        Let 'im Out,
                        w bd, 1914
                                                        Lottery
                                        Lengsfeld
                                                        Gaysfield
        Na Boc Lei,
        w bd, 1921
                                                        Friendly Joe
                                        Coming Tide
                                                        Fast Waves
                        Talbotstown III,
                        Be, 1916
                                                        Merry Miller II
                                        Bag o'Slack
                                                        Royal Jessie
```

INDEX

The index is arranged alphabetically except for subheadings, which appear in approximate chronological order as appropriate.

INDEX